Literary Loneliness in
Mid-Eighteenth-Century
England

Literary Loneliness in Mid-Eighteenth-Century England

JOHN SITTER

Cornell University Press

ITHACA AND LONDON

First published 1982 by Cornell University Press.
Published in the United Kingdom by Cornell University Press Ltd.,
Ely House, 37 Dover Street, London W1X 4HQ.

International Standard Book Number 0-8014-1499-7
Library of Congress Catalog Card Number 82-5105
Printed in the United States of America
*Librarians: Library of Congress cataloging information
appears on the last page of the book.*

*The paper in this book is acid-free and meets the guidelines for permanence and
durability of the Committee on Production Guidelines for Book Longevity of the Council
on Library Resources.*

For Vivian Sitter
and in memory of
E. B. and B. E. Sitter

Contents

Preface   9

PART I. WRITING AND BELIEF

1. Hume's Stylistic Emergence   19
2. William Law and the "Fiction of Behaviour"   50

PART II. TOWARD A POETICS OF CONVERSION

3. The Flight from History in Mid-Century Poetry   77
4. Ambition, Conversion, and Lyric Grace   104

PART III. NARRATIVE DIFFUSION

5. The Long Poem Obstructed   157
6. The Final Novels of Fielding and Richardson   189

Conclusion: Literary Loneliness
  and the Historical Moment   214

Index   227

Preface

Much commentary on eighteenth-century English literature and most teaching of it splits the century into an "Age of Pope and Swift" and an "Age of Johnson," the first ending about 1740, the second beginning in earnest somewhere in the 1750s. This book might be regarded as an attempt to understand what happened between terms.

The middle of the eighteenth century is an interesting, confusing, and relatively neglected literary period. It is conspicuously a time of experiments. The most successful of them, such as *Tom Jones* and *Clarissa,* are part of its meaning—the best known part; but its failed experiments are, or ought to be, historically central as well. The period is one in which many apparently eternal premises seem to have shifted with surprising speed and in which a few of our own seem to have first emerged. One major shock of recognition for the modern observer is the discovery, made in the 1740s, that poetry, if it is to be "pure poetry," should be about a lonely poet surrounded by "nature"—an idea hardly pure or natural but inherited today by almost any beginning writer of verse. It is primarily this new assumption and its variants in the particular consciousness mid-eighteenth-century authors had of themselves as solitary writers for solitary readers that I have tried to characterize as "literary loneliness."

The period has been neglected, I think, because understanding it requires studying a number of minor writers. We study minor writers to understand any period, of course, but we are habitually more comfortable doing so when we can group them around a great author, who then serves as literal or imaginative spokesman for a real or hypothetical collaboration. Thus the "Augustans" or "Johnson and his Circle." The generation of writers immediately after Pope and Swift is not dominated by a single voice, however, and the problems of trying to give it one—usually the rising one of "pre-romanticism"—have long been recognized. (They are reviewed again briefly in chapter 3 and, in terms of recent biases, in the conclusion.)

But historical skepticism is not the proper response to the problem unless one's interest is in compiling its logical product, a chronological chart. As my title suggests, I have tried to discover some unity in the period's preoccupations and problems while acknowledging at every turn discontinuity and divergence. My procedure has been to select works and dilemmas which seem to have been ignored or underestimated and which suggest the period's deeper strains. The goal, then, is not explanation but emblematic and empathetic description, something like the phenomenology of a generation.

In trying to write literary history from, as it were, the inside out, I have been challenged by contradictions that many students of literature must feel. On one side are all the limitations and distortions of the single-author study and on the other all its obvious satisfactions. We write about individual authors, after all, not only because the life and death of Whomever offer us the pragmatic *some*where at which we must start and stop if books are to be finished and scholars sane, but also because personal identification is both animating at the first step and a vivid corrective at the last to the breezy formulas in which living specificity so easily evaporates.[1] Still, much literary scholarship seems to proceed too confidently on the premise that we can make history solely out of biography. In trying to balance the claims of identification and synthesis, I have sought a mode somewhere between the history of ideas (that is, images) and the history of

[1]Although Raymond Williams would likely find the following discussion more "Hegelian" than historically specific, I am indebted at several points to his emphasis in *Marxism and Literature* (Oxford: Oxford University Press, 1977), esp. pp. 121–35 and 171–98, on authorial "practical consciousness" as something that "cannot without loss be reduced to belief-systems, institutions, or explicit general relationships, though it may include all these as lived and experienced" (pp. 132–33).

persons, paying particular attention to individual careers as well
as to the life of some of the metaphors and postures that became
common property.

I have emphasized David Hume and William Law in the first
two chapters for different but perhaps symmetrical reasons.
The broad and initial assumption is simply that Hume, however
difficult it is to demonstrate his influence upon most of his literary contemporaries, defined rather than invented many of the
major mid-eighteenth-century problems of knowledge and belief—that Hume, in short, argued out problems under which
most thoughtful writers labored. This aspect by itself might well
be left to scholars more competent to deal with Hume's epistemology, but my primary concern is with Hume as a writer, and
particularly as a developing writer, whose attempts to find a
credible voice seem an essential part of his philosophical development and a rigorously revealing mirror of the literary
changes around him.

William Law, who happily and steadily moved further and
further from the literary mainstream Hume worked to find, is
clearly not a "central" figure in any usual sense. (His widely
discussed *Serious Call to a Devout and Holy Life* is a relatively small
part of his work.) But there seem to me to be three general
reasons for moving him to the center of our reconstruction. The
first is that his fideism balances Hume's skepticism both as coun-
terweight and as complement: beyond their obvious differences,
Hume and Law are equally at odds with the "commonsense"
pronouncements of their day and similar in their emphasis on
conversion as the model for understanding belief. (Hume would
of course not relish this comparison any more than Law would.)
Second, Law's career begins in pamphlet controversy and "Augustan" character sketching and ends in "Blakean" vision. To
attempt to understand his development, therefore, is to con-
front from within one writer's experience the felt insufficiencies
of sharply focused observation and the increasing attractions of
a dimly perceived wholeness, to which Law in his later years
liked to refer as an all-inclusive "magnetism." The third reason
for including Law is more frankly judgmental and polemical. Of
the religious writers of the period, he seems to me the brightest
as well as the most amiable critic of the period's compromises,

ecclesiastical as well as epistemological, and his own stylistic magnetism seems to merit much more literary attention than we have paid.

That more than half of this book deals with mid-eighteenth-century poetry can be explained genetically and I hope justified argumentatively. My interest in the period began with the poets because so many of the poems of the 1740s and 1750s seemed to express a puzzling but pronounced discontinuity with the immediate past. For the generation of poets writing just after the deaths of Pope and Swift, the resources of early-eighteenth-century irony and proportion seem suddenly to collapse. Perhaps because Pope moralized his song so well and so long that many individuals coming of age in his wake found Pope and culture the same, the problems of change that may exist for any generation stand here in sharper relief. The conscious rejection of Pope's achievement by Joseph Warton or by Edward Young is matched in poetic practice by striking and apparently unconscious reversals of his metaphoric values. Thus we find "Fancy" or "Concord," for example, praised in terms that only a few years earlier had been reserved for "Dulness." More broadly, the earlier eighteenth century's union of modern poetry and modern history dissolves quickly in the mid-century attempt to purify poetry of topicality and poets of typicality. In the increasing characterization of the poet himself as a sensitive fugitive from his society, we may have the best testimony to the violence of change.

Literary change in eighteenth-century England has been studied in our own century primarily through the history of criticism and the history of the novel. From the broad sweep of Samuel Monk's *The Sublime* (1935) to M. H. Abrams's *The Mirror and the Lamp* (1953), the discussion of eighteenth-century critical ideas has long taken place on a more sophisticated level than the study of poetic practice.[2] As much as possible, therefore, I have turned the present argument to the poetry itself.

[2] As later references will at least partly attest, a number of modern studies of eighteenth-century poets have helped me; my point is that for much of our century it has been easier to work from these unified views of eighteenth-century critical tendencies than to deal with many of the poets collectively. To sophisticated readings of mid-century critical theory and the novel, perhaps we may now

Preface

The novel, of course, is the eighteenth century's success story in more senses than one. The quantity and quality of modern commentary on the early novel determined me at first to exclude it altogether from this book. Gradually, however, I have begun to realize that the increasing differentiation of poetry and the novel in the period is part of the problem of change I am attempting to describe. More specifically, it now seems clearer to me that the narrative problems experienced in their last works by the period's greatest practitioners, Richardson and Fielding, are closely related to the impasses confronting mid-eighteenth-century poetic ambitions. While the problems of the poets and the novelists would seem to oppose each other—poetry attempting to dissociate itself from history and the novel representing itself as "history" undistorted by romance—the roads leading to what Joseph Warton called "pure poetry" and what Richardson called "sentiment" are paved, as I have tried to show in the final chapters, with similar intentions and exact similar tolls. Some of these tensions are still with us in the form of modern critical premises, and in the conclusion I have tried to suggest the more significant and problematic correspondences between mid-eighteenth-century literary practice and mid-twentieth-century literary reflection.

A book so small should not be embarrassed by so many debts; but it is a pauper's pleasure to acknowledge several of the individuals and institutions who helped it and its author along. Much of the thinking, reading, and writing for the first draft took place and shape during a year's residence at the National Humanities Center in Research Triangle Park, North Carolina. I am deeply grateful to the Center's trustees, staff, and fellows for their generous encouragement. The first director of the

---

begin to add the general area of popular expression: see Ronald Paulson, *Popular and Polite Art in the Age of Hogarth and Fielding* (Notre Dame: University of Notre Dame Press, 1979). It will be instructive to see whether mid-century poetry, which Paulson deliberately excludes (p. xiv), can eventually be studied usefully in terms of his suggestive discussion of cultural metaphors. One possibility is that Prior or Pope may come to seem closer than Collins or Gray to Paulson's group of texts in which there is a "strong sense of oral tradition being caught or fixed in print" (p. x); if so, conceptions of poetry of the earlier eighteenth century as characteristically "aristocratic" may need to be rethought.

Preface

Center, the late Charles Frankel, his successor William Bennett, and Kent Mullikin, the assistant director and a fellow traveler in the eighteenth century, were especially helpful at the outset. The daily conversational life at the Center during 1978–1979 was a continual education; with no more nostalgia than is due, I wish to acknowledge having learned things of use from all my fellow fellows and many from many. Joseph Beaty, Abraham Edel, and Elizabeth Flower kindly read early sections of the manuscript and brought philosophic eyes to bear on many Humean errors; they should not be implicated, of course, in errors which remain or which have found fresh "recruits of needful pride." Muriel Bradbrook and Ann Douglas lent encouragement at crucial points. In less identifiable ways I was helped by the peripatetic influence of some of the civilest of civil historians, John Agresto, William Leuchtenberg, Peter Riesenberg, and the late Jacob Talmon.

Even in such a colloquial garden, books cannot be made without books: for the resourcefulness of the Center's librarian, Allen Tuttle, and the cooperation of the libraries of the University of North Carolina, Duke University, and North Carolina State University I am very grateful. Former colleagues at the University of Massachusetts at Amherst gave support of many kinds. Morris Golden generously shared his encyclopedic knowledge of the period and offered helpful suggestions on matters large and small. Vincent DiMarco listened with medieval patience to many false starts and helped redeem some which appeared salvageable. J. Paul Hunter, formerly of Emory University, read the entire manuscript and asked many useful questions. Through confidence and provocation, Jerome Beaty helped me conclude, in both senses. Trudy Kretchman supervised the final preparation of the manuscript with professional efficiency and personal good humor. To the late Samuel Monk, with whom I began my study of the eighteenth century, and to Aubrey Williams, I owe older and increasing debts. Deborah Ayer Sitter encouraged, endured, and enlightened this book from beginning to end.

I am grateful to editors and publishers for permission to use previously published material. Passages from Gray follow the text of *The Poems of Gray, Collins, and Goldsmith*, ed. Roger Lons-

dale (London: Longmans, Green, 1969) and are quoted by permission of Longman Group Limited. Passages from *The Seasons*
and *Liberty* are quoted from *The Poetical Works of James Thomson*,
ed. J. L. Robertson (1908; reprint ed. London: Oxford University Press, 1965), and those from *The Castle of Indolence* are taken
from *The Seasons and The Castle of Indolence*, ed. James Sambrook
(London: Oxford University Press, 1972); passages from Collins
are from *The Works of William Collins,* ed. Richard Wendorf and
Charles Ryskamp (Oxford: Clarendon Press, 1979). I am grateful to Oxford University Press for permission to quote from
these three editions. Parts of chapter 4 are based on arguments
which originally appeared in *ELH* 44 (1977), 312–36, published
by The Johns Hopkins University Press, and in *Studies in Eighteenth-Century Culture,* vol. 10, pp. 181–89, published by the University of Wisconsin Press, copyright © 1981 by the American
Society for Eighteenth-Century Studies. Part of chapter 5 is a
revision of an article first printed in *Eighteenth-Century Studies* 12
(Fall, 1978), 90–106, published by the American Society for
Eighteenth-Century Studies. Some paragraphs from the conclusion appeared in *The Humanist as Citizen,* ed. John Agresto and
Peter N. Riesenberg (Research Triangle Park, N.C.: National
Humanities Center, 1981), pp. 94–116.

JOHN SITTER

Atlanta, Georgia

PART I

Writing and Belief

CHAPTER 1

Hume's Stylistic Emergence

David Hume spent much of the 1740s revising his thesis. *A Treatise of Human Nature,* his first work and the one philosophers generally regard as his greatest, fell "dead-born" from the press in 1739–1740. He recast most of it thoroughly as the *Enquiry Concerning Human Understanding* in 1748 and the *Enquiry Concerning the Principles of Morals* in 1751, the second of which Hume thought "incomparably the best" of his works. Unlike the philosophers, students of literature have generally followed Hume's advice to ignore the earlier work; they have looked instead to its more elegant descendants or have turned from Hume's technical works altogether in favor of the explicitly literary essays, the dialogues, and the *History of England.*[1]

---

[1] Notable exceptions on either side are A. D. Nuttall, who discusses the *Treatise* in *A Common Sky: Philosophy and the Literary Imagination* (Berkeley: University of California Press, 1974), esp. pp. 93–111, and Antony Flew, who conducts a thorough philosophical analysis of the *Enquiry Concerning Human Understanding* in *Hume's Philosophy of Belief* (New York: Humanities Press, 1961). I find myself in essential agreement with the contention of Michael Morrisoe, Jr., that it is misleading to continue to study Hume's "content" without attending to the "intellectual movement" of mind reflected in his style and that it is time to "look to Hume as a writer first and a philosopher second"; see "Linguistic Analysis as Rhetorical Pattern in David Hume," in William B. Todd, ed., *Hume and the Enlightenment* (Austin and Edinburgh: University of Texas and University of Edinburgh presses, 1974), pp. 72–82. Morrisoe has also written on style in Hume's later works in "Hume's Rhetorical Strategy: A Solution to the *Dialogues Concerning Natural Religion,*" *Texas Studies in Language and Literature,* 11 (1969): 963–74, and "Rhetorical Methods in Hume's Works on Religion," *Philosophy and Rhetoric,* 2 (1969): 121–38. Quotations from Hume's *Treatise* are from the edition of A. D. Lindsay (London: J. M. Dent, 1911); parenthetical references are to page numbers and, for convenience, to book, part, and chapter.

I hope it does not seem a fond paradox or the product of what Johnson would call a "love of singularity" to contend that Hume's *Treatise* deserves our careful reading because it is not very readable. Hume was at once one of the great thinkers of the eighteenth century, but he became one of its great writers. From our standpoint, he is one of a group of prose writers, including Fielding, Johnson, and Richardson, who diversely "came to power" during the 1740s. The fact that he did so while ostensibly articulating the same ideas over again offers us a unique chance to observe the interaction of stylistic and intellectual demands, and the story of his literary maturation should be instructive. His attitudes toward his audience, his experimentation, and his development should suggest a great deal about the versions of prose discourse, the pressures of voice, and the criteria of credibility which an extremely acute writer felt to be emergent during the mid-eighteenth century.

In the following sections I will try to suggest that Hume's gradual acquisition of an "easy" style during the formative phase of his philosophic career—from the *Treatise of Human Nature,* published in 1739–1740, to the *Enquiries* of 1748 and 1752— should be understood as inseparable from his continuing preoccupation with the idea of belief. It is necessary to begin, therefore, by attending to some of Hume's technical analyses and dichotomies (most of which stem from an effort to distinguish throught from feeling) as well as to his more accessible or "literary" overtures in the *Treatise.* In part I wish to contend that some of the ostensibly least personal sections of his work can instructively be read as unconscious autobiography and, in turn, that his stylistic development not only reflects but shapes new solutions to his original questions about the causes and nature of belief.

Since belief interested Hume both in private and public experience, and since writing is "in" both realms at once, we will also need to attend closely to the matter of how Hume found his voice in order to understand the difficulties that he and other mid-century writers encountered in establishing new grounds for believability. Earlier in the century Swift had defined good style as proper words in proper places. But for Hume and many of his contemporaries, the style of belief changed dramatically, and finding proper words and places became as problematic as finding proper truths which one might wear credibly at home or at large.

Rhetorical Process in *A Treatise of Human Nature*

To speak of credibility and problems of voice in the same breath is not to approach Hume's *Treatise,* as most commentary has; but it is particularly helpful to keep these concerns together when the philosopher is very self-conscious about making his philosophy into a book. We do not have to seek far to find this concern in Hume, certainly not as far as his later revisions. Hume's stylistic self-consciousness appears in the first sentences of the *Treatise.* His entering gesture is a wave to the grander gestures with which philosophers normally begin, in order to "insinuate the praises of their own systems, by decrying all those which have been advanced before them." These philosophers are frequently right about their predecessors' systems, Hume suggests, but are more frequently blinded by rhetorical posturing to the errors of their own. Anyone who troubles to look can see that philosophy does not have its house in order—"even the rabble without doors may judge from the noise and clamour which they hear, that all goes not well within"—but it requires greater discernment to understand the cause of confusion: "Amidst all this bustle, it is not reason which carries the prize, but eloquence; and no man needs ever despair of gaining proselytes to the most extravagant hypothesis, who has art enough to represent it in any favourable colours. The victory is not gained by the men at arms, who manage the pike and sword, but by the trumpeters, drummers, and musicians of the army" (Introduction, p. 4).

This distrust of eloquence is announced early and repeatedly, "trumpeted," one might say unkindly, as part of a contract with the reader for plain-style severity. Readers cannot expect colors or music, must in fact anticipate numerous "pains," but in return they will have the presumable satisfaction of real swordplay and security from extravagance or "art." Hume's attitude toward his reader and his subject is an interesting compound of wit and defensiveness, of hesitation (any still undiscovered truth "must lie very deep and abstruse") and optimism militant: "Here then is the only expedient, from which we can hope for success in our philosophical researches, to leave the tedious lingering method, which we have hitherto followed, and, instead of taking now and then a castle or village on the frontier, to march up directly to the capital or centre of these sciences, to human nature itself; which once being masters of, we may elsewhere hope for an easy victory" (Introduction, p. 5).

We might see Hume's shifting ground as a schoolmasterly maneuver by which he alternately warns his readers of the difficulties ahead and encourages them with promises of the "conquests" to be made. But the historical moment in which Hume situates himself suggests that the uncertainty of attitude is his own. In his hopefulness for the application of the "experimental method" to moral as well as to natural science, Hume calls the reader's attention to the fact that the "space of time" from Thales to Socrates is "nearly equal to that betwixt my Lord Bacon and some late philosophers in England, who have begun to put the science of man on a new footing, and have engaged the attention, and excited the curiosity of the public." The analogy cuts at least two ways. Hume may have some of the heady optimism of a man confident that he is riding a new wave; he must also recognize that he is plunging into waters already crowded by the sophisticated and formidable company of "Mr. Locke, my Lord Shaftesbury, Dr. Mandeville, Mr. Hutchinson, Dr. Butler, etc." (p. 6). The "et cetera" of this group is to include young David Hume, and it is interesting to compare the historical timeliness and tension of his announcement with Locke's mild and relatively ahistorical account introducing *An Essay Concerning Human Understanding*. For Locke the "history" of his work consisted of its origin in sociable conversation with "five or six friends, meeting at my chamber"; for Hume the historical situation of his undertaking is defined by his relation to five (or more) friends of sort, the "late philosophers" who meet not in his chamber but in the course of his *Treatise*.[2]

[2]Locke's remark is from the prefatory "Epistle to the Reader." Rosalie Colie studied Locke's style sensitively in "John Locke and the Publication of the Private," *Philological Quarterly*, 45 (1966): 24–45, and "The Essayist in His *Essay*," in John Yolton, ed., *John Locke: Problems and Perspectives* (Cambridge: Cambridge University Press, 1969), pp. 234–61.

The silent solitude of Hume's chamber is one of the more vivid "impressions" throughout the *Treatise,* particularly at those several points where Hume calls attention to his physical situation as thinker and writer. The most dramatic of these is the famous conclusion to Book I, but lesser moments of self-dramatization occur throughout the *Treatise.* Hume's first illustration of the distinction between "impressions" and "ideas" (a problem to which we will necessarily return) serves to remind the reader at once that he is reading a book: "By *ideas,* I mean the faint images of these [impressions] in thinking and reasoning; such as, for instance, are all the perceptions excited by the present discourse, excepting only those which arise from the sight and touch, and excepting the immediate pleasure or uneasiness it may occasion." Another illustration a few sentences later carries our attention from the present discourse to the present author: "When I shut my eyes, and think of my chamber, the ideas I form are exact representations of the impressions I felt. . . . In running over my other perceptions I find still the same resemblance and representation. Ideas and impressions appear always to correspond to each other. This circumstance seems to me remarkable, and engages my attention for a moment" (I, i, 1; p. 12).

The chamber and the moment are the boundaries of Hume's experience as writer, and both are invoked frequently in ways which emphasize the privacy of all experience. Instances range from the routine reference to "the table before me" (I, ii, 3; p. 41) to somewhat more arresting self-portraits:

> The paper on which I write at present is beyond my hand. The table is beyond the paper. The walls of the chamber beyond the table. And in casting my eye towards the window, I perceive a great extent of fields and buildings beyond my chamber. . . . My books and papers, present themselves in the same uniform manner, and change not upon account of any interruption in my seeing or perceiving them. . . . I am here seated in my chamber, with my face to the fire; and all the objects that strike my senses are contained in a few yards around me. [I, iv, 2; pp. 185–90]

Notable in each case is the appeal to the present. The present tense resonates in particular in the last sentence if one hears the echo of Descartes—as Hume at La Flèche most likely did—describing how his meditations ripened during a day spent in a "warm room." The emphasis on solitude and spatial confinement is one rhetorical similarity which draws Hume closer to the Cartesian meditation than to the "clubbable" conversation of Locke or the gardens of Shaftesbury. But in Descartes the warm room is invoked in the past tense, as the scene of his discovery, not as the condition of his discourse.[3]

Because all of our ideas are based on impressions, Hume has argued earlier, any apparently free thinking we do is confined to the "narrow compass" of our prior perceptions: "Let us chase our imagination to the heavens, or to the utmost limits of the universe; we never really advance a step beyond ourselves. . . . This is the universe of the imagination, nor have we any idea but what is there produced" (I, ii, 6; p. 72). Later, in the section "Of Personal Identity," he writes: "The mind is a kind of theatre, where several perceptions successively make their appearance; pass, repass, glide away, and mingle in an infinite variety of postures and situations" (I, iv, 6; pp. 239–40). The theatrical metaphor Hume warns us against extending, although not because it is too confining: it might be too comforting, persuading us that personal identity is more locatable than it is. But this metaphor for mind proves useful to Hume when—theatrically—he combines the process of rumination and rhetoric; musing on the problem of the "immateriality" of the soul, Hume begins by looking around at material objects. "Here Spinoza appears, and tells me that these are only modifications and that the subject in which they inhere is simple, uncompoundable, and indivisible." Next he considers his "universe of thought," and "upon my inquiring concerning these, theologians present themselves, and tell me that these also are modifications." Then comes act 3 of this miniature drama: "immediately upon which I am deafened

[3]Descartes's account of his "day alone in a warm room" occurs early in the *Discourse on Method* when he explains how, during a stay in Germany, he came to the conclusion that most of the knowledge which has "grown up little by little by the accumulation of the opinions of many different persons" ought to be rejected in favor of individual reason. See *Discourse on Method and Meditations,* trans. Laurence J. Lafleur (Indianapolis: Bobbs-Merrill, 1960), pp. 10–11.

with the noise of a hundred voices, that treat the first hypothesis with detestation and scorn, and the second with applause and veneration" (I, iv, 5; pp. 230–231).

Hume's mischief here is not fundamentally different from his tendency throughout the *Treatise* to stage for his audience the steps, including many of the false ones, of his approach. It is, however, more comically controlled and pedagogically deliberate than other interior dramas presented in these later sections of Book I, which take up major skeptical problems. Near the end of the long discussion "Of Scepticism with Regard to the Senses," Hume puts away his detachment disarmingly:

> Having given an account of all the systems, both popular and philosophical, with regard to external existence I cannot forbear giving vent to a certain sentiment which arises upon reviewing those systems. I begun this subject with premising that we ought to have an implicit faith in our senses, and that this would be the conclusion I should draw from the whole of my reasoning. But to be ingenuous, I feel myself *at present* of a quite contrary sentiment, and am more inclined to repose no faith at all in my senses, or rather imagination, than to place in it such an implicit confidence. [I, iv, 2; pp. 208–9]

The italics are Hume's and underscore his increasingly dramatic *present*ation of his sentiments at the instant of writing. At this particular instant, Hume allows himself to finish the chapter by arguing that since this "sceptical doubt" is a "malady which can never be radically cured, but must return upon us every moment, however we may chase it away," the only antidotes to the "profound and intense reflection" which give rise to it are "carelessness and inattention." This manner of concluding a difficult argument has much to do with Hume's nineteenth-century reputation as a cynical trifler, but there is no reason to doubt the sincerity—just now—with which he offers his remedies. "For this reason I rely entirely upon them; and take it for granted, whatever may be the reader's opinion at this present moment, that an hour hence he will be persuaded there is both an internal and external world" (I, iv, 2; p. 210).

Hume's rhetoric here becomes the philosophical equivalent of what Richardson would call writing "to the Moment."[4] I do not mean to suggest that *A Treatise of Human Nature* is really the first great English epistolary novel or that it contains urgent sketches of partial perceptions, dashed off breathlessly while a would-be interrupter waits outside the door. Hume never appears to be writing against time (as do Pamela or Clarissa or, later, Tristram Shandy), but he frequently appears to be writing *in* it. Hume shares with Richardson not the drama of potential interruption but the melodrama of momentary intensities, sequences of self-revelatory appeals to the writer's sentiments "at present" as a means of validation.

The melodrama is most complex in the Conclusion to the first book. In a sense it is an emotional rather than a logical completion, since, officially at least, Hume claims already to have "finished" his most critical work at the end of the preceding section. He does not yet seem ready, however, to release his reader or to halt his self-analysis. "But before I launch out into those immense depths of philosophy which lie before me, I find myself inclined to stop a moment in my present station. . . . methinks I am like a man, who having struck on many shoals, and having narrowly escaped shipwreck in passing a small frith, has yet the temerity to put out to sea in the same leaky weather-beaten vessel" (I, iv, 7; p. 249). The oceangoing conceit is conventional enough, but it quickly yields, as Hume decides to allow his "melancholy" its say, to two very powerful dreamlike vignettes. In the first of these Hume presents himself as "affrighted and confounded with that forlorn solitude in which I am placed in my philosophy" and imagines that he has become "some strange uncouth monster, who not being able to mingle and unite in society, has been expelled all human commerce, and left utterly abandoned and disconsolate. Fain would I run into the crowd for shelter and warmth, but cannot prevail with myself to mix with such deformity." These few words encompass

---

[4]For suggestive connections between Hume's theory of belief and later eighteenth-century interest in momentary perceptions, see John A. Dussinger, *The Discourse of the Mind in Eighteenth-Century Fiction* (The Hague: Mouton, 1974), esp. pp. 37–39 and 48–51, and Richard Kuhns, *Structures of Experience: Essays on the Affinity between Philosophy and Literature* (1970; reprint ed., New York: Harper, 1974), pp. 58–68.

a range of literary emotions, stretching from the imaginative starting point of *Robinson Crusoe* to Gulliver at the end of his travels. Hume goes on at this point to picture himself surrounded by controversy: "All the world conspires to oppose and contradict me; though such is my weakness, that I feel all my opinions loosen and fall of themselves, when unsupported by the approbation of others" (I, iv, 7; p. 250).

Between this self-portrait and the following one, Hume appears momentarily to have resolved the problem of the "total scepticism" and solipsism by a naturalistic appeal, that is, by noting that happily it is natural for us in practice to disregard elaborate arguments, however sound. In his later *Enquiry* Hume would say of skeptical arguments, such as Berkeley's, that "they admit of no answer and produce no conviction."[5] Nonetheless, *at this moment*, "Nature" is not so happily protecting the author:

> But what have I here said, that reflections very refined and metaphysical have little or no influence upon us? This opinion I can scarce forbear retracting, and condemning from my present feeling and experience. The *intense* view of these manifold contradictions and imperfections in human reason has so wrought upon me, and heated my brain, that I am ready to reject all belief and reasoning, and can look upon no opinion as even more probable or likely than another. Where am I, or what? From what causes do I derive my existence, and to what condition shall I return? Whose favour shall I court, and whose anger must I dread? What beings surround me? and on whom have I any influence, or who have any influence on me? I am confounded by these questions, and begin to fancy myself in the most deplorable condition imaginable, environed with the deepest darkness, and utterly deprived of the use of every member and faculty. [I, iv, 7; 253–54]

This nightmare of isolation and impotence is dissipated, Hume claims, by dinner, conversation, or a game of backgammon. He immediately labels it a piece of "philosophical melan-

---

[5]*Enquiries Concerning Human Understanding and Concerning the Principles or Morals*, ed. L. A. Selby-Bigge, rev. P. H. Nidditch (London: Oxford University Press, 1975), p. 155n. Parenthetical page and section numbers in text below refer to this edition. Hume's contention that Berkeley's arguments are ultimately skeptical occurs in his note near the end of the first part of section XII of the *Enquiry Concerning Human Understanding*.

choly and delirium," and six years later he was indignant that an opponent should quote this passage without noting that in context it is regarded as a "delusion" and is "positively renounced."[6] Any renunciation Hume may have had in mind is more wishful than real, however, for the simple reason that the "cure" which he attributes to "Nature herself" turns out to be as bad as the disease. If the author recovers the world by walking out of his chamber, he returns not refreshed but disgusted with his reflections, which now "appear so cold, and strained, and ridiculous, that I cannot find it in my heart to enter into them any further." Even having acquiesced in "indolent belief" in the ways of the world, Hume writes, "I still feel such remains of my former disposition, that I am ready to throw all my books and papers into the fire. . . . For these are my sentiments in that splenetic humour which governs me at present" (p. 254).

Feelings such as these are not to be "renounced" by argument, and in fact what Hume presents in the Conclusion is not a repudiation but a phenomenology of doubt. He broods deeply, in his mood of "spleen and indolence," on his identity and vocation as a philosopher: why should he "seclude" himself, "torture" his brain, and wander into "such dreary solitudes"? The resolution of these doubts is more psychological than logical. As he further probes his moods and motives, Hume focuses on a point somewhere between study and conversation. Having left his chamber for society, and now being tired of company, he indulges in a "*reverie* in my chamber, or in a solitary walk by a river side," and it is at such a moment—relaxed but alone—that "I feel my mind all collected within itself, and am naturally *inclined* to carry my view into all those subjects."

I call this resolution psychological because Hume defines his relation toward his reader at this point not in terms of proving his system but as an obligation to explain its genesis: curiosity, concern, ambition "spring up naturally in my present disposition; and should I endeavour to banish them, by attaching myself to any other business or diversion, I *feel* I should be a loser in

---

[6]*A Letter from a Gentleman to his Friend in Edinburgh* (1745), ed. Ernest C. Mossner and John V. Price (Edinburgh: Edinburgh University Press, 1967), p. 20. Hume wrote this defense of the *Treatise* during his unsuccessful candidacy for the chair of ethics and pneumatical philosophy at Edinburgh.

point of pleasure; and this is the origin of my philosophy" (p. 255). Throughout his attempt to conclude this book, Hume moves back and forth uneasily between professions of impersonal high-mindedness and personal low spirits. As he loftily declares "Human Nature" to be the "only science of man" and himself as one whose goal is to bring it into the light, his discourse suddenly plummets to phrases reminiscent of another Swiftian speaker, the narrator of *A Tale of a Tub:* "The hope of this achievement serves to compose my temper from that spleen, and invigorate it from that indolence, which sometimes prevail upon me" (p. 257).[7]

The precariousness of Hume's rhetorical situation is most apparent in such innocent lapses, when the confessional impulse of writing to the moment may suggest the merely momentary self-referential preoccupations of Swift's garreteer rather than the reliable observations of the philosopher in his study. It would be unfair to use Swift "against" the young Hume—his fine-spun parodies of clichés and postures would catch many a more mature author—were it not that Hume was soon to become a writer of ironic capacity close to Swift's own. Whatever the bathetic possibilities of Hume's remark, uttering it seems to enable him at last to conclude. The self-dramatizing writing to the moment turns into a program for thinking to the moment: a willingness to take any felt certainties which come our way regarding "particular points" at a "particular instant" and, more importantly, a readiness to pursue philosophy whenever so "inclined." Should the reader's inclination run otherwise, he is invited to follow it "and wait the returns of application and good humour," for "the conduct of man who studies philosophy in this careless manner, is more truly sceptical than that of one who, feeling in himself an

7Cf., e.g., Swift's narrator's protestation at the end of section VIII of the *Tale* that "I think it one of the greatest, and best of humane Actions, to remove Prejudices, and place Things in their truest and fairest Light; which I therefore boldly undertake without any Regards of my own, beside the Conscience, the Honor, and the Thanks," and his confession at the close of section IX (the Digression concerning Madness) that "even, I my self . . . am a Person, whose Imaginations are hard mouth'd, and exceedingly disposed to run away with his *Reason*, . . . upon which Account, my Friends will never trust me alone, without a solemn Promise, to vent my Speculations in this, or the like manner, for the universal Benefit of Human kind . . . " (*A Tale of a Tub,* ed. A. C. Guthkelch and D. Nicol Smith, 2d ed. [Oxford: Clarendon Press, 1958], pp. 161, 180).

inclination to it, is yet so overwhelmed with doubts and scruples, as totally to reject it" (pp. 257–58).

Here Hume has managed to evolve a rationale for and a re-definition of "carelessness," a more serious carelessness than backgammon and more responsive to one's "present view" (p. 258) than systematically careful application. Carelessness is not, in this reformulation, simply a concession to one's weakness or spleen but the most appropriate way for a skeptic to do philosophy. Like the solitary walk or indulgent reverie, it is the closest thing to a "method" for an essentially unmethodological problem, namely how to restore and to focus one's energy.

The selection of passages examined so far should suggest that Hume's sylistic self-presentation, if not an aspect of his philosophy which philosophers normally discuss, is nonetheless an interesting condition for it and an important clue to his development as a philosophic writer. His self-consciousness regarding the strangely anonymous but private relationship between himself as author (at his table, facing the fire) and his reader (for whom the *Treatise* will be a series of "faint images") is reflected most clearly in the moments of self-dramatization and writing to the moment which occur throughout Book I of the *Treatise* and culminate in its Conclusion. It must be conceded at once, however, that these melodramatic moments are not entirely typical and that we have been concentrating on the more conspicuously autobiographical sections and ignoring most of the book. But it is interesting that in his later attempt to make the treatise more literally attractive, Hume omitted all of these passages. He cannot have omitted them for the same reason that he excised or compressed several of his more technical arguments. Why, then, did he do so?

We are dealing with motives and an image of self which may well have remained partly unconscious, but I believe that when Hume revised his *Treatise* a decade later he very likely heard in it a voice which did not accord with his own ideals of discourse, with his developing sense of how best to speak to an invisible audience and of how best to write philosophy. Moreover, it is a voice which he would have had good personal reason to suppress, which perhaps helps explain his insistence later in life that the *Treatise* should not be taken as representative of his thought.

30

Hume, as we have seen, resolves the first book of his *Treatise* by locating the "origin" of his philosophy in his temperament. We can follow his lead and go one step further in order to see the emergence of his particular kind of philosophy against a background of particular psychological circumstances.

Carelessness and Crisis

In 1734 Hume wrote a long letter to the famous Dr. Arbuthnot describing an episode, somewhat analogous to John Stuart Mill's, of depression and mental inertia. Hume explains his sudden alternation from intellectual optimism to apathy.

> After much Study, & Reflection . . . when I was about 18 years of Age, there seem'd to be open'd up to me a new Scene of Thought, which transported me beyond Measure, & made me, with an Ardor natural to young men, throw up every Pleasure or Business to apply entirely to it. . . I was infinitely happy in this Course of Life for some Months; till at last, about the beginning of September 1729, all my Ardor seem'd in a moment to be extinguisht, & I cou'd no longer raise my Mind to that pitch, which formerly gave me such excessive Pleasure. I felt no Uneasyness or Want of Spirits, when I laid aside my Book; & therefore never imagind there was any bodily Distemper in the Case, but that my Coldness proceeded from a Laziness of Temper, which must be overcome by redoubling my Application. In this Condition I remain'd for nine Months, very uneasy to myself, as you may well imagine, but without growing any worse, which was a Miracle.[8]

Hume naturally describes his condition in terms of "the spleen" rather than in Victorian or modern terms of "crisis"; but like Mill he reaches ruefully for a religious analogy, comparing his situation with the "Coldness and Desertion of the Spirit" frequently described in the autobiographies of the "French Mysticks" and "our Fanatics here." Hume has no doubt that his

[8]For the complete letter see *The Letters of David Hume*, ed. J. Y. T. Greig (Oxford: Clarendon Press, 1932), I, 12–18. The circumstances surrounding its writing and the identification of Arbuthnot rather than George Cheyne as the intended recipient are discussed by Ernest Mossner in "Hume's Epistle to Dr. Arbuthnot, 1734: The Biographical Significance," *HLQ*, 7 (1943): 135–52, and *The Life of David Hume*, 2d ed. (Oxford: Clarendon Press, 1980), pp. 83–85.

"distemper," whether bodily or not, is secular, but he regards his own "coldness" or "weakness" of spirits as a reaction to the "warmth or Enthusiasm" caused by overstrenuous meditation.

> I was continually fortifying myself with Reflections against Death, & Poverty, & Shame, & Pain, & all the other Calamities of Life. These no doubt are exceeding useful, when join'd with an active Life; because the Occasion being presented along with the Reflection, works it into the Soul, & makes it take a deep Impression, but in Solitude they serve to little other Purpose, than to waste the Spirits, the Force of the Mind meeting with no Resistance, but wasting itself in the Air, like our Arm when it misses its Aim.

This letter apparently was never sent, probably, as Ernest Mossner cogently suggests, because the act of writing it was therapeutic in itself.[9] Reviewing it, Hume might see that he had already answered several of his questions about the possibility of a cure. He has resolved on his own to diversify his study with a "more active Life" of "Business and Diversion," and he has previously discovered the usefulness of studying more "moderately, and only when I found my Spirits at their highest Pitch, leaving off before I was weary, and trifling away the rest of my Time in the best manner I could."

Both the dilemmas and the solutions which Hume describes in this account are reenacted in the course of the first book of his *Treatise,* particularly in the Conclusion. There, as in his letter to Arbuthnot, the feelings of isolation and "forlorn solitude," of intellectual impotence and cold disgust, are introspectively orchestrated and are resolved into a program of relaxation and "careless" pursuit, of following one's inclination and waiting for good humor to return. Far from trifling, Hume is struggling to transform what he at first regarded as weakness and laziness in himself into a way—the best, most "truly sceptical" way—of philosophic behavior.

The emphasis of the Conclusion is a long way from the point

9Mossner, *Life,* p. 86. John A. Dussinger discusses the letter from a psychoanalytic standpoint in "David Hume's Denial of Personal Identity: The Making of a Skeptic," *American Imago,* 37 (1980): 334–50, questioning Mossner's interpretation of its "cathartic" effect as final (pp. 341–43).

where the *Treatise* began, with images of military marches upon the citadel, promises of a complete system of the sciences, and the immediate bifurcation of experience into impressions and ideas. The Conclusion does not, however, bring to a full stop Hume's more doggedly systematic analysis, his hierarchical arrangement of the *Treatise* as a whole (into books, parts, and sections), or his reliance upon dichotomies—a fondness for the "bipolar oppositions" which Earl Wasserman has described as characteristic of the era.[10] Just after the Conclusion, for example, the reader arrives at Hume's discussion of the passions in Book II and finds a virtual banquet of two-pronged forks: mental experience divides into ideas and impressions, impressions into those of sensation and those of reflection, impressions of reflection into the calm of the violent; and finally, the violent reflective impressions may be either direct or indirect. It is difficult to imagine a more cumbersome taxonomy (joy, for example, would be a direct violent reflective impression) or to believe that Hume's dogmatism of the dichotomy does not represent an earlier stage of his thinking than the Conclusion of Book I, which precedes it. If the Conclusion were in fact written late, this fact would help explain why its prescriptions seem to have had so little influence on the shape of most of the remainder of the *Treatise*. Whatever the actual stages of composition, one frequently feels throughout the *Treatise* a tension between (to indulge in still another dichotomy) some of Hume's most fluidly introspective descriptions of experience and his insistence upon the solidity of distinctions in experience.

The most basic of these distinctions involves impressions and ideas, to which I would now like to return because it is the starting point which commits Hume to certain concerns and procedures and because I believe the analogy between it and Hume's account of his "distemper" may again be instructive. Impressions are primary perceptions, such as sensations or emotions; ideas are "faint images of these in thinking and reasoning." When we look at an object or feel pain, we have an impression; when we close our eyes and recall the object or the pain, we have an idea. For Hume, ideas are always ideas *of* something;

[10]"Johnson's Rasselas: Implicit Contexts," *JEGP*, 74 (1975): 1–25.

specifically, they are ideas of impressions. An idea of pain may in fact cause new pain, which Hume would then call an "impression of reflection," but we need not follow Hume past his initial dichotomy to sense a problem. Although Hume declares impressions and ideas to be two "distinct kinds" of perceptions, the distinction is a matter of degree, namely "the degrees of force and liveliness, with which they strike upon the mind" (I, i, 1; pp. 11–14). The distinction is obvious, Hume says, and need not be labored. "Everyone of himself will readily perceive the difference betwixt feeling and thinking" (p. 11).

This statement is hardly as clear as Hume would have it. If we frequently "perceive" such a distinction, presumably we should be able to say whether we think it or feel it, rather than having to use the word which covers both experiences. Hume is willing to allow that the distinction may be problematic in exceptional cases: "Thus, in sleep, in a fever, in madness, or in any very violent emotions of the soul, our ideas may approach to our impressions: as, on the other hand, it sometimes happens, that our impressions are so faint and low, that we cannot distinguish them from our ideas." Unlike Locke, however, Hume is not inclined to regard exceptional cases as relevant, and he resorts to insisting that the two experiences are "in general so very different" that surely "no one can make a scruple" to distinguish them categorically (I, i, 1; pp. 11–12).[11]

Now, Hume's own lack of "scruple" at this point is enough unlike his usual meticulous meeting of foreseeable objections to make one wonder why so conspicuous a blind spot should occur just here. It seems to me that there are two general ways to approach the question, and they need not be mutually exclusive. The first would stress the philosophic tradition Hume inherits and would see this dichotomy as forced upon him by a basically materialistic orientation or, perhaps more particularly, as merely a displaced version of a distinction which influenced Hume

[11]Commenting on Locke's discussion of an acquaintance who was persuaded that "his had been the *soul* of Socrates" (*Essay*, II, xxvii, 14), Antony Flew observes that Locke "seems to have been the first to appreciate the relevance of such puzzle cases." Flew's essay, "Locke and the Problem of Personal Identity," first appeared in *Philosophy*, 26 (1951), and is reprinted in revised form in C. B. Martin and D. M. Armstrong, eds., *Locke and Berkeley: A Collection of Critical Essays* (London: Macmillan, n.d.): 154–78; see esp. pp. 157–58.

more than he knew, that between "primary" and "secondary" qualities. But a more personal approach leads to a simpler-minded yet perhaps clearer question: whether Hume, in light of his condition during much of the formulation of the *Treatise,* is not protesting too much? The difference between thinking and feeling seems to have been deeply problematic for Hume at this spiritless period of his life, as was the distinction between impressions and ideas. Passages from the old moral philosophers, he tells Arbuthnot, might make a "deep Impression" on a reader leading an active life, but in solitude such as his own, they "serve to little other Purpose, than to waste the Spirits, the Force of the Mind meeting with no Resistance, but wasting itself in the Air, like our Arm when it misses its Aim." In short, the condition which Hume in the *Treatise* dismisses as a temporary or irrelevant aberration—the effect of fever or madness, for example— characterizes his mental state for some time just before he dismisses it in print. Whatever else it may be, this declaration is a piece of wishful thinking, or wishful feeling.

Before deciding what the biographical connection has to tell us, we need to recall the internal relation of Hume's categorical distinction between impressions and ideas to a second distinction, between memory and imagination, which leads in turn to what Hume himself considered most original in the *Treatise,* his discussion of belief. "Imagination" is a very elastic term in Hume, stretching at times to become the apparent basis of all experience. When opposed to memory, however, imagination belongs to the realm of fiction (the "loose reveries of a castle-builder"), while memory is truth. Like impressions as compared with ideas, memories are more "lively," have more force than imaginings. The latter we merely entertain, but the memories we believe. When we believe something, Hume says, running out of terms, it "*feels* different," and this "different feeling I endeavour to explain by calling it a superior *force,* or *vivacity,* or *solidity,* or *firmness,* or *steadiness*" (I, iii, 7; p. 120). The conversion of an idea of imagination into a memory begins in fact to sound like a religious conversion experience: "the very same ideas now appear in a new light, and have, in a manner, a different feeling from what they had before" (I, iii, 5; p. 88).

The remarkable similarity between Hume's formulation of

belief and his personal preoccupation with vivacity, with the lack of firmness or solidity in his own experience—the "Force of the Mind meeting with no Resistance, but wasting itself in the Air"—is instructive in at least three ways. To begin with, it offers an interesting example of the intersection of historical and personal requirements in the formulation of hypotheses, an intersection somewhat analogous to T. S. Eliot's declaration of a "dissociation of sensibility" in literary history (a separation, in fact, of thought and feeling) at a time when his own sensibility seems to have been most dissociated. A theory should not, of course, be discarded because it happens to have been therapeutic for the theorist. Neither of these theories occurs in a vacuum: the influence of each can be seen as jointly sponsored by the recent past of the group (the shared assumptions which make the formulation possible), by the author's personal present (which makes it necessary), and by the future readers who agree to find it therapeutic for them as well (which makes it historically significant).

A second and perhaps more manageable lesson to be read from the relation of Hume's state to his statements concerns the rhetoric of Book I of the *Treatise* itself. It helps explain why, despite all Hume's apparently strict organization, the subject of belief keeps appearing throughout the book. Officially Hume devotes two chapters (I, iii, 7–8) to an analysis of the causes and effects of belief, but attempts at such an analysis are everywhere, from the earliest sections to the final chapter on personal identity, and as we have seen, Hume is still seeking to describe accurately the feeling of belief in the conclusion. Even the appendix to Book III circles back for a last look at the "greater firmness and solidity" of the "objects of conviction." At such points Hume most feels and shows linguistic strain, complaining of the limitations of "common language" (I, iii, 8; p. 107).

A third direction indicated by Hume's crisis leads us to consider the implications of making vivacity the criterion of belief for Hume's rhetorical conduct after the *Treatise*. Vivacity, as Hume conceives it, is necessarily a temporary feeling, defined largely by its difference from the faintness, or weakness, or lowness, which it replaces when we come to believe something. We have seen how in his personal development Hume found it necessary to shorten his periods of concentration in order to avoid losing

conviction all together. We see in the *Treatise* a nagging suspicion
that prolonged and abstruse arguments may, despite their inge-
nuity or integrity, fail not only to be believed but to be believ-
able, according to the criterion Hume himself has established.
Difficult problems require rigor, belief requires vigor, and within the framework of the *Treatise* these two characteristics are not
easily reconciled. If Hume is to act as a writer on his own recommendation, to follow shifting inclination and to philosophize in a
vividly "careless" manner, then he will need to abandon the
treatise for the essay as his most appropriate form and to surrender his defensive distrust of "eloquence" for a new rhetoric.

The *Essays* and Eloquence

Hume's work immediately after the *Treatise* is the two-volume
collection *Essays, Moral, Political, and Literary,* published in 1741
and 1742. When he recast the first book of the *Treatise* for publication in 1748, he called the new work *Philosohpical Essays Concerning Human Understanding.* The similarity to Locke's title—
Hume later altered it to *An Enquiry,* perhaps to mark his distance—is less significant formally than the difference; Hume's
work is not an essay but a dozen essays, many of which are
comparatively self-contained. It has been suggested that Locke's
use of the work "essay" is the first step in a rhetoric of humility;[12] Hume's use of "essays" announces a series of short, accessible works in the same genre with which he had identified himself at the start of the decade in his bid for common readers.
  Several of Hume's earliest essays are concerned with problems
of style and with the form itself. In the Addisonian and affable
"Of Essay Writing," Hume proposes to use his essays, perhaps
on a periodical basis, to help unite the "learned" and "conversible" worlds. This echoes the *Spectator* program for bringing philosophy out of colleges and into coffeehouses, but it is interesting to see Hume so shortly after the *Treatise* offering himself as
an ambassador from the learned land of solitude and severe
labor, whose scholarly inhabitants fall prey to their "moping
recluse method of study" and to "chimerical' conclusions unless

---

[12]Colie, "The Essayist in His Essay," pp. 237–42.

they maintain full diplomatic relations with polite society.[13] According to Mossner, Hume's claim that the "balance of trade" between the two countries will be equal is more gallant than accurate, but it seems that Hume is bringing to the problem a personal need which Addison did not share and that for him the project is not so much how to philosophize society as how to socialize the philosopher.[14]

Hume in any case goes out of his way in these essays to become an eminently sociable creature, leaving far behind him any traces of that "forlorn solitude" and the picture of himself as a "strange uncouth monster" in the conclusion of Book I of the *Treatise*. In "Of the Dignity of Meanness of Human Nature," the essayist comes down cheerfully on the dignified side, casting a benevolist eye, for example, even on the motives of the anti-benevolists. Far from attributing "any bad intention" to the harsher critics, Hume says, he understands that a "delicate sense of morals, especially when attended with a splenetic temper, is apt to give a man a disgust of the world, and to make him consider the course of human affairs with too much indignation." In this statement and in the essay as a whole, Hume is at once disowning and sentimentalizing his own posture of alienation from "all human commerce" in the conclusion of the *Treatise,* where he had written, "Fain would I run into the crowd for shelter and warmth, but cannot prevail with myself to mix with such deformity." But the maneuver in this essay which most reveals Hume's stylistic reorientation is his decision to begin the analysis of this perennial debate from a fundamentally literary standpoint. It is not religion or philosophy which separates those who praise human nature from those who blame it but stylistic disposition: "If an author possess the talent of rhetoric and declamation, he commonly takes part with the former: if his turn lie toward irony and ridicule, he naturally throws himself onto the other extreme."

[13]"Of Essay Writing" appeared in the second volume (1742) of *Essays* and was not reprinted by Hume thereafter. See *The Philosophical Works*, ed. T. H. Green and T. H. Grose, Vol. 3 (London, 1882), pp. 42–44, and (for the essay) 4:367–70. For the essays quoted in the following paragraphs, "Of the Dignity or Meanness of Human Nature" and "Of Eloquence," see 3:150–56 and 163–74.
[14]Mossner, *Life*, p. 142.

Now, the cool quickness of this reduction might cause us to expect aloof neutrality from our author, unless its fine irony suggests such an aptitude for ridicule that deflation of the claims of "dignity" is sure to follow. In fact, either expectation proves wrong, and Hume proceeds to argue for the most generous interpretation of human motivation. In doing so he allies himself not only with the benevolists but with "rhetoric and declamation" as well. We can note another influential dichotomy here in Hume's separation of rhetoric from ridicule. Traditionally rhetoric had been regarded as the art of praise and blame; by making it the art of praise, Hume signals both the general distrust of satire which begins to appear in the mid-eighteenth century and his personal conception of eloquence as something salutary and uplifting.

Hume's essay "Of Eloquence" looks nostalgically to ancient oratory, comparing its sublimity and pathos with the "mediocrity" of modern discourse. Contemporary eloquence at its best is like Attic oratory—"calm, elegant, and subtile, which instructed the reason more than affected the passions"—but this is a mode much inferior to the more passionately elevated style which "commanded the resolution" of the hearers of Demosthenes or Cicero. The best eloquence is the most powerful, and Hume's real question is why advances in learning have not brought more rhetorical strength; for "if we be superior in philosophy, we are still, notwithstanding all our refinements, much inferior in eloquence." Why should so much knowledge, as Wordsworth would put it, be purchased with the loss of power?[15] Hume never poses the question directly here (it occupies a larger place in the essays on "refinement" and "progress" in the arts), but his notion of ancient oratory suggests that an answer must lie in the problem of belief. The "vehemence" of old depended not on "artifice" but on conviction: "The orator, by the force of his own genius and eloquence, first enflamed himself with anger, indignation, pity, sorrow; and then communicated those impetuous movements to his audience." If modern

[15]*The Prelude* (1850), V, 423–25: "May books and Nature be their early joy! / And knowledge, rightly honoured with that name— / Knowledge not purchased by the loss of power!"

39

speakers have less command and authority in their speeches, it would seem to be because they have less belief in their ideas.

Belief in ideas, the central problem of the *Treatise*, is central as well, then, to much of Hume's literary theory and practice as an essayist. The most conspicuous change is in the upward valuation of eloquence—disdained at the outset of the *Treatise* as mere color and trumpetry—to a cultural and personal ideal. Far from interfering with truth, eloquence is now nearly its test. This is a dramatic shift in the space of a few years, and I do not believe that Hume ever quite made up his mind on the subject. But it does not seem that his praise of eloquence in the essays can be regarded simply as the protestation of the would-be man of letters, a writer whose ambition is now primarily literary rather than philosophic and who is thus prepared to abandon truth for popularity.

Hume's concern for the success of his works no doubt had much to do with authorial vanity, but it is also congruent with his theory of belief. If one side of Hume's skepticism leads him to distrust popular views, another side logically leads him to question whether any view which cannot be rendered with enough vivacity or force to win belief can be true. Elaborated without qualification, this question could lead to the position that the most popular statements must be the truest. That Hume never seriously entertains such a position indicates that he continued to regard philosophy as distinct from oratory, where the position *does* apply, since there is no such thing as a great but unpopular orator. The orator's business is to move masses, here and now; but in other areas of aesthetic activity, Hume does not hesitate to designate a less democratic jury the "fit judges" of polite society and sufficient education. But just as clearly, the fit judges are not to be drawn only from the ranks of the "learned" and must include most of the "conversible" world as well. Very quickly after the *Treatise*, Hume begins to broaden his idea of the audience he feels his philosophy not only could have but should have. When he comes to recast it as the "Philosophical Essays" later in the decade, it is not surprising that he begins from a profoundly literary point of view. Gone is the defensiveness of his earlier remarks on eloquence; gone, too, is the priority given

to the "distinct" dichotomy of impressions and ideas. In their
stead is a preliminary distinction of another order, a discussion
of two different ways of writing philosophy.

The Style of the *Enquiries*

The two kinds of moral philosophy which Hume first divides
according to their "manner" also differ in their emphases. The
"easy and obvious" philosophy, which includes most of traditional ethics, considers man "chiefly as born for action; and as
influenced in his measures by taste and sentiment," while the
"accurate and abstruse" philosophy ("or what is commonly
called metaphysics") studies man primarily as a "reasonable
rather than an active being," endeavoring to "form his understanding more than cultivate his manners" (*Enquiry Concerning
Human Understanding*, I; pp. 5–6). The distinction is less invidious than it sounds, despite Hume's own announced focus on
the understanding. "Easy" is no longer the loaded word it was in
the *Treatise,* and "abstruse" turns out not to be honorific; after
this initial description Hume stops applying "abstruse" to what he
is doing—retaining "accurate," of course, and occasionally im-
porting "profound"—and links it instead with the pseudophilos-
ophy and "metaphysical jargon" of superstitious web-spinners
(I; p. 12).

The distinction actually seems weighted in favor of the "easy"
philosopher. He deals in "colors," to be sure, and borrows all he
can from "eloquence and poetry"; but if Hume in the *Treatise*
harbored a residual Presbyterian distrust of music and painting
in the temple of philosophy, he is now high church by comparison. Not only does the easy philosopher, Hume says, usually
gain more fame but he deserves it, for he generally falls into
fewer "dangerous illusions." Hume's examples of the two traditions are revealing: "The fame of Cicero flourishes at present;
but that of Aristotle is utterly decayed. La Bruyère passes the
seas, and still maintains his reputation: But the glory of Male-
branche is confined to his own nation, and to his own age. And
Addison, perhaps, will be read with pleasure, when Locke shall
be entirely forgotten" (I; p. 7).

Much can be said on the other side (anatomy is less elegant than painting, for example, but useful in its own right and useful for painters), but what is interesting is how undefensively Hume asserts his view. Perhaps the most notable claim made for the "easy" philosophy is that "it enters more into common life; moulds the heart and affections; and, by touching those principles which actuate men, reforms their conduct." It sounds, in other words, very much like belief; meanwhile its speculative counterpart "vanishes when the philosopher leaves the shade, and comes into open day" (I; p. 7).

But Hume's project in the *Enquiries* is to reconcile the "speculative" and "active" philosophic traditions, much as he had undertaken to join the "learned" and "conversible" worlds in his earlier essays, a project he now urges in high oratorical style: "Happy, if we can unite the boundaries of the different species of philosophy, by reconciling profound enquiry with clearness, and truth with novelty! And still more happy, if, reasoning in this easy manner, we can undermine the foundations of an abstruse philosophy, which seems to have hitherto served only as a shelter to superstition, and a cover to absurdity and error!" (I; p. 16). Despite such rhetorical flourishes (section VIII, for example, ends with a nearly identical "Happy if" peroration), Hume's suspicion of eloquence reappears at intervals to the end of the *Enquiry Concerning Human Understanding* and in the *Enquiry Concerning the Principles of Morals*. Passages of deliberately enthusiastic writing and bids for the approbation of "the public" (IV; p. 26) exist side by side with sarcastic dismissals of the "eloquence" which "every *Capuchin,* every itinerant or stationary teacher" can use to sway his believers (X; p. 118) and with recommendations that the sensible philosopher leave the "more sublime topics" to the "embellishment of poets and orators, or to the arts of priests and politicians" (XII; p. 162).

But Cicero, La Bruyère, and Addison are hardly Capuchins for Hume, and his attitude toward them and their "manner" of philosophy is steadily wistful and at times frankly imitative. The essential role of the "easy" philosopher who considers man as an "active" being is to paint amiable pictures of virtue and thus to engage our affections for it (I; p. 5), precisely what Hume claims to have accomplished at the end of the second *Enquiry:*

But what philosophical truths can be more advantageous to society, than those here delivered, which represent virtue in all her genuine and most engaging charms, and make us approach her with ease, familiarity, and affection? The dismal dress falls off, with which many divines, and some philosophers have covered her; and nothing appears but gentleness, humanity, beneficence, affability; nay, even at proper intervals, play, frolic, and gaiety. [*Enquiry Concerning the Principles of Morals,* IX, part ii; p. 279]

In terms of Hume's own dichotomy of discourse his problem is simple enough. He aspires to make his main contribution to "speculative" philosophy, yet he wants to write like a "practical" philosopher. According to his speculative principles, eloquence has the unfortunate quality of appealing to the "affections" rather than the "understanding," and he must therefore indulge in ritual disavowals of it. But in fact Hume's problem runs deeper because his philosophy leaves less and less room in which to "consider man as a speculative being" and progressively emphasizes the "active" being. As early as Book II of the *Treatise*, Hume had declared that "reason is, and ought only to be, the slave of the passions" (II, iii, 3), but the real undermining of the function of "speculative" discourse comes at the end of the first *Enquiry:* "Morals and criticism are not so properly objects of the understanding as of taste and sentiment" (XII, part iii; p. 165).

This reformulation of what moral philosophy is properly about is more radical than Hume seems fully to have recognized, given his persistence in dividing rhetoric and truth in the second *Enquiry;* but it is compatible with a subtle and profound shift of metaphorical emphasis which begins to occur early in the *Enquiries.* Put most simply, Hume's movement toward the "active" philosophy begins in the first *Enquiry* with the use of more active metaphors than appear in the *Treatise.* Whereas the *Treatise* depended heavily from the outset on a theory of mental imagery, the *Enquiry* begins from a conception of mental operations, "acts of the mind." We can think of this provisionally as a change from a philosophy based on "perceptions" to one based on "conceptions," though it must be granted at once that Hume uses the terms somewhat interchangeably. The characteristic metaphor of the *Treatise,* however, construes mind as a passive object, upon which, for example, some impressions "strike" with more force, while in the *Enquiry* mind implicitly becomes an active subject, "taking hold" of some perceptions more firmly than others. One pair of contrasting descriptions may suggest the role of style in the earlier and later formulations. First, from the *Treatise:*

> The mind is excited by the lively impression, and this vivacity is conveyed to the related idea, without any great dimunition in the passage. . . . Our memory presents us with a vast number of instances of perceptions perfectly resembling each other. . . . If sometimes we ascribe a continued existence to objects, which are perfectly new to us, of whose constancy and coherence we have no experience, it is because the manner in which they present themselves to our senses, resembles that of constant and coherent objects. . . . The imagination is seduced into such an opinion only by means of the resemblance of certain perceptions. [I, iv, 2; pp. 201–2]

From the *Enquiry Concerning Human Understanding:*

> The *imagination* of man is naturally sublime, delighted with whatever is remote and extraordinary, and running, without control, into the most distant parts of space and time in order to avoid the objects, which custom has rendered too familiar to it. A correct *Judgement* observes a contrary methods, and avoiding all distant and high enquiries, confines itself to common life. . . .
>
> Reason here seems to be thrown into a kind of amazement and suspence, which . . . gives her a diffidence of herself, and of the ground on which she treads. She sees a full light, which illuminates certain places; but that light borders upon the most profound darkness. And between these she is so dazzled and confounded, that she scarcely can pronounce with certainty and assurance concerning any one subject. [XII, parts ii–iii; pp. 157–162]

The most significant features are the prevalence of passive grammatical constructions in the first passage and the tendency toward personification in the second. In the section from the *Treatise,* things impinge upon the subject. In the *Enquiry* the mind's "powers" are personal agents, whether technically neuter, as in the case of imagination and judgment, or ironically feminine, as in the brief allegory of reason. Personification is for Hume an important way to make his writing not only more "literary" but more "active" or "practical" or "easy." As he gravitates toward the ideal of a more sociable prose, Hume moves as well toward a less passive and solitary description of mind.

The shift is fundamentally metaphorical, and it is not clear how consciously Hume made it when he began the *Enquiries*. His distinction between impressions and ideas is in many ways identical to the corresponding discussion in the *Treatise*. But at least two significant differences in his rhetorical posture prepare the ground for a less static and passive conception of mental behavior. The first is Hume's confident alignment with Newton, not simply as an "experimental" heir of Bacon but as the discoverer of principles of *motion*. "At last," Hume writes, a philosopher arose who "determined the laws and forces, by which the revolutions of the planets are governed and directed. . . . And there is no reason to despair of equal success in our enquiries concerning the mental powers and economy." Hume had spoken of the mind's "powers" earlier, but it is revealing to compare this phrase —"mental powers and *economy*"—with its closest counterpart in the introduction to the *Treatise*, where Hume refers to the difficulty of knowing the mind's "powers and *qualities*." The atomistic emphasis of the earlier work, where the mind finally is a bundle of perceptions, begins to yield to an implicit model of mind as an integrated system, its several "operations" all existing as "forces" of a single "economy."[16] The second important shift in direction is Hume's casual use (beginning with section II of the *Enquiry Concerning Human Understanding*) of the word "sentiment" as a synonym for "impression." As long as Hume continues to speak only of impressions, the mind is wholly a thing to be "impressed" from without; "sentiments," however, suggests an important change of focus away from the supposed atoms of experience to an experiencing mind, actively grasping its world.[17] In the *Treatise* the word appeared only in the sense of "moral sentiments," that is, as virtually instinctive aesthetic judg-

[16]For these phrases see especially section I of the *Enquiry Concerning Human Understanding*, pp. 13–14.

[17]In "'Sentiment': Some Uses of the Word in the Writings of David Hume," R. F. Brissenden points out that Hume employed the term in ambiguous and sometimes contradictory senses, especially in *An Enquiry Concerning the Principles of Morals;* see Brissenden, ed., *Studies in the Eighteenth Century* (Toronto: University of Toronto Press, 1968), pp. 89–107.

ments. By bringing it into play much earlier in his analysis of experience, Hume now suggests that experience may be selective and judgmental at even the most basic level.

It is difficult to know whether these shifts are entirely conscious. Hume either does not recognize or does not choose to point out, for example, a significant technical change in which belief, awkwardly but consistently an "idea" in the *Treatise,* suddenly becomes the "sentiment of belief."[18] The implications of this change are fully apparent only at the close of the second *Enquiry,* where it is clear that the logic of Hume's analysis would move nearly all mental activity from the realm of reason to that of "taste": "The former conveys the knowledge of truth and falsehood: the latter gives the sentiment of beauty and deformity, vice and virtue. The one discovers objects as they really stand in nature, without addition or diminution: the other has a productive faculty, and gilding or staining all natural objects with the colours, borrowed from internal sentiment, raises in a manner a new creation" (appendix I; p. 294). To appreciate how far that statement is from the world of the *Treatise,* we need only compare with it a description in similar language from the earlier work, of a faculty which "opens a world of its own, and presents us with scenes, and beings, and objects, which are altogether new" (I, iv, 7). The "productive" faculty so described in the *Treatise,* however, is not taste but superstition.

The similarity is not one with which Hume would be pleased. Had it been pointed out, he might have attempted a distinction between superstition and taste along the lines of his characterization of societal virtues such as justice (*Treatise,* III, ii, 1), that is, that taste may be "artificial" without being "arbitrary." But this position is easier to defend when "artificial" can plainly mean "in accord with human nature as manifested in society" than when the phenomenon under analysis is taken to be a

[18]*Enquiry Concerning Human Understanding,* section V, part II, esp. pp. 48–50. When Hume argues that the ideas of belief "take faster hold of my mind, than ideas of an enchanted castle" (p. 50), he relapses momentarily into the "passive" model of mental experience used in the *Treatise;* but in most of his accounts in the *Enquiry,* it is the mind which takes hold of ideas rather than the other way around. Belief is, for example, a "process of the mind," a "progress of the mind," an "operation of the soul," and an "act of the mind" (*Enquiry Concerning Human Understanding,* section IV, part II, pp. 33, 37, and section V, part II, pp. 46, 49).

"power" or "operation" of the individual mind. We have already seen how in the *Treatise* Hume's emphasis on the "vivacity" of belief leads to a quasi-religious description of conviction as a change of view in which things suddenly appear "in a new light." But the difference between a new light and the new creation now attributed to "taste" is one which Hume had wrestled to maintain in the *Treatise* in distinguishing legitimate belief from poetry and madness, conditions similar to each other in that the "vivacity they bestow on ideas is not derived from the particular situations or connections of the objects of these ideas, but from the present temper and disposition of the person" (I, iii, 10). The distinction presupposes a knowledge of "objects" which Hume had already foreclosed, so it is not surprising that this untenable dichotomy was eliminated in the *Enquiries*.

The problem it was meant to dispose of remains, however, and Hume's deepest recognition of it in his work may lie in the rules he establishes for his discourse in the *Enquiries,* where madness and poetry are no longer uttered in the same breath. From the "carelessness" and pursuit of "inclination" recommended for therapeutic reasons in the conclusion of the *Treatise,* Hume moves, in the opening chapter of the first *Enquiry,* to a statement of procedures grounded on essentially artistic intuition. The conventional "eye" cannot distinguish on its own the dynamic "faculties," the "powers," and "operations of the mind" which we most wish to study: "The objects are too fine to remain long in the same aspect or situation; and must be apprehended in an instant, by a superior penetration, derived from nature, and improved by habit and reflexion" (I; p. 13). Hume's description of the work and the worker sounds like a description of poetry and the poet. "In all abstract reasonings there is one point of view which, if we can happily hit, we shall go farther towards illuminating the subject than by all the eloquence and copious expression in the world" (VII; p. 79).[19]

This surprising claim comes close to saying that there is only one way to express the truth, that manner and matter cannot be

---

[19]Hume's description is particularly close to Pope's emphasis, in the *Epistle to Cobham* and the *Epistle to a Lady,* on the quick perception and "flying stroke" as preferable to "sedate reflections" in the analysis and representation of human motivation.

separated. Despite his pejorative use of the word "eloquence" here, Hume is actually providing his rationale for a different eloquence, one quicker, easier, and therefore more accurate. Hume is still writing to the moment, but it is now the reader's moment rather than his own, that "one point" or happy hit which is not exhaustive but suggestive. However much Hume's "easy" manner in the essays comprising the *Enquiries* may be calculated to catch a wider audience, its suppleness, deliberate brevity, and penetrating grace are designed as well to catch the fine and elusive acts of minds.

Hume's shift of emphasis in the *Enquiries* is major, and as a philosophy of mind it suggests at least a partial anticipation of Reid's objections (launched in the 1760s and directed entirely at the *Treatise*) that Hume lacks an adequate theory of concept formation.[20] The shift seems to have been made, however, largely in response to literary needs. As Hume's ideas of audience and eloquence change, his philosophic formulations tilt toward the "easy" or "active" philosophy which is likelier to secure and sustain belief. The belief in question is that not only of the audience but of the author as well.

For our purposes, then, Reid's criticism of Hume's logic is less interesting than his response to Hume's voice, when he observes laconically, "It is probable that the 'Treatise of Human Nature' was not written in company."[21] The *Enquiries* are written in company in the sense that Hume's overtures to his audience's requirements take the place of his solitary self-dramatization. The direction of Hume's rhetorical career is steadily toward "company" and away from the "chamber" which had dominated and perhaps focused the "new scene of thought" that Hume discovered at eighteen. In that chamber, he had complained, the "Force of the Mind" wasted itself because it met with "no Re-

[20]For a discussion of concept formation and Reid's attack on earlier versions, see Norman Daniels, *Thomas Reid's "Inquiry": The Geometry of Visibles and the Case for Realism* (New York: Burt Franklin, 1974), esp. chap. 4.

[21]Reid, *An Inquiry into the Human Mind* (1974), chap. 1, sec. v: "It is probable that the 'Treatise of Human Nature' was not written in company; yet it contains manifest indications that the author every now and then relapsed into the faith of the vulgar, and could hardly, for half a dozen pages, keep up the sceptical character."

sistance." The young Scot who warmed himself by a French fire to write the *Treatise of Human Nature* became the historian of England, finding in the recalcitrance of historical documents something to resist the mind.

CHAPTER 2

William Law and the "Fiction of Behaviour"

Theophilus: Everything, Academicus, is, and must be, its own
Proof. . . . Life, and every Kind and Degree of Life, is only known
by Life; and so far as Life reaches, so far is there Knowledge, and
no further. . . For nothing that is brought into the Mind from
without, or is only an Idea beheld by our reasoning Faculty, is any
more *our Knowledge,* than the seeing our natural Face in a Glass, is
seeing our *own Selves.* . . . for Knowledge can only be yours, as
Sickness and Health is yours, not conveyed into you by a Hearsay
Notion, but the Fruit of your own Perception and Sensibility of
that which you are, and that which you have in yourself.
William Law, *The Way to Divine Knowledge* (1752)

So playful are the ways of fame to men that it is through
Boswell or Gibbon that most students of eighteenth-century literature first hear of William Law. Everyone knows Boswell's
account of how Johnson picked up *A Serious Call to a Devout and
Holy Life* (1728) while at Oxford, expected to find it dull ("as
such books generally are"), expected to laugh, and instead
"found Law quite an overmatch for me." Gibbon did not feel
overmatched by Law's arguments, but he was impressed by both
his character and his characters, those vivid prose portraits
which Gibbon was the first to compare with La Bruyère's.
Wesley credited Law with "sowing the seed" of Methodism.
Whitefield spoke of the change of heart he underwent while
reading *A Serious Call* and *On Christian Perfection.* Pope probably
learned from Law's character sketches, Johnson almost certainly
acquired from them a few strokes of parodic psychologizing

which he could use in the *Rambler,* perhaps, too, the would-be
flyer in Rasselas, and Fielding may well have borrowed an emphasis from the *Remarks upon . . . "The Fable of the Bees"* for his
final rejection of Mandeville's claims in *Amelia.* Blake could have
come to German pietism through Law, as Coleridge certainly
did, thanking Law later as one of the writers who helped him
"keep alive the heart in the head" and convinced him that "all
the products of the mere *reflective* faculty partook of DEATH, and
were as the rattling twigs and sprays in winter."[1]

But finally Law is more interesting as an index than as an
influence. Not that he is "typical," any more than Hume is, but
in his own restless, rigorous analysis of the meaning of human
behavior—and especially that behavior known as belief—he offers a fundamentally religious commentary on some of the
deepest ethical and epistemological problems of the period.
Law's religious perspective is a particularly compelling one because unlike many of his clerical contemporaries, he gives testimony throughout his life that he actually believes everything he
says and evidence throughout his works that he actually understands its implications. His writings span a long career, stretching through nearly a half century, bounded at one end by the
glittering forfex of the *Rape of the Lock* and at the other by the
hesitant forceps of *Tristram Shandy.* It is also a career of dramatic
change, beginning in a somewhat earnest but still recognizably
Augustan world of urbane discourse, a mode of argument in
which his readers need to be "reasonable" and attentive to the
"God of Reason," to a later universe where "all is magnetism,"

---

[1]Boswell, *Life of Johnson,* ed. R. W. Chapman (London: Oxford University
Press, 1960), pp. 50–51; Gibbon, *Memoirs of My Life,* ed. George A. Bonnard
(New York: Funk & Wagnalls, 1969), pp. 22–23; Wesley, quoted in Leslie Ste-
phen, *English Thought in the Eighteenth Century,* 3d ed. (London: John Murray,
1902), II, 416; Whitefield quoted in A. Keith Walker, *William Law: His Life and
Thought* (London: S.P.C.K., 1973), p. ix. Also instructive on the relation of Law
to the Methodists are Eric W. Baker, *A Herald of the Evangelical Revival* (London:
Epworth Press, 1948), J. Brazier Green, *John Wesley and William Law* (London:
Epworth Press, 1945), and Robert Jude Cascio, *Mystic and Augustan: A Study of the
Impact of W. L. on John Wesley, Edward Gibbon, and John Byrom* (Ph.D. dissertation,
Fordham University, 1974), esp. chap. 1. For Coleridge's account see *Biographia
Literaria,* ed. J. Shawcross (London: Oxford University Press, 1907), p. 98 (chap.
9).

where reason leads to spritual death, where God is the "Fire of Love," and where the readers are his flames.

Law's "conversion" to a more mystical or visionary faith is usually attributed to his discovery of Jakob Boehme sometime in the mid-1730s. While Law's enthusiasm for the untutored theosopher who is sometimes called the father of German philosophy was eventually boundless, and while he spent several of his last years learning German and planning a new translation of Boehme, the shift in his thought is more gradual and complex than this explanation suggests.[2] It was necessary for Law to revise his psychology considerably before he could discover in Boehme's vision anything other than the rhapsodies of a self-deluded enthusiast. Law's championing of Boehme cut him off from the Evangelicals as well as from the Establishment, but the fact and the manner of his coming to such an "eccentric" position may tell us a great deal about something more central, a general uneasiness on the part of some of the best writers of the mid-century in the face of increasingly strident appeals to reason and "sense" as monitors of moderation. In his critique of impure reason (the only kind he recognized) or "corporeal understanding," Law frequently moves close to Hume, and in his steadily greater preoccupation with the apocalyptic visions attending "new birth," he shares the metaphorical focus of many of the mid-century poets. But he is too atypical, too original and forceful a writer, to appear to us simply a reed in the wind, useful for showing its direction. In the sequence of fresh convic-

[2]The most helpful treatment of Boehme's possible influence on and similarities to various later philosophers and to German idealism in particular is Howard H. Brinton's *The Mystic Will* (New York: Macmillan, 1930). For the Behmenistic explanation of Law's development as a thinker, see, e.g., J. H. Overton, *W. L.: Non-Juror and Mystic* (London: Longmans, 1881), chaps. 10–11; J. Brazier Green, *John Wesley and W. L.*, chap. 6, and Peter Malekin, "Jacob Boehme's Influence on W. L.," *Studia Neophilologica*, 36 (1964) 245–60. Stephen Hobhouse (whom Malekin attacks) assesses Boehme's influence more moderately in *Selected Mystical Writings of W. L.* (London, C. W. Daniel, 1938), as does Henri Talon in *W. L.: A Study in Literary Craftsmanship* (New York: Harper, n.d. [1948]), chap. 5. There is no consensus. In the following discussion I will emphasize the importance of Law's treatise, *The Case of Reason*, published in 1731, which most commentators ignore but which most would agree antedates his study of Boehme (see especially Hobhouse, *"Fides et Ratio*, the Book which Introduced Jacob Boehme to William Law," *Journal of Theological Studies*, 37 [1934]: 350–68).

tions that form his imaginative life we feel something of the
wind itself.

1

Law's first publication, his *Letters to the Bishop of Bangor*
(1717–1719), confirms his status at the start of his career as a
nonjuror and signals an authorial career to be spent in the minority "opposition." Law remained a good controversialist right
into his last years, taking on Warburton as easily as he had coun-
tered Hoadly, but in a sense his career can be seen as a deepening of his minority position and a broadening of his sense of the
opposition so completely as to impersonalize it and thereby to
make Law's own position nearly nonsectarian. Thus when Law
writes against Hoadly again in 1737, twenty years later (in *A
Demonstration . . .*), in reply to Hoadly's *"Plain Account . . . of the
Lord's Supper*, he has much less respectable company on his side
than when he entered the "Bangorian" lists and much less interest this time in the political stakes of the controversy itself
than in the competing visions of spiritual psychology which it
reveals. Without irony Law tells his reader, "Now I desire you to
know no Books, but this Book of your own Heart, nor to be well
read in any Controversy but in that which passes within you" (V,
102).[3] The distrust of argument grows in Law's later works.
Since there are signs of an analogous retreat in the poetry of the
mid-century from argumentative "essays," "witty warfare," and
what might more generally be called an "opposition" literary
contract,[4] an effort to reconstruct Law's development may help
us understand changing ideas of written truth during the mid-
eighteenth century.

[3]References are to *The Works of W. L.*, reprinted in 9 volumes from J. Richardson's ed. of 1762 (New Forest: G. Moreton, 1892–93) with the exception of
references to the following works more readily accessible in modern editions: *A
Serious Call to a Devout and Holy Life* (London: J. M. Dent, 1967) and *The Spirit of
Love and the Spirit of Prayer*, ed. Sidney Spencer (Cambridge: James Clarke,
1969). I have considerably reduced the italics in quotations from the *Works*.
[4]Joseph Warton objected to the prevailing taste in poetry for "essays on moral
subjects" in the preface to his *Odes on Various Subjects*, published in 1746. William
Whitehead hoped to see "Critics grow mild, life's witty warfare cease, / And true
good-nature breathe the balm of peace," in "On Ridicule" (1743).

Law's best-known work, *A Serious Call to a Devout and Holy Life* (1728), comes at the end of what I regard as his early period. In addition to the Bangorian letters, Law's other works during this period are the *Remarks upon a late Book, entitled, 'The Fable of the Bees,'* 1723, *The Absolute Unlawfulness of the Stage Entertainment,* and *A Practical Treatise upon Christian Perfection* (both 1726). Both Leslie Stephen and Mandeville's modern editor have called Law's *Remarks* the "ablest" of the many replies to him, and it is as good an example of Law's early argumentative style as it is of controversial expertise generally.[5] Law begins with a problem to which we will return later because it occupied Fielding in his last novel, namely Mandeville's definition of man as a "Compound of various Passions," all of which "as they are provoked and come uppermost, govern him by turns whether he will or no" (Law, II, 4). This definition and the consequent historical account of moral virtue (as the "political offspring which flattery begot upon pride") are presumably the premises of Mandeville's analysis which constituted his modernity in Hume's eyes, and they are precisely the premises Law regards as most pernicious.

Law's objection to Mandeville's political theory of virtue is telling because it attacks Mandeville not as cynical but as credulous for believing in an original virtueless state of whose existence he has no proof at all. Law's argument anticipates Adam Ferguson's objections forty years later to state-of-nature accounts which, he says, confuse history and poetic fiction.[6] "For how," Law asks, "can your observations upon them, under the Power of Education, Custom, Laws, and Religion, tell you what man is, in a supposed state, where all these are wanting?" (II, 9). Even if we imagine, for the sake of argument, that Noah's descendants degenerated to the state described by Mandeville and then had to be "wheedled" back into virtue, we are still describing only the restoration of morality, not its origin: "To make the taming of some such Savage Creatures the Origin of Morality, is just a way of thinking as to make the History of the Curing of People in Bedlam, a true Account of the Origin of Reason" (II, 8).

[5]*English Thought in the Eighteenth Century,* II, 42; *Fable of the Bees,* ed. F. B. Kaye (Oxford: Clarendon Press, 1966), II, 401.
[6]Ferguson, *An Essay on the History of Civil Society* (1767), ed. Duncan Forbes (Edinburgh: Edinburgh University Press, 1966), pp. 2–10.

Law clearly regards Mandeville's argument for the political or artificial origin of virtue as the most dangerous one, and he reserves for it his most energetic ironies. "Could it be supposed, that an Understanding so fine as yours, could be conveyed to your Descendents, and that you should ever have a Grandson as wise as yourself, it may be expected that he will be able to teach that Generation of Men, that Seeing was first introduced into the world by Sir Isaac Newton's Treatise upon *Optics*" (II, 13). Law insists upon an innate moral optics, a geometry of ethics wholly outside Mandeville's historical genealogies—for the difference between a good action and a bad one is as "immutable and eternal as the Difference between one line and another"— just as it is beyond Mandeville's experiential range. Mandeville's description of the pleasures of humility, Law claims, must be "owing to such a feeling Sense as the blind Man had of Light, who being asked what it was like, answered it was like the Sound of a Trumpet" (II, 18).

Law's position in this work is essentially rationalistic: Reason is eternal; humans are rational and therefore capable of and obligated to follow virtue; an act is virtuous because it is "an obedience to Reason"; Reason links us to God and the angels; "Cool Reason" is the basis for religious thinking; and so on. If the remarks on the blind man's trumpet remind us of Fielding as well as of Locke, Law's geometry may at this point remind us of the philosopher Square as well as of Samuel Clarke or Thomas Chubb: "In these immutable Qualities of Actions, is founded the fitness and reasonableness of them, which we can no more alter than we can change the Proportions of Relations of Lines and Figures. And it is no more the Pride of Man that has made this Difference between Actions, than it is the Pride of Man, that makes the Difference between a Circle and a Square" (II, 12, 13).[7]

Law's restatement of Clarke's rationalism is not remarkable in

---

[7]Fielding twice alludes in *Tom Jones* to Locke's blind man who imagined the color red to be like the sound of a trumpet (*Essay*, III, iv, 11). Like Law and unlike Locke, Fielding uses the anecdote to illustrate moral insensitivity: "To treat of the Effects of Love to you, must be as absurd as to discourse on Colours to a Man born blind . . ." (*Tom Jones*, VI, i; cf. IV, i). For Square, Clarke, and Chubb, see J. Paul Hunter, *Occasional Form* (Baltimore: Johns Hopkins University Press, 1975), pp. 120–30, 239–40.

itself. What is intriguing is how thoroughly he rejects it in his later works, where reason and religion are usually at odds: "For Reason, or a Faculty of Reasoning . . . upon the moral Proportions of Actions, has no more of the Nature and Power of Religion in it, than so much Reasoning upon the Relations of Squares and Triangles" (*A Demonstration*, 1737: V, 81). The turn toward such a position begins with *The Case of Reason* in 1731, but before exploring it, we need to consider some of the ways in which Law's most popular books—*A Practical Treatise upon Christian Perfection* (1726) and *A Serious Call* (1728)—remain tied to rationalistic appeals at the same time they reveal some of the fundamental tensions in the idea of rational devotion.

2

During a rare skeptical moment in the otherwise intellectually confident reply to Mandeville, Law had noted that "there are nothing more various, imperceptible, or more out of our Sight than the Motives of human Actions" (II, 28). His next works are in large part meditations on motivation, less explicitly epistemological than, for example, Pope's *Epistle to Cobham* ("On the Knowledge of the Characters of Men"), but like Pope's poem they approach their subject by means of character analysis and individual psychology. So great is the reliance upon biographical character sketches in these works that Law's characters in fact seek out characters themselves in their own reading. When the idealized Miranda of *A Serious Call* seeks books which "enter into the heart of religion, and describe the inward holiness of the Christian life," she finds that "of all human writings, the lives of pious persons . . . are her greatest delight" (p. 79). By the late 1740s Law seems to have in mind something very different from biography for his model—and for the use of his speakers—when he has Theophilus describe "truly spiritual" writers as "Friends of God, entrusted with his Secrets, and Partakers of the Divine Nature" (*Spirit of Prayer*, p. 70).

Both *A Practical Treatise upon Christian Perfection* and *A Serious Call* are handbooks which suggest their own limits; for as Law says near the end of *Christian Perfection*, that prayer which his manual is meant to encourage "stops not at Forms and Manuals of Devotion, but is a Language of the Soul, a Judgment of the Heart" (III, 196). In this sense all of Law's devotional writings, early and late, are about the "spirit of prayer" or the "spirit of love" and are as suprarational as the two works (1749–1750, 1752–1754) bearing those titles. The difference is that the works preceding *A Serious Call* invoke "reason" as at least an official norm and use a rhetorical "realism" of character presentation as their way to "enter into the heart of religion." Reason's normative function in *A Serious Call* shares ground with Pope's Horatian world of "ethick epistles," where an unobtrusive but self-evident measure is used by writer and reader to gauge the compulsive characters whose actions, if observed carefully enough, embody a fascinating monomania. This inner motivation Pope refers to in ironic bemusement as "Some Revelation hid from me and you" (*Epistle to Bathurst*, 1.116).

We can imagine that much of what Johnson felt "overmatched" by in *A Serious Call* was Law's use of biographical logic to make his doctrines persuasive. Law's argument is simple: a person is living either according to his own will or according to God's, and the clues as to which will is operative lie not in his professions of faith, in his attendance at public worship, or in any extraordinary acts of piety but in "all the ordinary actions" of "common life" (6, 9, and passim). In a way that later becomes characteristic of Johnson, Law combines the high demands of an either/or "devotion" with a commonsense emphasis on daily behavior that excludes moral melodrama. On one hand, the reader is repeatedly called on to "regulate" his actions (an emphasis which would have had special appeal for the "violent" young Johnson), even the "innocent and lawful parts of our behaviour."[8] On the other hand, such regulation is beyond no one's capacity; it is no martyrdom but a heroism of accretion, a realistic response to a world where, after all, "more people are kept from a true sense and taste of religion by a regular kind of

[8]Katherine Balderston, in "Doctor Johnson and William Law," *PMLA*, 75 (1960): 389–94, suggests that Johnson's statement may pertain to his depression shortly after reading *A Serious Call* and a sense of failure at not meeting Law's high standards. For Johnson's characterization of himself as "violent" during this period, see *Life of Johnson* for the year 1729.

sensuality and indulgence, than by gross drunkenness" (72, 122).

Many of Law's most effective portraits combine careful construction of a whole character out of several habits with a stark, even arithmetical, reduction of the whole back to its behavioral "parts":

> Thus lives Flavia; and if she lives ten years longer, she will have spent about fifteen hundred and sixty Sundays after this manner. She will have worn about two hundred different suits of clothes. Out of these thirty years of her life, fifteen will have been disposed of in bed; and, of the remaining fifteen, about fourteen will have been consumed in eating, drinking, dressing, visiting, conversation, reading, and hearing plays and romances, at operas, assemblies, balls and diversions. [69]

Like Pope's sketches, Law's usually grow in poignancy as more details are added.[9] It is only in the briefer caricatures that simple contempt dominates, as in Law's "vain and senseless flyer" who is an emblem figure for ambition: "What can you conceive more silly and extravagant, than to suppose a man racking his brains, and studying night and day how to fly?—wandering from his own house and home, wearying himself with climbing upon every ascent, cringing and courting everybody he meets to lift him up from the ground, bruising himself with continual falls, and at last breaking his neck?" (119). The episode may still have been in Johnson's mind three decades later when he wrote *Rasselas,* although he treats his aviator a bit more gently than Law does, whose comic phrasing—"cringing and courting everybody he meets"—is here closer to Swift's rhythms than to Johnson's.

The character sketch of Flatus does seem wholly Johnsonian, however, perhaps because it is just about the right length for a *Rambler* profile and because its introduction anticipates the opening of *Rasselas:* "Look at Flatus, and learn how miserable they are, who are left to the folly of their own passions" (134).

---

[9]Benjamin Boyce discusses the likely influence of Law's portraits on Pope's in *The Character-Sketches in Pope's Poems* (Durham: Duke University Press, 1962), pp. 49–54, 68–69.

Flatus restlessly pursues one "new project" after another, his "wandering imagination" each time getting "sight of another happiness" (again the language suggests the inner vision of Pope's "some Revelation hid from you and me"), and at each stage of this career Law dramatizes Flatus with a piece of indirect discourse. Flatus not only tired of his gun and dogs, he "hated the senseless noise and hurry of hunting"; he not only makes building his new avocation, he "wonders at the dulness of the old builders"; and, nicest of all, when he undertakes Italian grammar, he does it to understand opera, "and not be like those unreasonable people, that are pleased with they know not what." When we last see Flatus, he is a vegetarian jogger, "living upon herbs" and living up to his name by "running about the county to get himself into as good wind" as any footman (135–37).

Law continues to invoke reason in the face of such unreasoning conduct, equating sin with disregard for the "God of reason" and finally equating reason with God's will, against which "no actions have any honour" and bold conduct is "no more true bravery than sedate malice is Christian patience" (352). But it appears that Law, like Pope, has trouble maintaining the categories of his psychology as his analysis deepens. These characters seem to move and be moved by forces that have little to do with reason, even potentially, and in fact Law's emphasis on habits, on childhood education, on the "natural" desire to sing, on the contagion of example, and on the effect of actions on the state of mind all reflect implicit recognition of reason's limitations. But Law's explicit formulations are in this work still closer to traditional Christian Stoicism, and one example will suggest the strain: "For all the wants which disturb human life, which make us uneasy to ourselves, quarrelsome with others, and unthankful to God; which weary us in vain labours and foolish anxieties; which carry us from project to project, from place to place, in a poor pursuit of we know not what, are the wants which neither God, nor nature, nor reason, hath subjected us to, but are solely infused into us by pride, envy, ambition, and covetousness" (121–22). At such moments Law invokes the compound satiric norm—God-reason-"nature"—which makes his character sketches possible. But in his desire to prize reason, God, and nature, Law is also at such moments in the unsatisfactory posi-

tion of having to maintain that pride, envy, ambition, and covetousness are not "natural" realities in the lives of human beings.
Beginning with *The Case of Reason* in 1731, Law begins to develop a less complacent account of reason and a more inclusive view
of nature. These developments alter both God's place and Law's,
carrying the writer from the theater of observed conduct into
theories of depth psychology.

3

If a recent church historian is correct in describing the Evangelical movement of the 1740s as in large part a response to the
increased influence of official deism and public anticlericalism
in the 1730s, then Law's response to Matthew Tindal's *Christianity as old as the Creation* is paradigmatic and anticipatory.[10]
Law generally regards Tindal's confidence in the self-sufficiency
of reason as dangerous presumption, and he particularly objects
to the claim that duty is obvious to reason, since, in Tindal's
words, "a Mind that is attentive can as easily distinguish fit from
unfit, as the Eye can beauty from deformity" (Law, II, 62). The
universe is mapped out not according to a self-evident geometry
but according to the will of God: "The pretended *absolute independent fitnesses,* or *unfitnesses* of actions therefore *in themselves,*
are vain abstractions, and philosophical *jargon,* serving no ends
of morality, but only helping people to wrangle and dispute
away that sincere obedience to God, which is their only happiness" (II, 89).

Law's attack on the physicotheological premises is less remarkable for originality than for the turnabout it signals. The positions Law repudiates here sound very similar to his own insistence in 1723 that actions are clearly fit or unfit "by their own
proper Natures, independent of our Wills" (II, 13–14). The
change is striking, second, because it apparently precedes rather
than reflects his sympathetic reading of Boehme; in other
words, Law's "mysticism" begins in response not, ironically, to
the "Teutonick Philosopher" but to the English deist. And final-

[10]John Walsh, "Origins of the Evangelical Revival," in G. V. Bennett and J. D.
Walsh, eds., *Essays in Modern Church History* (London: Oxford University Press,
1966), pp. 132–62.

ly, Law's change of thought is compelling in itself because of the thorough critique of reason, the shift to theological voluntarism, and the growing interest in the mystery of the Creation it entails. These are by no means neatly separate elements in Law's thought; each is extended somewhat independently of the others. From the initial premise that "we can be no farther competent judges of the fitness of the conduct of God, than we are competent judges of the divine nature," Law goes on to define that nature as essentially will; Law has in mind not the angry will of the Calvinists but a continually creative God who is loving and lovable: "People imagine that *will alone* is not so adorable . . . because they consider it as a blind imperfect faculty that wants to be directed. But what has such a will as this to do with the will of God?" (II, 86).

If Law's voluntarism can be seen as a response to deistic tendencies rather than to Boehme—of whom there are no visible traces yet in Law's work—it can also be seen as one logical outgrowth of his original nonjuring principles.[11] Being a nonjuror in the eighteenth century could mean many things, but we can be fairly confident that for a thinker of Law's sort, refusal to swear allegiance to the Hanoverian establishment would involve a strong belief in the principle of royal prerogative, earthly and divine. That the latter should have chosen to manifest itself through such an unlikely succession as the later Stuarts might strain human convenience and common sense, but the choice only points up the inadequacy of "reasonableness" as a norm: "We will not allow a Providence to be right, unless we can comprehend and explain the reasonableness of all its steps; and yet it could *not* possibly be right, unless its proceedings were as much above our comprehension as our wisdom is below that which is infinite" (II, 99). And significantly, Law grounds his skepticism regarding reason on the analogy of our limited understanding of power: "As our enjoyment of power is so limited, so imperfect, so superficial as to be scarce sufficient to tell us what power is, much less what omnipotence is; so our share of reason is so

---

[11]Useful background for Law's generation is contained in Henry Broxap, *The Later Non-Jurors* (London: Cambridge University Press, 1924) and, more recently, in W. A. Speck, *Stability and Strife: England, 1714–1760* (London: Edward Arnold, 1977), chap. 4.

small, and we enjoy it in so perfect a manner, that we can scarce think or talk intelligibly of it, or so much as define our faculties of reasoning" (II, 92).

This is one of many points where Law's skepticism is as uncompromising as Hume's, and there is in fact an aversion to "reasonable" compromise which links the two men in what we might think of as a broader fraternity of intellectual "nonjurors." I do not mean to confuse matters needlessly by momentarily extending the term beyond ecclesiastical recognition, but I believe our understanding of the eighteenth century might benefit at present from some confusion of the usual boundaries. We need, most simply, a comprehensive term which allows us to appreciate the fact that despite our emphasis on the "age of compromise," most of the writers whom we still read from the period were in some sense "dissenters" who stood apart from the newly established centers of power, who were voluntarily or involuntarily alienated from the mainstream of mercantile orthodoxy, and who consciously or unconsciously declined to swear allegiance to a patched-up compromise of prudential conveniences. This is of course not to say that there are no great minds among the moderates. In this scheme, for example, Locke would be the archbishop of Latitudinarianism, for there is no necessary contradiction between a sense of epistemological limitation and optimistic or "progressive" moderation. But while Hume and Law would agree with Locke that we are surrounded by mysteries, they are not quick to share Locke's confidence that we nevertheless have clear knowledge at least of those things which "concern our conduct."[12] It is precisely the everyday world of thinking and acting which is most mysterious and is likely to remain so, not despite but because of man's "need" to infer more coherent laws from his fragmentary experience than it warrants. Until, Law says, we can account for God's act of Creation on principles of "fitness" and the "reason" of things, "no revealed mysteries can more exceed the comprehension of man, than the state of human life itself" (II, 63).

Law's next major step will be to discuss the condition of everyday life in terms of the Creation, projecting his analysis of psy-

[12]Locke, *Essay*, I, i, 1.

chological experience as a reinterpretation of the Books of Genesis and Nature. It is a step which he does not take for several years, but it is forced upon him by his own sophisticated and anthropological critique of intellectual premises. We speak, he argues, of judging according to one's "own" reason, but in fact reason has "very little that can be called *its own.*" We come to our so-called natural knowledge just as we come to language, adopting it the way we adopt the customs and "modes of behaviour" of what happens to be our "native" land. "Nothing seems to be our own but a *bare capacity* to be instructed. . . ." Law immediately asserts that he is not suggesting a relativistic view of good and evil, but certainly his argument that we learn to distinguish them the same way we learn cultural conventions (the "rules of civil life") is itself difficult to distinguish from full-scale relativism (II, 117–18).

A natural outcome of Law's voluntaristic theology will be a greater emphasis on human will as well. The faculty of Reason virtually disappears from Law's discourse except as an obstacle to insight. The most interesting thing about God's will is the Creation; the most interesting thing about man's will is his continual creation of his experience, the *"Imaginations"* and *"Desires"* which by 1740 Law terms the "greatest reality we have" (VI, 134). In 1731 Law's analysis is still primarily negative, largely an assault on the supposed autonomy of reason. (Law describes the final chapter of *The Case of Reason* as "Shewing that all the *mutability* of our tempers, the *disorders* of our passions, the *corruption* of our hearts, all the *reveries* of the imagination, all the *contradictions* and *absurdities* that are to be found in human life, and human opinions, are precisely the mutability, disorders, corruptions, and absurdities of human reason." [II, 55]) The logic of the assault on traditional distinctions between reason and passion and particularly the persuasiveness of his description of reason as a cultural acquisition must have provided Law with at least glimpses of Hume's abyss of skepticism. His next book did not appear for six years. When it did, Law continued his attack on the "Religion of Reason,"[13] but he also began to construct in

[13] In *A Demonstration* Law defines the "Religion of Reason" as a doctrine denying the "*Necessity*" of a Savior" and calls it the "Religion of Hell, or that very State of Mind which reigns and governs there" (V, 83–84, cf. 87).

the place of its "fictions" a mythopoeic vision of the ongoing creation called Nature and a new, more deeply poetic theory of interpretation, of how to take figurative language seriously.

4

Law's fusion of controversial and devotional interests is suggested simply by the titles of his next several books: *A Demonstration of the Gross and Fundamental Errors of a late Book, called, A Plain Account of the Nature and End of the Sacrament of the Lord's Supper, &c.* (1737); *The Grounds and Reasons of Christian Regeneration, or, the New-Birth* (1739); *An Earnest and Serious Answer to Dr. Trapp's Discourse of the Folly, Sin and Danger of Being Righteous Over-Much* (1740), and in the same year, *An Appeal to all that Doubt, or Disbelieve the Truths of the Gospel, whether They be Deists, Arians, Socinians, or Nominal Christians.* This flurry of activity is again followed by a period of relative silence, lasting through most of the 1740s this time, until the publication of Law's two best known "mystical" works, *The Spirit of Prayer*, 1749–1750, and *The Spirit of Love*, 1752–1754, and his most Behmenistic one, *The Way to Divine Knowledge*, 1752, written as a preface to a projected new edition of Boehme's works.

As a religious rhapsode Law does some of his strongest writing in these last works.[14] But we must go back to *A Demonstration* of 1737 and the treatise on *Regeneration* of 1739 to see the decisive working out of the positions first hinted at in *The Case of Reason*. Although he is nearly a quarter century older than Hume, the 1730s also mark for Law the period in which a "new scene of thought" opens before him, demanding of its witness a new method of inquiry and exposition.

Near the middle of *A Demonstration*, Law pauses in the midst of a reflection of God's mercy to explain his procedure: "You must forgive these little Digressions; for I want so much to touch the

---

[14]There are few wholly secular evaluations of Law's literary power. Helpful commentaries on the later writings are contained in Henri Talon, *W. L.: A Study in Literary Craftsmanship*, esp. chap. 5, and John Hoyles, *The Edges of Augustanism* (The Hague: Martinus Nijhoff, 1972), pp. 81–150; Hoyles gives more emphasis to Byrom than to Law, but his remarks frequently illuminate their similar implied aesthetic.

Heart of my Reader, and make him in love with God, and his own Salvation in Christ Jesus, that I know not how to content myself with bare Arguments" (V, 72). Law's sense of discrete argumentative and hortatory roles may remind us of Hume's distinction in the *Enquiries* between speculative and practical philosophy, the latter consisting largely of persuasive descriptions of moral virtue. As we will see, Law is not at all interested in moral virtue as an end in itself, but like Hume he is increasingly drawn to a rhetoric of "sentiment," and on very consistent intellectual principles. His "digression" in *A Demonstration* is barely a digression at all, for it turns on the three themes which dominate his new disagreement with Hoadly from the outset of the treatise: (1) the limits of reason, with a corresponding appeal to the "inward sentiment" (V, 93) of the reader, (2) the need for the experience of regeneration, and (3) the proper use of language in religious understanding. Since we have already seen the main lines of Law's attack on rationalistic claims in *The Case of Reason* and since we will have a better look at his view of "new birth" in *Regeneration,* it will be useful to concentrate for the moment on his remarks on language, though again we will find that the themes overlap.

Hoadly as construed by Law in *A Demonstration* appears much like a caricatured New Critic in the positioning of late twentieth-century hermeneutical controversy. Law's argument is of course hermeneutical in the original sense, with the debate over scriptural interpretation centering on the biblical warrant for the sacrament of the Lord's Supper. Hoadly, says Law, would have us interpret the passage as an autonomous text, apart from the author and apart from its "relation" (V, 9) to other parts of the Bible (ignoring what would now be called "intertextuality"). Anyone who proceeds in this uncontextual way is no better off than a heathen who simply reads the words on a scrap of paper: "The words of the Institution are as unintelligible and useless to him, as if he had found them by chance; they relate to he knows not what, they may be all Fiction and Invention for aught he knows; they cannot possibly be understood as having any Truth or Reality in them, till he knows the chief Articles of Christian Salvation." To understand a text one genuinely needs to understand the belief system which is part of its language: "Now a

Scripture-Christian Institution must necessarily be understood according to Scripture and Christian Doctrine, as an Hebrew Proposition must be understood according to the Hebrew Language" (V, 12–14).

Hoadly's biggest mistake is his reliance upon literally conventional wisdom, his attempt to understand the biblical text in terms of ordinary language conventions, or "according to the common rules of speaking in like cases." "But, pray Sir," asks Law, "where must a Man look for a *like case?*" Words mean differently, depending on the nature of their Speaker, and so the "words of God are of the Nature of God, Divine, Living, and Powerful." The "common rules of speaking" are "like other things common amongst men, *viz.*, poor, empty, and superficial, hardly touching the Outside of the mere human things we talk about" (V, 6–7). To reach the inside for Law means to recognize the insufficiency of commonsense deductions in the face of the unique and to repudiate the sort of moderation which would turn a sacrament into a "bare act of memory." Those who emphasize the sacrament as a mere "remembrance" mistakenly regard it as the memory of "something that is absent," of things "done and past." But what is needed is precisely a theology of presence, attentive to our "vital Sensibility" or "Instinct of God" and freed from the limits of reason and memory, each of which is a "bare" activity of solipsistic reiteration. Reason is inferior to sentiment because "this Faculty of Speculating and arguing is only the Activity of the mind upon its own Images and Ideas, and is only the same bare Activity, whatever the Images be that exercise it." The least "stirring" of sensibility is more valuable than this "Painter of dead Images, which leave the Heart in the same State of Death in which they find it" (V, 19–20, 89–94). Real knowledge must be more vivid—must, in Hume's terms, have more "vivacity,"—than such images because, as Law would put it some years later, a "distant absent, separate God is an unknown God" (*Way to Divine Knowledge*, 1752: VII, 202).

The characterization of reason as a kind of sterile imagination—something like Blake's circular mills and Coleridge's mechanical fancy—is a new element in Law's skepticism, not part of the antirational arsenal of *The Case of Reason* but repeated in roughly similar terms from *A Demonstration* onward. So, in the *Spirit of Prayer*, for example, "all real Knowledge" is equated with feeling, while "all after this is only the Play of our Imagination, amusing itself with the *dead Pictures* of its own Ideas" (*Spirit of Prayer*, 115–16). Reason, memory, imagination all are used interchangeably by Law during this period to denote the mind's capacity to keep and to form images—"Fictions of our Minds" (V, 90; cf. V, 93–94, 141; VI, 94–96)—which prevent true feeling. To put it schematically, sight blocks sentiment. Were we not busied with our visualized mental fictions, we would be aware of the world's "magnetism" (V, 90). And were we not beguiled by the "outward Things" which feed the fancy, our "sensibility" of our true condition would be undeniable: "This wandering of the Imagination through its *own Invention* of Delight, hinders the poor soul from feeling *what it is*, in its own Nature" (*Regeneration: V*, 151). Equally strong during this period is Law's insistence on a theory of interpretation which will not domesticate or naturalize the language of revelation so thoroughly as to tame it into mere similitude. His dispute with Hoadly about the Lord's Supper began over a notion of language which would, he claimed, reduce the Sacrament to an "Act of Memory upon something that is absent," and in *An Appeal to all that Doubt*, Law extends his warning against any academic readings of the Bible which turn it into a merely "figurative, historical system of things, that has no Ground in Nature," a "dead Letter"(VI, 82) serving only as an arena for the critical skirmishes of learned clerics.

The academic approach is seen by Law as a travesty of proper reading for two reasons. The first is his conviction that Scripture, if read right, is a personal phenomenology: "It is only the Description of that which passes within you. It is the Book of yourself" (V, 103). The second is that merely figurative or conventional readings of Scripture are inappropriate because the author is one whose text is made up of deeds, of literal "speech-acts":[15] "For his Words are Power, and what he speaks he acts" (V, 73).

Both of these positions are central in Law's theology, and I

[15]"Speech-act" here is a pun on the term for any act performed when we use language, as discussed by J. L. Austin in *How to Do Things with Words* (1962; reprinted ed., Galaxy, 1965) and John R. Searle, *Speech Acts: An Essay in the Philosophy of Language* (London: Cambridge University Press, 1969). I will return later to Austin's distinction between constative and performative utterances; roughly, the difference is between a statement ("He married her") and an act performed by saying ("I marry you").

believe they also go to the heart of a great deal of mid-eighteenth-century poetry. The relevance of the first stance lies in the increasing poetic preference for a retreat from the world of ordinary images and the similes based on them in form of a world of feeling and direct vision. This preference frequently manifests itself as an aversion to light, the medium of sight, and a turning toward personified forces.[16] The second emphasis, on God's words as acts rather than as descriptions of acts, has its secular counterpart in a conspicuous fascination with verbal power on the part of the authors of sublime odes. It is perhaps not accidental that Longinus's best remembered example of the sublime was one in which the gap between word and deed had been closed: "God said, Let there be light, and there was light; let there be land and there was land." The example no doubt sponsored many bombastic echoes of Genesis, but it also points to subtler attempts to place the poet himself into the godlike position where "his Words are Power, and what he speaks he acts."

Such poems would include Collins's construction of visionary shrines within his odes, the fatal speech act of Gray's bard, the word-woven reality of his fatal sisters, the self-completing *Song of Smart* ("DETERMINED, DARED, and DONE!"), and later Coleridge's use of the poem to "decree" reality in *Kubla Khan*. These are important preoccupations beginning in the mid-eighteenth century, and we will return to them in considering the poets in more detail. For now I want simply to suggest the similarities between Law's desire to replace the conventional theology with a theology of presence, or presences, a world consisting, in Thomas Warton's words, of the "actions of spirits."[17] The spiritual action crucial to both worlds and the force which animates the

[16]These tendencies will be described more fully in the following chapters. Pertinent discussions are Martin Price, "The Sublime Poem: Pictures and Powers," *Yale Review*, 58 (1968–69): 194–213, and Jonathan Culler, "Apostrophe," *Diacritics*, Winter 1977, pp. 59–69, esp. p. 61: "The apostrophizing poet identifies his universe as a world of sentient forces."

[17]Warton characterized the new poetry of his day as imitating the "actions of spirits" rather than human characters or natural events, in the fragmentary manuscript essay on a "Romantic Kind of Poetry," quoted in David Fairer, "The Poems of Thomas Warton the Elder?", *Review of English Studies*, n.s., 26 (1975): 287–300, 395–406.

realm of nature is the experience of conversion, or what Law analyzes variously as "regeneration" or "new-birth." I would like to consider this last important theme in his work before turning to the poetics of conversion in poetry itself.

5

Law's *Regeneration* (1739) begins with the statement that man was made in God's "own Likeness," and much of Law's career can be thought of as centering on the meaning of likeness, a concept which for Law is not, as we have seen, merely a matter of similitude or figurative resemblance but of identity or participation in the same vital nature. If man is like God, it is because he is part of God. If man's internal disturbances are like the disturbances in the external world, that is, increasingly in Law's thought, because man and nature are parts of each other. "For the outward World is but a Glass, or Representation of the inward; and everything . . . must have its Root or, hidden Cause, in something that is more inward" (V, 172). In Law's terms this statement means that the dichotomy between "outward," or physical, nature and "inward," or subjectively human, nature nearly ceases to exist. In the *Appeal*, for example, he argues that the "wrath" of a man and of a tempest do "one and the same thing to outward Nature, alter its State in the same Manner," differing only in the degree of their effects, and that it would be perfectly plausible to imagine "that if all human Breath was become a mere, unmixed Wrath, that all the Fire in outward Nature would immediately break forth, and bring that Dissolution upon outward Nature, which will arise from the last Fire" (VI, 112). If this manner of thinking reminds us of Blake's habit of merging subject and object, perhaps it also illustrates the underlying "logic" of Pope's last work, the *Dunciad* of 1743, in which collective human breath is pooled and homogenized until it is strong enough to bring on the apocalypse.[18] And it points as well to the happier human-caused apocalypses of other

[18]Cf. VI, 116: "For Hell and Evil are only two words for one and the same Thing," and *Spirit of Prayer*, 31: "The Angels that extinguished the Birth of Heaven in themselves, fell directly into the horrible Depths of their own strong self-tormenting Nature, or their *own Hell*."

poems which we will turn to shortly, such as Thomson's *Liberty* and several of Collins's and Akenside's odes.

The principle of likeness which leads Law to conflate the conventionally inner and outer worlds leads him also to imagine personal "new-birth" in terms of the birth of external nature. When Law remarks "what a harmonious Agreement" appears "between our Creation and Redemption" and "how finely, how surprisingly" the first birth illustrates the second, he is not simply finding happy similes. So completely have the two halves of the analogy been equated that any explanation of one must involve an explanation of the other. Law works the equation both ways, inferring at times his own gloss on Genesis from present introspection and then asserting that our most urgent questions about the present are answered "as soon as it is known that the *first State* of Things is quite altered." Or, more definitely: "we know nothing *truly* of the Nature of the Christian Religion, and our deep Concern in it, but so far as we see into the Nature of our *first* State, in the Creation, and our *present* State by the Fall" (V, 142–48).

Conversion for Law is an "Earthquake within," a frightened recognition of one's "inward Deformity," and anything less is "but a kind of Table-Talk" (V, 152). Law is less interested than many of the Evangelicals in the sudden "Flash of Conviction" (V, 179) and is more skeptical than Jonathan Edwards, for example, about the visible signs of conversion.[19] But he is insistent upon the difference between regeneration and reformation, or what he would call "only a *moral Change*," a "dead and superficial thing" (V, 159–61). As Law moves his analysis steadily inward he begins to speak not only of the "fictions of reason," a phrase used frequently from 1731 onward, but of the "fiction of behaviour." He means works without faith, a "Virtue of Art and human contrivance" based on nothing higher than "Sense and Reason." This kind of moral virtue may result in civility but not in conversion; it is "little better than such a new Birth as may be

[19]Edwards's *Treatise Concerning the Religious Affections* (1746) is largely concerned with the "distinguishing signs" of grace, the significance and cultural background of which are discussed by John E. Smith in his introduction to the *Religious Affections* (New Haven: Yale University Press, 1959), pp. 1–73.

had from a Dancing-Master" (*Way to Divine Knowledge*, 1752; VII, 156–57).[20] Lacking radical change within, all of one's virtues are nothing more than "fine-painted Fruits hung upon a bad Tree" (*Spirit of Prayer*, p. 76).

The life of contrivance which Law describes here is close to Helene Deutsch's conception of the "as if" personality, a structure of appropriate learned responses, designed to meet the expectations of others, but fundamentally unreal and unfelt.[21] Like Deutsch, Law is analyzing self-delusion rather than hypocrisy, and his focus suggests the concern with felt authenticity which is a conspicuous part of the Protestant tradition generally and of existential-influenced psychoanalytic thinkers today (Erikson would be another instance) but which is most evident in England beginning with the prizing of "sincerity" in the eighteenth century. The fiction of behavior or mere practice of virtue is the individual version of merely "rational" or "historical" religion and of "formalism" (*Of Justification* . . . , 1760: VIII, 245–47) in the church, a preoccupation with external regularity at the expense of spirit. Authenticity is in the will, which has long replaced reason in Law's system as our link to God, a "genuine Birth of the eternal, free, omnipotent Will of God." Only the will *makes* anything, and in fact it makes everything. It is the "only Workman in Nature; and everything is its Work. It has all Power; . . . it carries all before it; it creates as it goes. . . . It enters wherever it wills, and finds everything that it seeks; for its seeking is its finding" (VII, 210–11). The will is godlike in its freedom and its transformational power, its transcendence of the conventional space between thought and deed. Like God's language of ultimate speech acts—"for his words are Power, and what he speaks he acts"—which had fascinated Law since the thirties, the will makes its own reality.

It does so in a universe where "all is Magnetism, all is Sentiment, Instinct, and Attraction"—Law is using the terms syn-

---

[20]Values associated with dancing and dancing masters through the first half of the century are discussed by C. J. Rawson in *Henry Fielding and the Augustan Ideal under Stress* (London: Routledge & Kegan Paul, 1972), esp. chap. 1.

[21]Deutsch's "Some Forms of Emotional Disturbance and Their Relationship to Schizophrenia," is reprinted in her *Neuroses and Character Types* (New York: International Universities Press, 1965), pp. 262–81.

onymously—and where "Reason stands only as a Busybody, as an idle Spectator" (V, 90). Law is constructing a spiritual mechanics in which "attraction" is of course Newton's gravity.[22] This passage suggests two major similarities between Law's world and Hume's. The more obvious one is that between Law's characterization of reason is a powerless onlooker and Hume's cheerfully skeptical conclusion that "reason is, and ought only to be the slave of the passions" (*Treatise*, p. 127). The second and deeper link is between Law's "attraction" and Hume's description of the passions as the "cement of the universe," a phrase which, as Richard Kuhns explains, is also meant to invoke Newtonian gravity and internalize it.[23]

It is not entirely surprising that fideist and skeptical positions should overlap, but the more pertinent connection is that both Hume and Law turn from reason to models of sentiment, attraction, of unseen force or power, and that this is essentially the world of allegorical or visionary poetry in the mid-century.

There is an important difference as well. Hume's skepticism concerning a rational analysis on which to ground a system of the sciences leads him progressively away from introspective concentration and to the world of observable behavior. History is not a new interest for Hume, but the pressure of actors on the historical world more and more replaces the closet drama of internal impressions. Law's pilgrimage goes in the opposite direction. His growing skepticism concerning reason lessens his interest in the kinds of practical conduct which dominate his early work, and it brings him more deeply into a world of depth psychology where accounts of public actions fade almost entirely. History, observations, character sketches, even sacred his-

[22]Arthur Wormhoudt has noted that Law "seems to have thought it possible to enlist the tremendous prestige of Newton's scientific reputation behind a vitalistic and in his view essentially Christian world-picture" and has also remarked upon Law's "serious attempt to interpret the science of his day voluntaristically" ("Newton's Natural Philosophy in the Behmenistic Works of W. L.," *JHI*, 10 [1949]: 411–29).

[23]Richard Kuhns, *Structures of Experience: Essays on the Affinity between Philosophy and Literature* (1970; reprinted, New York: Harper, 1974), p. 58. Hume described the passions as "*to us* the cement of the universe" in *An Abstract of a Treatise of Human Nature* (1740), reprinted in *An Inquiry Concerning the Human Understanding* (New York: Liberal Arts Press, 1955), pp. 183–98.

tory by the end, are fictions, compared with the timeless and archetypal world revealed by introspection: "We do not want Moses to assure us that there was a First Man; that he had something from Heaven, and something from Earth in him. . . . For every man in himself is the infallible Proof of this; Moses is only the Historian that he recorded the When, and Where, and How." (VII, 164).

Again, these are changes of emphasis. Just as Hume is interested from the beginning in bringing his psychology to history, Law is interested in reaching the inner state in his earliest observations of behavior and character. Steadily, however, his loss of confidence in appeals to reason, in the efficacy of stricter external "regulation" and in the "common ways of speaking" of one's conduct, is counterbalanced by a stronger conviction that one can eliminate the "table talk" of surface behavior and go directly to the "Earthquake within," that the way to write the truth is to describe the contest of forces within the individual by retelling and reinterpreting the Creation story. In the difference between the responses of Hume and Law to the problems of their analyses, the one seeking greater certainty in observed social events and the other in visionary authenticity, we can begin to see the gulf developing in the mid-eighteenth century between the respective premises of novelists and poets.

PART II

Toward a Poetics
of Conversion

CHAPTER 3

The Flight from History
in Mid-Century Poetry

It is no doubt too simple to see the novelists of the 1740s and later as marching off in one direction—the road of Hume and historiography—and the poets as taking the "way" of William Law and vision. I will try to complicate this picture enough in the chapters ahead to do near-justice to the shared concerns of novelists and poets alike and to accommodate their influence on each other. Nonetheless, I hope to be able at the same time to preserve some of the simplicity that attends our fork-in-the-road model for the realities of mid-eighteenth-century literary life, merely because it suggests the either/or quality of certain artistic choices or means of finding and telling the appropriate truth. From our vantage point we could list some of these as solitary *or* social perspectives, the use of subliminal suggestion *or* visual "data," expressive description *or* narration of details generally regarded as sociologically accurate, and so on.

But a major problem concerns the extent to which we can trust models which depend on "our vantage point." The next question is whether we have any choice.[1] For example, the term

[1]The question is meant to be not whether final "objectivity" is available but what use is to be made of our own perspective when dealing with a "period of transition." This is much of the subject of Whitehead's *Adventures of Ideas*, written half a century ago, and a preoccupation of later "metahistory," including Hayden White's book by that title (Baltimore: Johns Hopkins University Press, 1973). Whitehead: "Knowledge is always accompanied with accessories of emotion and purpose. . . . In every age of well-marked transition there is the pattern of habitual dumb practice and emotion which is passing, and there is oncoming of a new complex of habit. Between the two lies a zone of anarchy, either

"preromantic," so often applied to the poets of this period, suggests a conspicuous question about retrospective distortion which remains, whether or not we avoid the term. The objections to the concept are obvious, and many of them have been made before. To regard the mid-century poets as "preromantics" is to evaluate their worth primarily in terms of values later established by the achievement of the romantic writers we happen to like most. To regard, say, Collins or Gray as a "preromantic" is to impose a false teleology on the past, one in which the poet is "trying" to be Wordsworth or in which he becomes a sort of John the Baptist heralding the redeemers to come. (Redemption is central enough to romantic mythology to have made this latter version particularly seductive.)

Problems of terminology are not in themselves very interesting, but much has been written during the last generation concerning the preromantic label as well as about designations often used more broadly, such as "classical," "Augustan," "Enlightenment," and of course the "Age of Reason."[2] Why not, if all of these are felt to carry too many preconceptions, throw them all out and start fresh? Terms are sometimes thrown out altogether. The "Age of Reason" is virtually dead now in serious discussions of the eighteenth century except as a phrase in curatorial quotation marks. Others remain, voiced or unvoiced, because they represent a way of generalizing which still seems interesting and plausible. For all its problems, "Augustan" is not only a convenient but a provocative term, suggesting self-conscious wishes and fears on the part of many of the figures grouped under its shade, and it allows (as Howard Weinbrot's

---

a passing danger or a prolonged welter involving misery of decay and zest of young life. In our estimate of these agencies everything depends upon our standpoint of criticism. In other words, our history of ideas is derivative from our ideas of history, that is to say, upon our own intellectual standpoint" (*Adventures of Ideas* [New York: Macmillan, 1933], pp. 5, 8).

[2]Donald Greene surveys the problems of these and other categories in "Augustinianism and Empiricism," *ECS*, 1 (1967): 33–68, and *The Age of Exuberance* (New York: Random House, 1970). For "preromantic" see, e.g., Bertrand Bronson, "The Pre-Romantic or Post-Augustan Mode," *ELH*, 20 (1953), reprinted in *Facets of the Enlightenment* (Berkeley: University of California Press, 1968), pp. 159–72; Northrop Frye, "Towards Defining an Age of Sensibility," *ELH*, 23 (1956): 144–52, and Joan Pittock, *The Ascendancy of Taste: The Achievement of Joseph and Thomas Warton* (London: Routledge & Kegan Paul, 1973), pp. 215–20.

work shows) new scrutiny of the historical material.[3] Other terms can be suppressed to occasional good effect, and I will for the most part attempt to suppress the term "preromantic" in favor of "post-Augustan." I do so not in the belief that the latter is without problems but in the simple hope that it calls more attention to the immediate past with which the writers themselves had to deal than to the future which preoccupies later critics. But if such a maneuver is a useful shift of emphasis, it would be wrong to exaggerate its novelty. We are still working with similar sorts of retrospective generalizations which will filter much of what we see in the available past. The alternative— and it exists more clearly in theory than in practice—would be to attempt no discriminations. Thus Josephine Miles's "samples" of poetry of various decades are selected more or less without regard to whether they represent new trends or lingering habits of the time. As soon as we begin to discriminate, to decide, for example, that some poems are more "of" the 1740s or 1750s than others also published then, we naturally begin to look for qualities which we believe to be important in the development of poetry. If we commit ourselves to the concept of preromanticism, in short, we will prize anticipation; if we see the mid-century as "post-Augustan" we will emphasize rejections of previous models. In either case we simplify, and our best method is merely to try to recognize the limits of our categories before we begin. Ernst Cassirer put the problem clearly in defending Burckhardt's generalized "Renaissance" type against the objections of scholars who claimed they could not find this type exemplified anywhere in their source material.

> What we are trying to give expression to here is a unity *of direction,* not *actualization.* The particular individuals *belong together,* not because they are alike or resemble each other, but because they are *cooperating in a common task,* which . . . we perceive to be new and to be the era's distinctive "meaning." . . . All genuine concepts of style in the humanities reduce . . . to such conceptions of mean-

[3]Weinbrot concludes his deeply provocative study of "Augustan" literature and political writing with the recommendation that the term be discarded: see *Augustus Caesar in "Augustan" England: The Decline of a Classical Norm* (Princeton: Princeton University Press, 1978), esp. pp. 229–41.

ing. The artistic style of an epoch cannot be determined unless we
gather into a unity all its divergent and often patently disparate
artistic expressions, unless . . . we understand them as manifestations of a specific "artistic will."[4]

Cassirer's formulation may be particularly useful for our purposes not only as a plea for certain kinds of generalizations but
because the sense of history to which it appeals—the idea of
history as secular "direction"—first became powerful in the middle of the eighteenth century.

The middle and later years of the eighteenth century have
been best studied in terms of the vast and sophisticated body of
critical theory the period produced. In the following pages I will
look more closely at poetic procedures than at critical ones, for
the simple reason that we now have more to learn from the
shared metaphors and period style or styles of the poetry itself
than from the aesthetic territory so well charted by, most promi-
nently, Samuel Monk, W. J. Bate, and M. H. Abrams. When we
look directly at the poetic procedures in the middle of the century, those which are often most interesting are procedures of
avoidance, and they show that the poets are seeking to avoid
history.

This claim requires much illustration to be convincing or of
help, but before proceeding to the poetry of the mid-century it
will be helpful to recall the single critical work of the period
which, while containing little that is profound, best suggests the
major discontinuity between the poetic assumptions of the period ending about 1740 and the generation or so following. The
work is Joseph Warton's *Essay on the Writings and Genius of Pope*,
volume 1 of which appeared in 1756. This book, along with
Thomas Warton's study of Spenser, his later history of English
literature, and the poems of both Joseph and Thomas—including the several poems they wrote "for" their deceased father—
show why the Warton brothers are so often singled out as the

[4]*The Logic of the Humanities* (New Haven: Yale University Press, 1961), pp.
139–40, For Miles's alternative approach see *The Primary Language of Poetry in the
1740's and 1840's* (Berkeley: University of California Press, 1950).

exemplars of preromantic taste.[5] Joseph's *Essay* is an attempt to put Pope in his place, which for Warton is clearly second place, behind Shakespeare, Milton, and Spenser. It is true that Warton's position is often taken to be more heterodox than it was and that his claim that Pope had not attempted the highest genres would have gone unchallenged by most readers.[6] Nevertheless, the decisiveness and explicitness with which Warton "places" Pope suggests a polemical stance, in fact a continuation of the miniature manifesto which had prefaced Warton's *Odes* a decade before the *Essay*, when he declared his intention to do what he could to detach poetry from the fashion of moralizing in verse and restore it to its "proper channel." While Warton would hardly go as far as Arnold a century later, there is a clear line between his premises and Arnold's opinion that Pope, like Dryden, is one of the classics not of our poetry but of our prose. Common to both is the assumption that there is something essentially unpoetic about Pope's subjects, that many of the poems are too didactic to enter the kingdom of "pure poetry."[7]

If we look at Warton's own poetry and much of what he praises in the newer poetry around him, we find in fact that he could tolerate quite a bit of didacticism and moralizing in verse, so that we need to push on a little further to see what the dividing lines really are. We gain a better idea from the following remarks concerning a poem Pope planned but never wrote, a nationalistic epic, *Brutus*. It would have been a failure, Warton decides, because Pope

[5]According to David Fairer, "The Poems of Thomas Warton the Elder?" *RES*, n.s., 26 (1975): 287–300, 395–406, Joseph and young Thomas wrote at least ten of the poems published in 1748 in the posthumous collection of their father's verse. The Wartons have been studied recently by Joan Pittock in *The Ascendancy of Taste*, by Arthur Johnston in his admirable brief survey "Poetry and Criticism after 1740," in Roger Lonsdale, ed., *History of Literature in the English Language: Dryden to Johnson* (London: Sphere, 1971), pp. 257–98, and by Wallace Jackson, *The Probable and the Marvelous* (Athens: University of Georgia Press, 1978), pp. 39–88.

[6]So argued George Sherburn in *The Early Career of Alexander Pope* (Oxford: Oxford University Press, 1934), p. 10.

[7]Joseph Warton first used the phrase "pure poetry" in his dedication (to Edward Young) of the *Essay on the Writings and Genius of Pope* (1756): "We do not, it would seem, sufficiently attend to the difference there is, betwixt a MAN OF WIT, a MAN OF SENSE, and a TRUE POET. Donne and Swift were undoubtedly men of wit and men of sense: but what traces have they left of PURE POETRY?"

would have given us many elegant descriptions and many general characters, well drawn, but would have failed to set before our eyes the *Reality* of these objects, and the *Actions* of these characters, so that it would have appeared . . . how much, and for what reasons, the man that is skillful in painting modern life, and the most secret foibles and follies of his contemporaries, is, THEREFORE disqualified for representing the ages of heroism, and that simple life, which alone epic poetry can gracefully describe, in a word, that this composition would have shown more of the *Philosopher* than the *Poet*. [1756 ed., p. 281]

This passage is interesting, first, because it is entirely in the subjunctive: like many present-day critics, Warton rises to high eloquence when unencumbered by a text. Interesting for our inquiry is the assumption that what disqualifies Pope for the epic is his modernity—his skill in "painting *modern* life." Warton views Pope as too historical, too much *in* history to rise above it. Warton does not put the emphasis squarely there and is not usually read the way I am reading him. In fact, he argues that poetry is likely to be better if it is historical, because "events that have actually happened are, after all, the properest subjects for poetry." But his examples of great works "grounded on true history" are revealing: *Oedipus, King Lear, Romeo and Juliet*, as well as Pope's own *Elegy to the Memory of an Unfortunate Lady*, all works based on very distant, obscure, or private history (253). Anything recent, documentable, and public will not have "poignancy" enough. Pope's later poetry will be judged inferior to his early work by posterity because it is more historically particular. "For Wit and Satire are transitory and perishable, but Nature and Passion are eternal" (333–34).

The oppositions are interesting—Wit versus Nature, Satire versus Passion—and of course sentimental. With too much wit and too little passion, Pope's writing presumably does not come straight enough from the heart; but more is going on here than the simple victory of bourgeois sentimentalism over Augustan satire.[8] Since satiric poetry is nearly always highly *historical* poetry, the battle is in large part over whether poetry should be

[8]Cf. Thomas Lockwood, "On the Relationship of Satire and Poetry after Pope," *Studies in English Literature*, 14 (1947): 387–402.

factual or fictional—that is, "romantic" in the old sense. When Warton says that Pope's epic would have shown more of the Philosopher than of the Poet, he means, I think, that Pope would have been not too logical but too accurate, too verifiable, and the antithesis anticipates Wordsworth's later declaration that the opposite of poetry is not prose but science.[9] Closer to Warton's own day, and closer to the terms of our discussion, we hear Adam Ferguson employing a similar distinction in *An Essay on the History of Civil Society*, published in 1767. The historian, he complains, who invokes a mythical state of nature to prove his points, "substitutes hypothesis instead of reality, and confounds the provinces of imagination and reason, of poetry and science." (Ferguson's zeal in exploding historical myths of societal origins is his generation's counterpart to Locke's zeal in exploding innate ideas.) For Ferguson, as for Hegel, history begins once myth and poetry have been cleared away. History is prose.[10]

And the poets would seem to agree. Whether by decision or default, from the 1740s on, most of the younger poets avoid direct historical treatment of the events of their day, even of their century. We can best appreciate how fundamental a shift occurs here by recalling that one of the deepest connections we can find between Dryden and Pope—and many of the contemporaries of each—is the shared sense of the poet's role as historian of his own times. That Dryden was for a time both poet laureate and historiographer royal was perhaps partially accidental, but it is also perfectly emblematic of his concerns from *Annus Mirabilis* to *Absalom and Achitophel* and beyond.[11] Pope's

---

[9]In a note to the preface to the second edition of *Lyrical Ballads* (1800), Wordsworth remarked that "much confusion has been introduced into criticism by this contradistinction of Poetry and Prose, instead of the more philosophical one of Poetry and Matter of Fact, or Science."

[10]Ferguson, *An Essay*, ed. Duncan Forbes (Edinburgh: Edinburgh University Press, 1966), p. 2, cf. pp. 6, 8, 10, 30. Hegel: "Myths, folk songs, traditions are not part of original history; they are still obscure modes and peculiar to obscure peoples. Here we deal with peoples who knew who they were and what they wanted. Observed and observable reality is a more solid foundation for history than the transience of myths and epics" (*Reason in History*, trans. Robert S. Hartman [Indianapolis: Bobbs-Merrill, 1953], p. 3).

[11]Earl Miner emphasizes Dryden's personal and public historicism persuasively in *Dryden's Poetry* (Bloomington: Indiana University Press, 1967), pp. 106–43.

historical commitment deepens throughout his career, though it is strong even in the resolution of *Windsor Forest* into current prospects for the engaged observation of *The Rape of the Lock* which, like Gay's *Trivia*, fondly records as it criticizes. Increasingly in Pope's later poetry the historical role impresses with more urgency; the decision to name names becomes not only a matter of satiric strategy but a determination to leave a record—the true record—for posterity, a record often spilling over into footnotes meant to outlast the pseudohistories of Walpole's propagandists. The catalog of corruption is wearying and perhaps futile, Pope concludes by 1738, "Yet may this Verse (if such a Verse remain) / Show there was one who held it in disdain" (*Epilogue to the Satires*, I, 171–72). The desire to reconcile poetry and history—which in the broadest sense is characteristic of most of what we think of as Augustan poetry from 1660 to 1740—is likewise the warrant for all those details of political history which Swift appends as footnotes for posterity to the *Verses on the Death of Dr. Swift*. Finally, the nightmare lurking behind the *Dunciad* is an Orwellian one of cultural amnesia: "O Muse! relate (for you can tell alone, / Wits have short Memories, and Dunces none)."

The specter which seems to be lurking behind much of the poetry of the generation after Pope's and Swift's, however, is the fear not of the loss of history but of its crushing presence, a subliminal version of Stephen Daedalus's vision where "history is a nightmare from which I am trying to awake."[12] If this is a correct interpretation of the underlying motivation of much mid-eighteenth-century poetry, as I will try to argue satisfactorily in what follows, it should be added at once that it is usually not conscious and that the poets frequently wake from history by turning to sleep. All of the symptoms of sleepiness which Pope attributed ironically to the dunces and to Dulness—lethargy, indolence, inertia, aversion to light, the blurring of perceptual and conceptual boundaries—begin to appear quickly in the 1740s as positive poetic values. One aspect of this change has been characterized by Martin Price as a shift from the "light-centered worlds of Spenser, Milton, and Pope" to the "asylum of

[12]James Joyce, *Ulysses* (New York: Random House, 1946), p. 35.

darkness."[13] Probably the most popular poem of the forties (and an extremely popular poem for another century) was *Night Thoughts*. Kindred but blessedly less sublime are the evening poems, of which Gray's *Elegy* and Collins's *Ode to Evening* are conspicuously the best.

That an atmosphere of melancholy gloom was cultivated during this period by solitary poetic wanderers has been well known since Eleanor M. Sickels wrote *The Gloomy Egoist* nearly half a century ago. Not explored in much depth since then is what might be regarded as the politics of melancholy, or perhaps more accurately, the politics of sensibility, of which melancholy is simply the commonest form in poetry. We will need to derive such a "politics" in most cases without the aid of the poets' explicit political statements, which are generally either lacking altogether in, or run contrary to what seem to be the likelier implications of, certain poetic decisions. To put these decisions into a context which clarifies their meaning, we need to consider them in continual relation to poetic procedures typified by Pope and Swift. Later I will contrast Swift and Gray in hopes of illustrating different sets of assumptions about the relation of public history and "poetic" privacy, but here the most useful general context may be suggested by considering Pope's career again. As Maynard Mack has pointed out, the vantage point from which Pope is able to tell his modern history is one of retirement.[14] This is a very complex stance, something achieved by living not merely in the country but close enough to the metropolis to be part of it (a sort of Connecticut of the soul); it must be achieved again and again in poem after poem, a vocal vision carefully and naturally "cultivated."

By the mid-century, retirement has hardened into retreat. The poet characteristically longs to be not only far from the madding crowd, which Pope had wanted as much as Gray, but far from everybody. Accordingly, many of the poems that most reflect the 1740s and 1750s are not epistles—that is, not poems with an explicit audience and implicit social engagement—but

[13]"The Sublime Poem: Pictures and Powers," *Yale Review*, 58 (1968–69): 194–213.
[14]*The Garden and the City: Retirement and Politics in the Later Poetry of Pope, 1731–1743* (Toronto: University of Toronto Press, 1969).

Toward a Poetics of Conversion

soliloquies or lyrics, usually blank verse musings or odes addressed to personifications. Conventionality again prevents us
from taking this vogue as seriously as we might; personification
is sometimes little more than capitalization, the echoes of Milton
grow tiresome, and the iconography of melancholy is all too
quickly learned in its entirety. (Parodies of melancholy poetry
were written as early as the fifties and sixties, many of them as
poetic recipes.)[15] But the fashion seems potentially revealing
largely because it becomes so fashionable so quickly. Moreover,
the melancholy poems seem merely to be part of a larger turning away from the social-historical world to which poetry traditionally belonged, and the deliberate break with and from the
past is sometimes just as evident in many of the more cheerful
poems of the period.

A signal example is the poem Joseph Warton placed at the
front of his volume of odes in 1746, the ode *To Fancy*, which
begins by saluting that visionary lady as the "Parent of each
lovely Muse" and goes on to celebrate her "magic" and "all-
commanding" power to alter the data of reality, for instance, to
make gardens bloom in Lapland. Traditionally, however, the
mother of the muses is not fancy but memory, whose magic is
bounded by mimesis. The link between poetry and memory is of
course more vivid in an oral culture than in a literate one, where
prose and print carry more of the burden of record keeping,
and it is true that the idea did not rest easily with Milton and
Blake, who complained of the confusion of true poetic "Inspiration" with the "siren daughters" of "Dame Memory."[16] But I
have tried to suggest how for most writers during the late seventeenth and early eighteenth centuries the conception of poetry
as a special form of memory is operative: the poet remembers
history and remembers it best. To make *fancy* the mother of the
muses is to sever by poetic fiat the link between poetry and
history and between the poet and the community.

We cannot place so much weight on the shoulders of Joseph

[15]Eleanor M. Sickels, *The Gloomy Egoist* (New York: Columbia University Press,
1932), pp. 67–68, 95–98.
[16]Milton, introduction to *Reason of Church Government;* Blake, preface to
Milton; cf. Northrop Frye, *Fearful Symmetry* (Princeton: Princeton University
Press, 1947), p. 163.

Warton, but the pattern is conspicuous elsewhere in the middle years of the century. When, from the late forties on, we find poems in praise of memory, they are likely to praise *private* memory; thus, Shenstone's *Ode to Memory* (1748) is largely an ode to childhood days and to "innocence." Whatever other motives may be involved, the act of prizing private memory and childhood innocence allows the poet to declare his innocence of history, that adult world of public contention. The innocence of childhood is something of a mid-eighteenth-century invention, and we can best grasp its political content by considering that to which it is frequently opposed, namely "Ambition." We will return to the theme of ambition directly below, but for now it is useful to recall that Shenstone uses memory as an explicit vehicle to transport him from the world of ambition, even purely literary ambition, to the careless world of his hobbyhorse and whistle. (It is pleasant to imagine Sterne deliberately placing Toby, his time divided between hobbyhorse riding and whistling, in a world of conventional childhood duties.)

A few years before Shenstone's *Ode to Memory*, Gray wrote the first important eighteenth-century poem which poses childhood scenes against the fallen world of adulthood, the *Ode on a Distant Prospect of Eton College* (1742). Gray's nostalgic praise of childhood joys, the "paths of pleasure" from which the speaker is separated by time and space, is all the more interesting as a period phenomenon, since Gray most likely had spent some miserable years on the edges of those celebrated playing fields. But after the gracefully awkward humor of pliant arms cleaving grassy waves and idle progeny urging the flying ball, the description of childhood is mostly in negative terms, in terms of its difference from the speaker's present condition:

> Gay hope is theirs by fancy fed,
> Less pleasing when possessed;
> The tear forgot as soon as shed,
> The sunshine of the breast. . . .

Only a powerful need to simplify childhood experience could prompt a poet of Gray's intelligence to say that the child's tear is forgotten as soon as shed or to sum up the world which includes adolescence—Gray himself left Eton at seventeen—as a guiltless succession:

> The thoughtless day, the easy night,
> The spirits pure, the slumbers light,
> That fly the approach of morn.

It is tempting to compare Gray's generalized "slumbers light" with the passage in *The Prelude* where Wordsworth describes the haunted slumbers following the boat-stealing episode:

> No familiar shapes
> Remained, no pleasant images of trees,
> Of sea or sky, no colours of green fields;
> But huge and mighty forms, that do not live
> Like living men, moved slowly through the mind
> By day, and were a trouble to my dreams.[17]

Thus far the temptation suggests much about the preoccupations of both poets, but it would not be useful to follow it a step further and to conclude that Wordsworth's lines are deeper because truer to experience. They are "truer" psychologically, and they depend less on conventional views of experience, or else on conventions closer to our own (the uninnocence of children); but the truth Gray is after here is, I think, more political than Wordsworth's and in fact more political than Gray himself likely would acknowledge:

> Alas, regardless of their doom,
> The little victims play!
> No sense have they of ills to come,
> Nor care beyond today:
> Yet see how all around 'em wait
> The ministers of human fate,
> And black Misfortune's baleful train!

[17]*Prelude* (1850), I, 395–400, in *The Prelude*, ed. Jonathan Wordsworth, M. H. Abrams, and Stephen Gill (New York: Norton, 1979). Quotations from Gray are from *The Poems of Gray, Collins, and Goldsmith*, ed. Roger Lonsdale (London: Longmans, 1969); Collins is quoted from *The Works of W. C.*, ed. Richard Wendorf and Charles Ryskamp (Oxford: Clarendon Press, 1979).

> Ah, show them where in ambush stand
> To seize their prey the murtherous band!
> Ah, tell them, they are men!

Gray's lament would seem to be wholly apolitical, since the woes which await the children are envisioned as human rather than historical evils, due, in other words, to the nature of things rather than to the nature of people's allotment of things. The children shall one day be torn by "fury Passions," those "vultures of the mind," which Gray catalogs iconographically ("pallid Fear," "pining Love," "Envy wan," and so on). Then Gray turns to a somewhat more social picture, though the images remain indistinct:

> Ambition this small tempt to rise,
> Then whirl the wretch from high,
> To bitter Scorn a sacrifice,
> And grinning Infamy.
> The stings of Falsehood those shall try,
> And hard Unkindness' altered eye,
> That mocks the tear it forced to flow;
> And keen Remorse with blood defiled,
> And moody Madness laughing wild
> Amid severest woe.

The most accurate thing we could say at this point of the politics of this particular melancholy is that Gray cannot or will not make a distinction between necessary and unnecessary human suffering, just as it is not clear a few lines later whether "Poverty" is as inevitable as "slow-consuming Age" or something which accompanies it because of human "Unkindness."[18] Gray offers no political platform, just as Johnson does not in *The Vanity of Human Wishes*. But what is politically significant from our position is simply the fact that childhood and rural innocence are being used as new norms by which to measure the passionate tragedy of the world adults make. The prepassionate, or innocent, state attributed to the schoolchildren is a kind of

---

[18]Cf. the "common lot" of political and natural ills in *Night Thoughts*, I, 237ff.: "War . . . volcano, storm . . . Oppression . . ."

internalized Golden Age, a prehistory of the sort which Adam Ferguson later complained belongs more to poetry than to truth. So, at the beginning of *The Seasons,* James Thomson lavishly describes the earliest stage of human life, when all was springtime harmony and vegetarian plenty, as a prepassionate childhood of the race. Now, however, "all / Is off the poise within: the passions all / Have burst their bounds," and the breeze of social feeling has given way to a psychic "storm" of "mixed emotions":

> Senseless and deformed,
> Convulsive Anger storms at large; or, pale
> And silent, settles into fell revenge.
> Base Envy withers at another's joy,
> And hates that excellence it cannot reach.
> Desponding Fear, of feeble fancies full,
> Weak and unmanly, loosens every power.
> Even Love itself is bitterness of soul,
> A pensive anguish pining at the heart;
> Or, sunk to sordid interest, feels no more
> That noble wish, that never-cloyed desire,
> Which, selfish joy disdaining, seeks alone
> To bless the dearer object of its flame.
> Hope sickens with extravagance; and Grief,
> Of life impatient, into madness swells. . . .
>
> [*Spring,* 281–95]

From this storm of violent and contending passions grows eventually the "listless unconcern" of modern life until (in phrases reminiscent of Book IV of the *Dunciad*) "At last, extinct each social feeling, fell / And joyless inhumanity pervades / And petrifies the heart" (301–7).[19]

One secular version of history which had been available to poets who wanted to retain the idea of a Golden Age was a correspondingly secular version of the Fortunate Fall: being expelled from a cultural Eden, or, as Thomson puts it, from "Na-

[19]Quotations from *The Castle of Indolence* are from *The Seasons and The Castle of Indolence,* ed. James Sambrook (London: Oxford University Press, 1972); *The Seasons* is quoted from Thomson's *Poetical Works,* ed. J. L. Robertson (1908; reprint ed., London: Oxford University Press, 1965).

ture's ample lap" (*Spring*, 182; cf. 351), leads man to exert his energies, learn, build, make laws, and so on. This is Pope's version of history in epistle 3 of the *Essay on Man*, and it is compatible both with traditional Christian patterns of theodicy and with the desire to posit a Lockean rather than a Hobbesean original state. But increasingly toward the mid-century the Fall into society and history is seen not as a fortunate fall but as a catastrophe.

To see this development accurately we need to distinguish "official" dogma for many of the poets from what emerges less consciously. Thomson is the best single example of the possible forms of ambivalence, probably because he is literally between the generation of Gay and Pope, for example, and that of Gray and Collins. (Gay was born in 1685, Thomson in 1700, Gray in 1716, Collins, the Wartons and Akenside in the early 1720s.) What I refer to as the official view in Thomson and later writers is one which endorses vigorous activity, commercial energy, social engagement, "worthy" ambition, and patriotism, which is merely a broadened form of benevolence, which in turn is virtue at its highest. Public life, hard work, technical progress are all good things, according to this view. We can see it embodied in the several mid-century adaptations of "The Choice of Hercules," the episode originally imagined by Prodicus, in which the young Hercules has to choose between Virtue and Pleasure. In Shenstone's rendition, "The Judgment of Hercules," it is clear that pleasure is suspect because it lies in "cloister'd" withdrawal from society, while virtue is tied to "industry," "Fame," "arts," and "arms." Officially, in short, virtue is public.[20]

But the increasingly commercial civilization in which public virtue would find its theater is at best problematic. Thomson is in the awkward position of celebrating the Golden Age, one of the traits of which is the absence of navigation, shortly before turning to praise the British navy and sea-connected empire—

---

[20]On the mid-century vogue of *The Choice of Hercules*, see Earl Wasserman, "The Inherent Values of Eighteenth-Century Personification," *PMLA*, 65 (1950): 435–63 (esp. 437–39), and Ronald Paulson, "The Simplicity of Hogarth's *Industry and Idleness*," *ELH*, 41 (1974): 291–320 (esp. 308–11). Shenstone's "The Judgment of Hercules" is quoted from *The Poetical Works of William Shenstone*, ed. George Gilfillan (1854; reprint ed., New York: Greenwood, 1968), pp. 186–201; the phrases are from lines 315–80.

and "Navigation bold," that "Mother severe of infinite delights!"
(*Summer*, 1,768–70). But if Thomson's mercantile muse praises
the "rising world of trade," sings the city as the "nurse of art,"
and sees "Industry" as its human prerequisite (*Summer*, 1,006;
Autumn, 113–41), Thomson repeatedly imagines his own inspiration as coming from solitary walks in the hills and longs for
the "deepending dale, or inmost sylvan glade" (*Summer*, 191–99,
560), for such precincts are

> the haunts of meditation, these
> The scenes where ancient bards the inspiring breath
> Ecstatic felt, and, from this world retired,
> Conversed with angels and immortal forms.
>
> [*Summer*, 522–25]

The opposition of poetic and political values animates Thomson's most powerful contrast of rural and urban life, contemplation and action, innocence and guilt:

> Let others brave the flood in quest of gain,
> And beat for joyless months the gloomy wave.
> Let such as deem it glory to destroy
> Rush into blood, the sack of cities seek—
> Unpierced, exulting in the widow's wail,
> The virgin's shriek, the infant's trembling cry.
> . . . . .
> Let this through cities work his eager way
> By legal outrage and established guile,
> The social sense extinct; and that ferment
> Mad into tumult the seditious herd,
> Or melt them down to slavery. Let these
> Ensnare the wretched in the toils of law,
> Fomenting discord, and perplexing right,
> An iron race! and those of fairer front,
> But equal inhumanity, in courts,
> Delusive pomp, and dark cabals delight. . . .
>
> [*Autumn*, 1,278–96]

Against this catalog of the woes of modern social life Thomson
places an image of individual retreat, a stoic figure who detaches
himself from the wreckage around him. This image we will find

again in Joseph Warton, where, too, the stoic protestations carry
overtones of desperation because the "philosophy" is so clearly
at odds with the emotionalism prized elsewhere in the poem.
Thomson's sage is one who,

> from all the stormy passions free
> That restless men involve, hears, and but hears,
> At distance sage, the human tempest roar,
> Wrapped close in conscious peace. The fall of kings,
> The rage of nations, and the crush of states
> Move not the man who, from the world escaped,
> In still retreats and flower solitudes
> To Nature's voice attends from month to month,
> And day to day, through the revolving year—
> Admiring, sees her in her every shape. . . .
> [*Autumn*, 1,299–1,308]

If this sage resembles a Roman philosopher at the beginning
of the passage, by its end he seems more like an English poet,
specifically, a poet who might write a poem on the "revolving
year." And if this poet is the laureate of "Nature's voice," it is
clear that Nature here does not include human nature. We have
entered the world of modern usage, where "nature" typically
means a place without people (or without any people but me)
and where "society" is seen as radically "unnatural." This is the
complex of assumptions which started becoming conventionally
"poetic" during the middle and later years of the eighteenth
century and which in Cowper apparently hardened into the ax-
iom that "God made the country, and man made the town" (*The
Task*, I, 749). One could add, of course that God made man and
so must have something to do with the town and with human
society generally; but the addition is not often made by the mid-
century poets.

Celebrations of solitary retreat are particularly arresting in
Thomson because they are very likely to follow, or be followed
quickly by, a call to art and arms, by praise of progress, or by
intimations of the providential role of British imperial policy.
But Thomson's most starkly ambivalent poem is *The Castle of
Indolence*, a work rather indolently composed beginning sometime in the thirties and ending with its publication a few months

before his death in 1748. Although Thomson uses his Spenserian idiom at several points for burlesque, it also calls attention to the similarity between the Castle and Spenserian seductions which must be destroyed or fled. Conceptually as well as chronologically, however, Thomson's Castle is closer to the Palace of Art than to the Bower of Bliss. Although sensually appealing, its lure is more intellectual than erotic: it is a retreat, offering uninterrupted solitude, freedom from any social responsibility, and absolution from all duties and from memory, and it is associated most persuasively with reverie and poetic imagination, "dreams that wave before the half-shut eye" (I, vi; cf. I, xxxvi–xlviii).

The castle is of course eventually broken up by the "Knight of Arts and Industry" in a kind of harrowing of hell, and the prisoners of sloth are set free. But more to the point for our inquiry concerning poetic alignment is the fact that this knightly paragon of social virtue is accompanied by a poet, the "little Druid wight" (II, xxxiii) usually identified as Alexander Pope (which might suggest that the Knight himself, who at his country seat combined the roles of "the chief, the patriot, and the swain," should remind us of Bolingbroke). Since it is the poet's song which breaks the enchanter's spell, Thomson is paying wistful allegiance to the notion of poetry as a political force, idealizing the collaboration of poet and patriot as Pope had done in his later poetry and as he himself had done in his most sustained political-historical poem, *Liberty* (1735–1736), where he commemorates the "recording arts" for their power to "rouse ambition" in a great nation (V, 374ff.).[21] But ambition is, as we have seen in *The Seasons*, likely to be delusive, dirty, and dangerous. In the *Castle of Indolence* there is a crystal ball called the Mirror of Vanity in which one can see the ambitious toiling at their getting and spending, at writing books—

> This globe pourtrayed the race of learned men,
> Still at their books, and turning o'er the page,
> Backwards and forwards: oft they snatch the pen
> As if inspired, and in a Thespian rage;

[21] *Liberty* has been quoted from the text of Thomson's *Poetical Works*, ed. J. L. Robertson, Oxford Standard Authors (1908; reprint ed.: London, Oxford University Press, 1965).

Then write, and blot, as would your ruth engage.
Why, authors, all this scrawl and scribbling sore?
To lose the present, gain the future age,
Praised to be when you can hear no more,
And much enriched with fame when useless worldly store!

[I, lii]

We next see those trying to make their way in the city, and then the politicians whispering and shrugging the "important shoulder" significantly.

But what most showed the vanity of life
Was to behold the nations all on fire
In cruel broils engaged, and deadly strife:
Most Christian kings, inflamed by black desire,
With honourable ruffians in their hire,
Cause war to rage and blood around to pour.
Of this sad work when each begins to tire,
They sit them down just where they were before.
Till for new scenes of woe peace shall their force restore.

[I, lv]

The Castle of Indolence can be read as a debate on the virtues of the stances I have characterized as Augustan retirement and post-Augustan retreat, with retirement the official winner: the rural but industrious Knight lives in "deep retirement" (II, xxvii), and he and his poet destroy the isolated and indolent world of the Castle. But at the same time much of the best energy of the poem is used to paint the futility of "industry" so convincingly that the world of reverie and retreat looks not only comfortable but potentially noble by comparison. Thomson might not agree with this reading of his unofficial sympathies, and some present-day students of his poetry certainly would not.[22] This reading, however, accords not only with much that is in the poem but with much that is around it, in the work of several writers of the mid-eighteenth century for whom the urgings of "ambition" and the promptings of "pure" poetry are felt as anti-

---

[22]E.g., Donald Greene, "From Accidie to Neurosis: *The Castle of Indolence* Revisited," in Maximillian E. Novak, ed., *English Literature in the Age of Disguise* (Berkeley: University of California Press, 1977).

thetical demands. This tension is of course especially difficult for anyone who might ambitiously want to be a pure poet, and we will examine its strains more closely in the next chapter.

In the mid-eighteenth century, history's metonymy is conflict. Very often it is the violent conflict of war, but it can also be the strife of competition. Not surprisingly, the retreat from history occurs in poems most dramatically when historical events and public actors are portrayed as hostile not only to the life of poetry (for example, as antithetical to Thomson's nature-loving solitary) but to the life of the poet himself. The very earliest major poems of William Collins and Thomas Warton the Younger are pastorals in which the youthful poetic speakers are victims of violence perpetrated by older, more public males. The speakers are fugitives from war, appearing in the poems at just the point where they are becoming refugees. The last of Collins's *Persian Eclogues* (published in 1742, but probably written when Collins was seventeen) ends with two shepherds fleeing the invading Tartar army—

> when loud along the vale was heard
> A shriller shriek and nearer fires appeared:
> The afrighted shepherds through the dews of night,
> Wide o'er the moonlight hills, renewed their flight.

Warton's *Pastoral Eclogues* (published anonymously in 1745) are set "during the wars in Germany," and his young swains are continually retreating from the clamor of war to the protection of groves and caves.

But the best example of such a collision between the poet-speaker and the hostile force of history is *The Bard*. Gray's poem is based on the appealing tradition that Edward I executed the Welsh bards once he had conquered that country—an appealing tradition because it suggests the poets were once too potent politically to be ignored—and the poem begins as the bard stands high on a cliff hurling prophetic curses down on the king like so many verbal boulders. Finally he hurls himself:

> ". . . with joy I see
> The different doom over fates assign.
> Be thine despair and sceptered care;

To triumph, and to die, are mine."
He spoke, and headlong from the mountain's height
Deep in the roaring tide he plunged to endless night.

To triumph and to die. The phrase seems more a definition
than a paradox in Gray's poetic world, where death, like childhood, can so readily become an emblem of innocence from history. The bard's suicide is both a badge of his sincerity (an association we have since tended to take more literally) and a final
exercise of the kind of linguistic power which William Law had
attributed to God: "What he speaks he acts."[23] To end his poet's
lyric and life in the same breath is Gray's sublime speech act. If
we visualize the dramatic moment Gray has frozen in the poem,
we may understand better the full significance of the encounter
and the redefinition of death as triumph. The fantasy on which
it turns is double. On the one hand, history must stop for the
poet, since this king, unlike George II, must actually listen to the
ode he has occasioned;[24] on the other hand, the forced march of
history will go on and, embodied in Edward and his army, will
kill the poet.

The collision between poet and history is less violent in the
Elegy Written in a Country Churchyard but no less fatal. The poem
ends with the imagined death of the poet himself, a death related in the subjunctive but converted into virtual fact in the epitaph, which I take to be the poet's own. Once we view the *Elegy* as
a poem in which the poet imagines the reaction to his own death,
a useful comparison comes to mind with Swift's *Verses on the
Death of Dr. Swift*. The poems are so obviously different in intent
and effect that most readers, not surprisingly, would not draw
the comparison; but it may help clarify some rapid changes in
poetry if we attempt to pinpoint some of the differences between these poems of the early 1730s and the late 1740s.

Both the *Verses* and the *Elegy* are poems of moral generalization. Swift's reflections are largely glosses on the maxim from La
Rochefoucauld which he translates in the epigraph as, "In the

[23]Law, *A Demonstration* . . . (1737), in *The Works of W. L.*, 9 vols. (New Forest:
G. Moreton, 1892–93), V, 73.
[24]Similar fantasies of the poet's access to his king and power over him are
enacted in Thomas Warton's *The Crusade* and *The Grave of King Arthur*.

97

Adversity of our best Friends, we find something that doth not displease us," and versifies as, "In all Distresses of our Friends / we first consult our private Ends." Gray's "maxims," on the other hand, are "The paths of glory lead but to the grave," and "Even from the tomb the voice of nature cries." The moral position implied by the *Elegy* as a whole is almost an inversion of La Rochefoucauld: we are so sympathetic, so tenderly framed, that even the imagined distresses of total strangers affect us feelingly. Not *every*one, exactly, but surely the speaker and the reader will appreciate the moral sentiments carved in the stones and trees of the churchyard in the innocent country.[25]

Distance from town is an important part of the moral atmosphere of Swift's poem, too, and so is the relative solitude of the speaker. If Swift is not quite as explicit about locating his world far from the madding crowd or about isolating his speaker ("And leaves the world to darkness and to me"), the ethos of his *Verses* is quite as dependent on the impression that the speaker is far from the center of power and that he is insulated by his integrity. The obvious difference on this count, however, is one between total and partial solitude. The simple and supposedly neutral speaker who characterizes Swift insists upon his social life: it is a contracted society, to be sure, but the friendships are as essential a part of the man as his pleasant stories of Whigs and Tories. Gray's speaker speaks to no one except the reader, and for the "hoary-headed swain" who describes him (a nice counterpart to Swift's coffeehouse judge) he is the silent image of "one forlorn."

The sympathies of Gray's poet are generalized to the while village and to the simpler folk everywhere ("mindful of the unhonored dead"), but he has no specific connection to anyone. The different attitudes toward the use of particulars is in fact the source of most of the other differences between the poems. For just as the expression of anger and humor in Swift's poem depends on the use of historical particulars, so Gray's melancholy and solemnity depend on the generalization of emotions

---

[25]The moral appeal of Gray's work has been reconsidered freshly and helpfully by Howard Weinbrot in "Gray's *Elegy:* A Poem of Moral Choice and Resolution," *Studies in English Literature,* 18 (1978): 537–51.

into a subjunctive world, a world where "*Perhaps . . . is laid*"
some potential hero to be mourned by a poet whom "*Haply* some
hoary-headed swain *may*" describe to "*some* kindred spirit" who
comes by "chance" to ask. Swift's poem is wholly without despon-
dency because its anger so clearly has particular limits; Gray's,
like the melancholy it marks as its own, is grief without an object.

While Swift's poem aims to make all of the people and events
it names into part of the historical record, much of the most
poignant musing in Gray's *Elegy* centers on the reflection that
the simple villagers buried in the churchyard are not part of
history. The "short and simple annals of the poor" are contrasted with the public "Memory" left by "Ambition," "Grandeur," and the "pomp of power." There is much melancholy in
their obscurity as it is translated into the speculative subjunctive:

> Perhaps in this neglected spot is laid
> Some heart once pregnant with celestial fire;
> Hands that the rod of empire might have swayed,
> Or waked to ecstasy the living lyre. . . .

> Some village-Hampden that with dauntless breast
> The little tyrant of his fields withstood;
> Some mute inglorious Milton here may rest,
> Some Cromwell guiltless of his country's blood.

But Gray insists upon having it both ways, as we have ever
since the mid-eighteenth century: the pathos of unrealized potential is balanced emotionally by the triumph of rural
innocence.

> The applause of listening senates to command,
> The threats of pain and ruin to despise,
> To scatter plenty o'er a smiling land,
> And read their history in a nation's eyes,

> Their lot forbade: nor circumscribed alone
> Their growing virtues, but their crimes confined;
> Forbade to wade through slaughter to a throne,
> And shut the gates of mercy on mankind. . . .

99

It is the conception of potential—unnurtured or thwarted talent—that is most remarkable in all of these reflections. What, after all, is a mute Milton? The fact that we are likely to read the lines hundreds of times without asking that question suggests how deeply the idea of potential is embedded in modern thought. A blind Milton we know, a deaf Milton we could imagine, but to conceive a mute Milton we need to conceive of the poet in a different manner; before the phrase can have any meaning, the poet must be no longer one who writes poetry but a sensitive person who has a poet's soul. In the *Ode to Fear* Collins prays that he will be allowed not to write like Shakespeare but "once like him to feel," the presumption being that all the rest will then follow.

Just after the stanzas from the *Elegy* which we have been considering the villagers are idealized for living "far from the madding crowd's *ignoble strife*," a phrase which suggests a vision like the one available in Thomson's little mirror of vanity. The emphasis is less on the crowd as an unruly or destructive mob—a traditional staple of satiric imagery—but on strife, the competition and ambition of city folk as "ignoble" virtually by definition. Gray's poet is not made for such a world, and even the subjunctive intrusion of history into the village where he has sought refuge is enough to kill him off. The mixture of defensive and superior feelings at being out of the public world and the historical mainstream crystallizes in the last line of a later poem, *The Progress of Poesy*, where the poet imagines his eventual place, "Beneath the Good how far—but far above the Great."

The suspicion of greatness is one of the few themes shared by early eighteenth-century satirists and later sentimentalists alike. *A Tale of a Tub, The Beggar's Opera*, and *Jonathan Wild* are largely treatises on the subject. If chronology did not discourage us, we might almost read the mock-heroic *Jonathan Wild* as an ironic commentary on Hegel's conception of heroism in his lectures on history. To juxtapose the two authors helps to measure the distance between either Augustan or post-Augustan attitudes and at least one strain of later romantic preoccupations with titanic figures. Hegel's world-historical individuals "must be called 'heroes,' insofar as they have derived their purpose and vocation not from the calm, regular course of things, sanctioned by the existing order, but from a secret source whose content is still hidden and has not yet broken through into existence." (Cf. Pope's ironic explanation in the *Epistle to Bathurst* that misers act upon "Some Revelation hid from me and you.") "Great men have worked for their own satisfaction and not that of others," Hegel explains, but when we consider their fate we find that

> they were not what is commonly called happy, nor did they want to be. . . . Thus they attained no calm enjoyment. Their whole life was labor and trouble. . . . They die early like Alexander, they are murdered like Caesar, transported to St. Helena like Napoleon. This awful fact, that historical men were not what is called happy— for only private life in its manifold external circumstances can be "happy"—may serve as consolation for those people who need it, the envious ones who cannot tolerate greatness and eminence.[26]

These are the terms in which Fielding's Jonathan Wild soliloquizes over his punch on the motives of "priggery" (that is, thievery):

> "'tis the inward glory, the secret consciousness of doing great and wonderful actions, which alone can support the truly GREAT man, whether he be a CONQUEROR, a TYRANT, a STATESMAN, or a PRIG. . . . For what but some such inward satisfaction as this could inspire men possessed of power, wealth, of every human blessing which pride, avarice, or luxury could desire, to forsake their homes, abandon ease and repose, and . . . at the hazard of all that fortune hath liberally given them, could send them at the Lead of a multitude of *prigs*, called an army, to molest their neighbours; to introduce rape, rapine, bloodshed, and every kind of misery among their own species? . . . let me then hold myself contented with this reflection, that I have been wise though unsuccessful, and am a GREAT though an unhappy man."[27]

A second, briefer pairing of ideas will underscore the difference between pathos based on heroic faith and irony based on a colder estimate of individualistic "greatness." Of heroes Hegel says, "Once their objective is attained, they fall off like

[26]Hegel, *Reason in History,* trans. Robert S. Hartman (Indianapolis: Bobbs-Merrill, 1953), p. 41; page numbers in text refer to this edition.
[27]Fielding, *Johnathan Wild and a Voyage to Lisbon,* ed. A. R. Humphreys and Douglas Brooks (London: J. M. Dent, 1973), pp. 58–59; page numbers in text refer to this edition.

empty hulls from the kernel" (41); they are dropped, in other words, when "Reason" no longer needs them. Fielding puts it this way: "There seems to be a certain measure of mischief and iniquity which every great man is to fill up, and then fortune looks on him [as] of no more use than a silkworm whose bottom is spun, and deserts him" (126).

But now let us turn the commentary and allow Hegel to serve as critic of some of the dominant chords in mid-eighteenth-century writing. We can indeed, says Hegel, dwell with melancholy, lamenting the decay of kingdoms and "contemplating history as the slaughter-bench at which the happiness of peoples, the wisdom of states, and the virtues of individuals have been sacrificed." But, he insists, "we have purposely eschewed that method of reflection which ascends from this scene of particulars to general principles. Besides, it is not in the interest of such sentimental reflection really to rise above these depressing emotions and to solve the mysteries of Providence presented in such contemplations. It is rather their nature to dwell melancholically on the empty and fruitless sublimities of their negative result" (27).

Hegel is not but easily could be describing in this meditation on melancholy the "fruitless sublimities" of Gray's *Elegy* or Johnson's *Vanity of Human Wishes*. We have seen how the conflict and violence of public history as it is conceived metonymically by many of the poets leads to images of Retreat, images of shepherds fleeing as they sing, for example, hurrying toward the shelter of shady groves or the protection of caves, and we have seen that these images of seclusion are also metaphors for the solitary poetic imagination itself. In one of the most radical of retreats, Joseph Warton imagines himself at the end of *The Enthusiast* secured from the ravages of historical reality, like Thomson's sage in his distance from disaster but unlike him in that he does not even hear the disturbance:

> So when rude Whirlwinds rouse the roaring Main,
> Beneth fair THETIS sits, in coral Caves,
> Serenely gay, nor sinking Sailors Cries
> Disturb her sportive Nymphs. . . .

[1744]

The imagined shipwreck is suggestive, for it is the image Hegel invoked to characterize one response, an inadequate response, in his view, to historical misery: "And at last, out of the boredom with which this sorrowful reflection threatens us, we draw back into the vitality of the present, into our aims and interests of the moment; we retreat, in short, into the selfishness that stands on the quiet shore and thence enjoys in safety the distant spectacle of wreckage and confusion" (27).

What is the nature of the world into which the poets retreat and which they pose as an alternative history? It is not in general a world of romance, although that is the term usually opposed to "history" in eighteenth-century criticism. The successful assimilation of romance material into poetry really *is* a romantic achievement. The post-Augustan poetic world first evident in the 1740s is typically less rich in narrative analogues and more abundant in detached images of seclusion and protection; it is a world which is often visually indistinct or darkened; and it is a world where consolation is prized over confrontation, stasis over strife. To understand it more fully we need to turn to one of its most problematic intruders, the specter of "Ambition," and to the miniature ahistorical drama which it often offers, a drama of conversion. And we will need to begin by considering what a contemporary had in mind when he defined the new poetry of the mid-century as "romantic."

CHAPTER 4

Ambition, Conversion,
and Lyric Grace

We have seen how, from the churchyard of the *Elegy*, "Ambition" is virtually synonymous with public history and with the "Pomp of Power" which lures the Cromwells and Hamdens of the world onto its high stage. And we recall how from the Castle of Indolence the motive of Ambition is what leads men—and Ambition is usually a male problem in these poems—into the series of civil disturbances making up the history of nations. When in the *Vanity of Human Wishes* (1749) Johnson personifies History ("Let Hist'ry tell . . ."), he is both calling in a second muse to assist "Observation" and generalizing public history into a series of ill-conceived and ill-fated ambitions. During the 1740s Shenstone as well turns to Johnson's Wolsey and others to point the perils of "fair Ambition," and in 1750 in an *Ode to Indolence* Shenstone chooses "gentle Sloth" over the complicity and compromise demanded of the "busy" people who would succeed at "ambition's guilty shrine."[1]

Even Mark Akenside, who, like Young, is less ambivalent than most of the other mid-century poets about the attractions of glory, begins his volume of *Odes* (1745) by preferring the "lowly, sylvan scenes" of poetry to the paths of "fond ambition." Akenside's most insistently "ambitious" poem in tone, as in scope, is *The Pleasures of Imagination*, which we will consider separately in

[1] *The Poetical Works of William Shenstone*, ed. George Gilfillan (1854; reprint ed., New York: Greenwood, 1968), pp. 11–14 (for *Elegy VII*, in which Wolsey appears) and pp. 135–36 (*Ode to Indolence*). Cf. *The Ode to Memory, 1748:* "But let me chase those vows away, / Which at Ambition's shrine I made" (p. 117).

the next chapter, but the notes of ambition, energy, patriotism, and public engagement are rung frequently in his odes as well. They are sounded in the odes of Joseph Warton and Collins and in much of Thomson's poetry; but the difference is that in these poets the call to public action is conspicuously in tension with other values associated with retreat, indolence, or purity. Akenside's problem is not a lack of conviction concerning ambition (when his calls to action fail to move, they do so less because of a confusion of beliefs than because of a diffusion of diction), for he generally shares the progressive optimism of the day, which we now regard loosely as Whiggish, though of course it sometimes cut across the shifting lines of party allegiances. The essential premise is perhaps best expressed by Adam Ferguson in *An Essay on the History of Civil Society* when he says that the human creature is "destined, from the first age of his being, to invent and contrive," that his "emblem is a passing stream, not a stagnating pool," because he "has in himself a principle of progression." The world of human art and industry is "natural," in other words, and should not be contrasted with some primitivistic myth of Rousseauvian return.[2] This is the context in which ambition is laudable, in which James Thomson praises navigation and imperial energy, for example, or in which Thomas Warton urges the sons of Isis to rush into politics, Collins rouses the new generation of patriots to public action, and Joseph Warton not only praises famous tyrant killers but sees the human imperative to "be free" reflected mightily in England's "busy towns."[3]

[2]*An Essay on the History of Civil Society* (1767), ed. Duncan Forbes (Edinburgh: Edinburgh University Press, 1966), pp. 5–8. Near the end of the *Essay* Ferguson urges satirists and moralists to stop attacking ambition, arguing that they have not been "duly aware of the corruption they flattered by the satire they employed against what is aspiring and prominent in the character of the human soul" (p. 257). Akenside assumes a similar position in ode 17 of Book I (*On a Sermon against Glory*, 1747). and in ode 5 of Book II (*Of Love of Praise*).

[3]Thomson's inconsistent treatment of ambition is discussed in chapter 5; the other references in this sentence are to Thomas Warton's *The Triumph of Isis* (1749; see also his *Ode for Music*, 1751), Collins's odes to Mercy and Liberty, and Joseph Warton's *To Liberty*. Editions used here and elsewhere unless otherwise cited: *The Works of William Collins*, ed. Richard Wendorf and Charles Ryskamp (Oxford: Clarendon Press, 1979); Joseph Warton, *Odes on Various Subjects* (1746), reprinted with an introduction by Richard Wendorf (Los Angeles: Augustan

But in the more usual context for the poets, Ambition is associated with either War or Commerce. From this perspective Joseph Warton's busy towns become—for Joseph Warton himself—the "tradeful city" which speaks with "one deep-swelling hum" of the "feverish luxury," "avarice," and "business" of a hostile culture. From such a "folly-fettered world" of noise and activity (thus described in the ode *To Solitude* and *The Enthusiast*) Collins withdraws in most of his odes to dwell quietly and singly with his visionary lady, much as Gray's poetic speakers withdraw from active contamination to the purity of death. And in this context, too, Thomas Warton contrasts rural life with "guilty gain," religious life with "guilty state," innocence with "busy scenes," and poetic inspiration with "industry," "commerce," and "pollution."[4]

1

Let us return now to the "politics of melancholy." On one level the phrase seems wholly contradictory, since one of the characteristics of melancholy laments—the "fruitless sublimities" of Hegel's description—is the apparent inability or refusal to differentiate between natural and political evils. Things are bad not because the Whigs or the Tories are in power, or because the standing army is too large or too weak, or because the ministry is corrupt, but because that is the Way Things Are. The paths of glory lead but to the grave because life is short. Human wishes are vain because human knowledge is narrow and the imagination hungry. Penury is likely to attend old age for the same reason that pain is, because happiness and health are fleeting. Such is the melancholy mood at its least political.

And yet when we look to much of the literature of the period, a cluster of political preoccupations does emerge. In general, success is suspect, as is the "ambition" required to achieve it. Commerce is unattractive, as is the city in which it is most in

---

Reprint Society, 1979); *The Works of the English Poets,* ed. Alexander Chalmers (London, 1810), vol. 18, for Thomas Warton and poems of Joseph Warton not in the *Odes* of 1746.

   [4]The phrases of Thomas Warton are quoted from *The Hamlet, In a Hermitage,* and *The Complaint of Cherwell.*

evidence. War, although occasionally fought in defense of "Liberty," which can be a poetic subject, is generally antipoetic, hostile to the peaceful spirit of poetry and poets. The best people do not often, perhaps not usually, rise to the top, because the competition for "places" in society and in history is ruthless and demeaning. "Slow rises worth by poverty depressed," Johnson wrote in *London*, a less melancholy and more angry poem than *The Vanity of Human Wishes*,[5] but the conclusion increasingly in the mid-century years is that worth is also by modesty depressed. Both Hume and Fielding explicitly address as a social problem the fact that "impudence" will generally outstrip modesty" in the competition of modern life. The liabilities of modesty and morality in such a world make up much of the action of Fielding's *Jonathan Wild* and *Amelia*, Sarah Fielding's *David Simple*, and Goldsmith's *Vicar of Wakefield*. (Thomas R. Preston has recently noted that the period interest in the "man of feeling in an unfeeling world" tends to make "prudence" an ambiguous value.) Goldsmith elsewhere weighs the "great and the avaricious of this world" against "harmless" scholars whose work may help repair "the breaches caused by ambition."[6]

All of these concerns would seem to add up to at least a general protest against various capitalistic tendencies, if not an analysis of them. If one socially acceptable avenue after another is portrayed as poetically unacceptable, we may infer a shared attempt to differentiate the world of poetry from the world of political and economic behavior. In other words, the very calls to depoliticize poetry and to lift it "above" the conflicts of modern history constitute a new politicization of poetry. We frequently fail to recognize it as such simply because it accords with many popular premises of our own concerning the separation of art and state, such as the expectation that artists will be "alienated" and too "sensitive" to be comfortable in "society." To see just

5In "To *The Vanity of Human Wishes* through the 1740s," *Studies in Philology*, 74 (1977): 445–64, I have tried to show that the latter peom is affected more by the melancholy of mid-century poetics than by the "Juvenalian" tones of Pope's *Imitations of Horace*, which seem to provide the immediate model for *London*.

6Preston, *Not in Timon's Manner: Feeling, Misanthropy, and Satire in Eighteenth-Century England* (University: University of Alabama Press, 1975), esp. pp. 20–28; Goldsmith, *An Enquiry into the Present State of Polite Learning* (1759), in *Collected Works*, ed. Arthur Friedman (Oxford: Clarendon Press, 1966), I, 286.

what kind of unconscious politicization of poetry was occurring in the middle decades of the eighteenth century we need again to rely on a post-Augustan rather than a preromantic context.

For we can characterize much of the best literature of the 1720s and 1730s as a literature of Opposition.[7] The major writers are sympathetic to the aims of the Opposition to Walpole's government, and while we are now fond of saying that the important works "transcend" their topicality, the fact is that they depend on an atmosphere of historical particularity *against* which to work. This vital tension between the writer and particular political actors comprises what I will call the Opposition literary contract. We can see it come apart when, just after Walpole's fall and just before the deaths of Pope and Swift, William Whitehead deplores the spirit of faction in literature and, in a poem "On Ridicule" (1743), wishes that life's "witty warfare" would cease. Or when Joseph Warton puts Wit and Satire in one column and Nature and Passion in another. For what begins to replace the opposition literary contract is a new agreement with the reader in which poetry will be opposed not to a particular politics but (ostensibly) to all politics. Such a shift dramatically restricts the province of poetry while at the same time severely limiting the legitimacy of political or economic activity as a theater for any sort of ambition on the part of the intellectual or artist.

The parallels with our own era are inescapable, and I would like to pursue them further after we have looked more closely at the poetry which reflects the problems of ambition not simply in "life" but as a literary value. We do not know, cannot know, that life suddenly became crasser in the 1740s and 1750s than in the first decades of the century. We can realize that the conventional representation of possible political and economic counterparts to "poesy" or "Contemplation" began to change, so that the idea of ambitious activity became poetically suspect despite the fact that, officially, most of the writers continued to endorse "indus-

[7]By the phrase I mean to suggest not only specific allegiances but an allegiance to the specific, i.e., an assumption of direct and usually combative referentiality. For the former sense, see Isaac Kramnick's discussion of Pope as the "Opposition Laureate" in *Bolingbroke and His Circle* (Cambridge, Mass.: Harvard University Press, 1968), pp. 217–23.

try" and to condemn idleness. We could discern many instances of this change, cases in which practical success and ambition are characterized as sordid, venal, or mean. But the more interesting problem lies not so much in the bare fact of such pronouncements as in the way the suspicion of worldly ambition affected poetic ambition. Since the mid-century ode is at once a characteristic form for the new poetry of the period and a repository for many of the poets' most ambitious hopes, we will look next at three volumes of odes which appeared in less than two years: Mark Akenside's *Odes on Several Subjects* (March 1745), Joseph Warton's *Odes on Various Subjects* (December 1746), and William Collins's *Odes on Several Descriptive and Allegoric Subjects* (dated 1747 but published in December 1746).

These are the poems Thomas Warton would have had chiefly in mind (along with several of his own, no doubt) when he began to sketch an essay on new tendencies in the poetry of his day, which he characterized as a "Romantic Kind of Poetry." The essay was never finished and the manuscript is not dated, but it is likely that Warton wrote it during the 1750s, the period in which he was preoccupied with Spenserian romance. To see what struck him as distinctive in the new poetry is to sense more fully the climate in which the odes appeared:

> The principal use which the ancients made of poetry, as appears by their writings, was to imitate human actions and passions, or intermix here and there descriptions of Nature. Several modern authors have employed a manner of poetry entirely different from this, I mean in imitating the actions of spirits, in describing imaginary Scenes, and making persons of abstracted things, such as Solitude, Innocence, and many others. A kind of Poetry, as it [is] altogether in the spirit, (tho with more Judgement and less extravagent) and affects the Imagination in the same Manner, with the old Romances.[8]

Now, in fact the effect of the modern poetry of the mid-eighteenth century on the imagination hardly at all resembles

[8]Quoted by David Fairer from the Trinity College, Oxford, ms. in "The Poems of Thomas Warton the Elder?" *Review of English Studies*, n.s., 26 (1975); 401–2.

that of the old romances. But what Warton finds similar, I believe, is the attempt to make poetry nonreferential, to free it
from the realm of memory and mimesis, at least from the mimesis of verifiable events and things. This new manner of poetry
imitates instead the "actions of spirits" as performed by personified abstractions upon imaginary stages. We may suspect that
Solitude and Innocence are not merely incidental examples of
appropriate personifications, and indeed they must loom large
in any attempt to generalize the action and atmosphere of many
mid-century poems, in which a solitary speaker quests after
some form of radical innocence.

How the Wartons' interest in romance could translate into a
polemical poetic and their interest in solitary innocence into a
rejection of current political relationships is best suggested by
Thomas's contrast of Spenser's and Pope's impressionistic effect
on the melancholy reader:

> Yet does my mind with sweeter transport glow,
> As at the root of mossy trunk reclin'd,
> In Magic SPENSER'S wildly-warbled song
> I see deserted Una wander wide
> Through wasteful solitudes, and lurid heaths,
> Wear, forlorn; than when the fated Fair
> Upon the bosom bright of silver Thames
> Launches in all the lustre of Brocade,
> Amid the splendors of the laughing Sun.
> The gay description palls upon the sense,
> And coldly strikes the mind with feeble bliss.
> [*The Pleasures of Melancholy,* 1747]

Warton has drawn a nice contrast here, although we need to
understand what else is involved besides a preference for darkness over brightness. Much of what makes Belinda less attractive
than Una is her brilliance of another sort, her ability to shine
within a social world of complicated compromises, glittering
gamesmanship, verbal competition, and wit. Spenser is an alternative to such a world not only in Warton's mind but in that of
any of the eighteenth-century writers who, somewhat be-
wilderingly, speak repeatedly of his "simplicity." Thus William
Thompson, for example, praises Spenser because in his work

there are "no ambitious ornaments, or epigrammatical
turns . . . , but a beautiful simplicity: which pleases far above the
glitter of pointed wit."9

Ambition and wit are associated, to the suspicion of each,
more and more toward the middle of the century. To be too
witty is to be insincere and combative. One can see something of
this dichotomy in Pope, but significantly it is in his life rather
than in his poetry that wit and "simplicity" or "truth" are felt as
contrary standards. In later years Pope tells a correspondent
that he strained to write witty letters when he was young but that
he has since determined to write with more simplicity and can-
dor.10 In his poetry, on the other hand, Pope makes a distinction
between "*fancy*" and truth: if anything, telling the truth appro-
priately demands more wit in the later poetry than before.

But Fielding is more typical of the increasing reservations of
the next generation concerning wit and the brittle ambition
coming to be associated with it. In one of the wittiest novels in
the world, Fielding goes out of his way to tell us twice that the
heroine has no "Pretence to Wit" and no capacity for repartee
(XVII, 3 and 6). The path from Congreve's Millamant to Fielding's Sophia suggests the drift of increasingly sentimental conceptions of heroines, but most important for our purposes is the
fact that the avoidance of wit and verbal ambition contributes to
a new ideal not limited to women. Fielding's authorial pursuit of
his own feminine ideal in *Amelia* is perhaps the novelistic counterpart to the strong tendency in mid-eighteenth-century poetry
to "feminize" the model for poetry. Like a sentimental heroine,
the perfect poem would be unambitious, tender, simple, and
more interested in the obscure shade of private life than in the
glare of public ambitions. We shall turn to the role of feminine
personifications in embodying the values of mid-eighteenth-cen-

9William Thompson's preface to *An Hymn to May* (Chalmers, *The Works of the
English Poets*, XV, 32–37). Ironically, Chalmers (XV, 5) found too many "glittering epithets" in the *Hymn* and judged that Thompson's memory had not been
sufficiently "chastened into simplicity by the example and encouragement of the
moderns."

10*The Correspondence of Alexander Pope*, ed. George Sherburn (Oxford: Clarendon Press, 1956) III, 79; see also James Winn, *A Window in the Bosom: The Letters
of Alexander Pope* (Hamden, Conn.: Archon Books, 1977), esp. pp. 153–64,
199–201.

tury poetry as we look now to Akenside, Joseph Warton, and Collins.

2

The study of mid-eighteenth-century poetry has been shaped far too greatly by the happenstance of twentieth-century editing. Collins and Gray are frequently discussed because there are good editions of Collins and Gray, including good paperback texts.[11] Many of their contemporaries live only by anthological respiration at present and so are rarely taught or written about. They are indeed minor figures, but their historical importance is recognized, almost litanized, much more often than even a few of their poems are actually examined. So the Wartons, for example, are repeatedly said to somehow reflect the "new sensibility," while they have still not—as Wallace Jackson has noted in a fine exception to the critical rule—received the "decent burial of a modern edition."[12] The same is true for Mark Akenside, as it is for Edward Young, whose letters happen at present to be accessible and well annotated, while *Night Thoughts* has not been edited for a century. For whatever reasons, discussions of Collins, whose importance now seems to be generally recognized, characteristically make little reference to the odes of Joseph Warton or Mark Akenside, despite the facts that Warton and Collins clearly influenced each other—they originally planned a joint volume—and that Akenside was an essential example for both of them. Because two of the three volumes of odes to be considered together are not widely accessible, it may be helpful simply to list their contents before comparing the arrangement of poems and the range of concerns.

[11] In addition to the *Works of Collins* edited by Wendorf and Ryskamp and the edition of Gray by H. W. Starr and J. R. Hendrickson (London: Oxford University Press, 1966), useful and accessible editions include Roger Lonsdale's *The Poems of Gray, Collins, and Goldsmith* (London: Longmans, 1969) and Arthur Johnston's *Selected Poems of Thomas Gray and William Collins* (London: Arnold, 1967).

[12] *The Probable and the Marvelous: Blake, Wordsworth, and the Eighteenth-Century Critical Tradition* (Athens: University of Georgia Press, 1978), p. 81; chapter 3 of Jackson's book is especially helpful on Collins and the Wartons as poets of the "passions."

Akenside added greatly to the number of his lyrics over the years, but the 1745 edition of *Odes on Several Subjects* consisted of these ten odes:

    I. Allusion to Horace
   II. On the Winter Solstice, 1740
  III. Against Suspicion
  IV. To a Gentleman whose Mistress had married an Old Man
   V. Hymn to Chearfulness, the Author Sick
  VI. On the Absence of the Poetic Inclination
 VII. To a Friend, on the Hazard of falling in love
VIII. On Leaving Holland
  IX. To Sleep
   X. On Lyric Poetry

Joseph Warton's *Odes on Various Subjects* are:

    I. To Fancy
   II. To Liberty
  III. To Health, Written on a recovery
  IV. To Superstition
   V. To a Gentleman upon his Travels
  VI. Against Despair
 VII. To Evening
VIII. *To a Fountain*
  IX. To the Nightingale
   X. On the Spring, To a Lady
  XI. To a Lady who hates the Country
 XII. On the Death of ——— [Thomas Warton, Sr.]
XIII. On Shooting
XIV. To Solitude

Collins's *Odes on Several Descriptive and Allegoric Subjects* bears several resemblances in scope to both of the volumes which preceded it:

    I. Ode to Pity
   II. Ode to Fear
  III. Ode to Simplicity
  IV. Ode on the Poetical Character
   V. Written in the Beginning of the Year, 1746

VI. Ode to Mercy
VII. Ode to Liberty
VIII. Ode to a Lady on the Death of Colonal Ross
IX. Ode to Evening
X. Ode to Peace
XI. The Manners: An Ode
XII. The Passions: An Ode for Music

Personifications, or what Thomas Warton called "abstracted things," are the explicit subject of many of the odes of each of the poets, but Collins's volume is the only one conceived so strictly on "allegoric" principles, and as a consequence, it is the least autobiographical of the three. The two occasional poems which are not wholly to or about personifications, *Written in the Beginning of the Year, 1746* ("How sleep the brave . . .") and *Ode to a Lady on the Death of Colonel Ross,* are impersonal statements as compared with the privately occasional and epistolary poems included by Akenside and Warton. To recognize this difference is to understand something of the terms of Collins's achievement and to be reminded that the poles "classic" and "romantic" are likely to be of little help in trying to grasp either the quality of inspiration or the quality of execution shown by these three poets.

For example, Akenside's volume is in some respects the most Augustan in allegiance. His mode is self-consciously Horatian from the beginning, two of the odes are virtually verse epistles, and one (*On Leaving Holland*) is primarily satiric (a note heard loudly in Warton's *To a Lady who hates the Country* but not at all in Collins). Akenside's volume is not only the most "Augustan" but also the most personal, locating several particular moments, describing various crises involving friends, and suggesting loosely autobiographical "progress" from, say, the statements of 1740 to a more mature declaration—at least one sickness and a foreign sojourn later—of poetic loyalty. The combination of Augustan and autobiographical qualities is not unprecedented, of course, for Pope's *Horatian Imitations* are probably his most personal poems; the combination simply suggests once again the difficulty with the idea of preromanticism, especially if a "preromantic" is assumed somehow to mean less classical allusion and (therefore) more self-revelation.

The personal journey which Akenside's volume describes is defined from beginning to end by classical allegiances.[13] His first poem, an *Allusion to Horace*, declares his intent to emulate the Horace of the odes:

> Amid the garden's fragrance laid
> Where yonder limes behold their shade
>   Along the glassy stream,
> With Horace and his tuneful ease
> I'll rest from crouds, and care's disease,
>   And summer's piercing beam.

The last poem, *On Lyric Poetry*, is a self-consciously Pindaric ode both in form and in aspiration. Akenside is not simply Pindaric, however, for he is interested in synthesizing the entire Greek lyric tradition (his ode is an interesting anticipation of Gray's *Progress of Poesy*) and appropriating it for modern needs ("While I so late unlock thy purer springs, / And breathe whate'er thy ancient airs infuse . . ."). And he wants to go further on his own wing than even the eaglelike "man of Thebes":

> But when from envy and death to claim
> A hero bleeding for his native land;
> When to throw incense on the vestal flame
> Of Liberty my genius gives command,
>   Nor Theban voice nor Lesbian lyre
>   From thee, O Muse, do I require;
>   While my prophetic mind,
>   Conscious of powers she never knew,
> Astonished, grasps at things beyond her view
> Nor by another's fate has felt her own confined.

The high-flown ambitions of this poem appear in various forms in several of the other poems in the volume. *Against Suspicion* aligns poetry with "universal candor" and the poet's resolute faith in the dignity of humankind. *To a Gentleman whose Mistress*

---

[13]It is possible that Akenside intended the arrangement of his odes in the 1745 volume to suggest an autobiographical subplot or personal "progress," in which the poet moves from the Rome of "free Horatian song" (see the first two odes especially) to the Greece of Pindaric prophecy in search of a satisfactory identification.

had married an Old Man attempts to dissociate the true poetic
world from one where it is common to "barter vows for gold,"
just as Joseph Warton in *The Enthusiast* imagines a nobler era
when "beauty was not venal." The ode *On Leaving Holland* chas-
tizes the Dutch women for their "sober care of gain" and the
men for their "slow-eyed" and "passive" lack of "daring."

Although the theme of patriotic ambition recurs often in
Akenside's poetry, he is probably most persuasive when he
sounds less assured. In the ode *To Sleep*, for example, he retreats
from senatorial daydreams as "too grand for fortune's private
ways,"

> And though they shine in youth's ingenuous view,
> The sober gainful arts of modern days
> To such romantic thoughts have bid a long adieu.

The renunciation is all the more poignant for the close resemblance of the "sober gainful arts" which control modern reality to the "sober care of gain" elsewhere dismissed as a merely
Dutch disease. At the end of the seventeenth century Locke had
said that in the beginning all the world was America; Akenside
suggests that it is now all Holland.

I do not mean to say that we can or should take Akenside
seriously only when he is not optimistic. He never really resigns
his optimism entirely, and most of the poems make some men-
tion of the progress of Liberty, of the mind's dignity and power,
of the benevolent future of man. But most of the poems also
pose problems concerning the province of poetic ambition, and
we are likely to feel—and I do not think this is our own obligatory pessimism intervening—that the doubts are more genuinely
expressed than the resolutions. The short ode *On the Absence of
the Poetic Inclination* (later called *To the Muse*) is a good example
and can be quoted whole:

> Queen of my songs, harmonious maid,
> Ah! why hast thou withdrawn thy aid?
> Ah! why forsaken thus my breast
> With inauspicious damps oppress'd?
> Where is the bold prophetic heat

With which my bosom wont to beat?
Where all the bright mysterious dreams
Of haunted groves and tuneful streams,
That woo'd my genius to divinest themes?

Say, can the purple charms of wine,
Or young Dione's form divine,
Or flatt'ring scenes of promis'd fame
Relume thy faint, thy dying flame?
Or have melodious airs the power
To give one free, poetic hour?
Or, from amid the Elysian train,
The soul of Milton shall I gain,
To win thee back with some celestial strain?

O mighty mind! O sacred flame!
My spirit kindles at his name;
Again my lab'ring bosom burns;
The Muse, th' inspiring Muse returns!
Such on the banks of Tyne confest,
I hail'd the bright, etherial guest
When first she seal'd me for her own,
Made all her blissful treasures known,
And bade me swear to follow Her alone.

The invocation of Milton as a surrogate muse points to the
period preoccupation with Milton generally and in particular to
the Milton that Collins imported into the *Ode on the Poetical Character*.[14] Unlike Collins, Akenside does not defer to Milton, but
neither does he make much poetry of him. When Collins thinks
of Milton he immediately starts to rebuild Eden in his own
poem; for Akenside, Milton is relatively abstract, a "mind," a
"name," which "kindles" his own aspiration, although the only
visible effect of the muse's return is to end the poem. "Milton"
has a similar function in the ambition-haunted ode *To Sleep*,

[14]Akenside's Milton, like Collins's, is not the Wartonian Milton of *Il Penseroso*
but the "ambitious" visionary of *Paradise Lost*. In Collins's poem Milton's "Glory"
is the alternative to "Waller's Myrtle Shades" (1.69), suggesting a literary "Choice
of Hercules" in which the poet presumably must choose strenuous Virtue over
Pleasure. I discuss Akenside's use of the Hercules pattern in *The Pleasures of
Imagination* in chapter 5.

where dreams of political ambition, courtship, and court are rejected for Miltonic dreams of poetic fame:

> But, Morpheus, on thy balmy wing
> Such honourable visions bring,
> As soothed great Milton's injured age
> When in prophetic dreams he saw
> The race unborn with pious awe
> Imbibe each virtue from his heavenly page. . . .

Much of the difficulty seems to lie in the idea of a Milton "soothed" by his prophetic power. A soothed Milton is not as problematic a conception as a mute Milton, but the notion epitomizes one of the strongest tensions in mid-eighteenth-century poetry and poetics—confusion as to whether poetry should "rouse" or "soothe." If it rouses, presumably what it rouses *to* is ambition, energetic action or passionate intensity of some sort. If it soothes, then the goal of the poem will be peace, contemplation, even the radical detachment imaged at the end of *The Enthusiast.* One finds both conceptions frequently in the period and frequently expressed by the same poet—whereas Pope, for example, spoke only ironically of "soothing" and poetic "peace," as in the *Dunciad*—but even so republican and libertarian a poet as Akenside more often lands on the side of the soothe-saying view when addressing his muse.

The Hymn to Chearfulness is particularly interesting as a dramatization of this problem, perhaps partly because the problem is not quite conscious enough to be allegorized as schematically as Akenside is sometimes fond of doing. The poem is also the longest work in his volume, and for the most part Akenside's handling of the octosyllabic couplet is graceful, fresh and light without a trace of the ludicrous, itself no small achievement in the period. The poem begins as an apostrophe spoken from the sickroom to Cheerfulness, a "kind power" who can "soothe affliction's lonely hour" and "compose" the poet to rest. Midway through the poem, the attempt to define the nature and scope of cheerfulness turns into a definition of poetry. Akenside wants to fuse the two abstractions by asserting that poetry is the voice of cheerfulness, or rather that it was so originally and should be so again:

> Let Melancholy's plaintive tongue
> Repeat what later bards have sung;
> But thine was Homer's ancient might,
> And thine victorious Pindar's flight:
> Thy hand each Lesbian wreath attired:
> Thy lip Sicilian reeds inspired. . . .
>
> [93–98]

But immediately after this assertion of poetic cheer, Akenside draws a full-length portrait of a "pensive sage," again rather like the careworn and enigmatic wanderer of the end of the *Elegy*— "Perhaps by tender griefs oppress'd, / Or glooms congenial to his breast"—and this solitary figure is in such melancholic turmoil that he too needs to be "composed" (105–27). By the end of the poem Akenside is again asking Cheerfulness to share in the control of his mind and to "soothe to peace intruding care" (144). More important, he wants the same things from poetry. Friendship would be better, but if, failing that,

> I court the Muse's healing spell
> For griefs that still with absence dwell,
> Do thou conduct my fancy's dreams
> To such indulgent placid themes,
> As just the struggling breast may cheer,
> And just suspend the starting tear,
> Yet leave that sacred sense of woe
> Which none but friends and lovers know.

The image of the poet as a wounded soul who needs the "healing" of his poetry is not one Akenside wants to relinquish, even in a poem which celebrates the value of good cheer in modern life and Attic literature. The idea of poetry as healing figures somewhat of course in Pope's *Epistle to Arbuthnot*, where the occupation of poetry has helped the author through the long disease of his life, but the differences are instructive. Whereas Pope hints that poetry is one occupation among many and that his circle of friends is his first audience, Akenside implies (and the same is true of Gray, Shenstone, and the Wartons) that the poet is a poet because everything else has disappointed him and he has no one to talk to but us. To describe the function of poetry as soothing or composing is, naturally, to dramatize the poet as one who is habitually discomposed and to suggest that "the world" outside the poem is a harsh and hostile place. And finally, this description turns poetry away from the role of mimesis or representation of such a world and into a refuge from it, an alternative world of "fancy" and "indulgent" themes. This view is the heavier half of Akenside's sense of his poetic vocation in his volume of 1745, and from this perspective Joseph Warton began when he placed the ode *To Fancy* at the front of his *Odes on Various Subjects* the next year.

3

The connection between Warton's volume and Akenside's is apparent at several points. The most deliberate alignment occurs when Warton praises Akenside in *To a Gentleman upon his Travels* as the lyric poet of true "Grecian strains" in present-day England. More general similarities appear in other ways. For example, it seems likely that Akenside's *Hymn to Chearfulness, the Author Sick* influenced Warton's decision to include an ode called *To Health, Written on a recovery,* or that Warton was motivated to write about a negative personification in *Against Despair* partly by the example of Akenside's *Against Suspicion* and the attempted resolution of similar emotions in *On the Absence of the Poetic Inclination.* The poems *To Liberty* and *To Superstition* celebrate (the latter by contrast) the free spirit of England much as Akenside had in *On Leaving Holland.* And the poem in which Warton singled out Akenside for praise, *To A Gentleman,* bears a strong thematic relation to Akenside's *On Lyric Poetry* in its attempt to appropriate the Greek tradition for contemporary English poetry. Of course Warton's volume points toward Collins's as well in its handling of "patriotic" and "poetic" themes, and we can take advantage of the more conspicuously similar topics of these would-be collaborators to consider both their shared concerns and their different abilities. Without making the comparison invidious, we may be able to understand the nature of Collins's genius better by comparing the poets' poems to Evening, Liberty, and Fancy.

If Warton's ode *To Fancy* is, like Akenside's introductory *Allusion to Horace,* a declaration of range and intent, it is also an extension of his declaration in the short prose preface to the *Odes* that he prizes "invention and imagination" above other poetic qualities. In the preceding chapter we considered briefly the separation of poetry and history which Warton signals by putting Fancy in the place of memory as mother of the muses. Warton is intent upon separating Fancy from any tradition and so clothes her in no more cultural an artifact than a wreath of "Indian" feathers and a few myrtle leaves to preserve her modesty. She is a primitivistic presence, whose address is unknown but who must—for she is a "lover of the desert"—live "where Nature seems to sit alone." Like so many of the mid-century odes, this is a poem about power, and through much of it Warton asks to be overpowered—"transported," "led," "hurried," even "drowned"—by Fancy.

In structure the poem is a tour and a tour de force, a survey and a trial of possible poetic emotions and subjects. These range from "sweetly-soothing" echoes of fairyland to landscapes of the "matron Melancholy," those

> gothic churches, vaults and tombs,
> Where each sad night some virgin comes,
> With throbbing breast, and faded cheek,
> Her promis'd bridegroom's urn to seek.
> Or to some abbey's mouldering tow'rs,
> Where, to avoid cold wintry show'rs,
> The naked beggar shivering lies,
> While whistling tempests round her rise,
> And trembles lest the tottering wall
> Should on her sleeping infants fall.[15]

From the iconic melodrama of these lines Warton hurries off to try his hand at war:

[15]It is interesting that even Warton's beggar must be female, which suggests that she is not simply a piece of melancholic iconography but a momentary proxy for the "matron Melancholy" herself. All of the significant personifications in the poem are feminine, with the exception of "Terror," whose brief appearance seems obligatory and disruptive. This passage and the four-line quotation following did not appear until the second edition (1747); see Joan Pittock's introduction to *Odes on Various Subjects (1746)* (Delmar, N.Y.: Scholars' Facsimiles and Reprints, 1977), pp. vi–vii.

Toward a Poetics of Conversion

> The trumpet's clangors pierce my ear,
> A thousand widows' shrieks I hear:
> "Give me another horse," I cry,
> Lo, the base Gallic squadrons fly.

then hastily retreats to scenes of love, then marches through a compressed survey of the seasons to a pledge of allegiance to Fancy and a petition for her "powerful, vital aid," her "energy divine." The ode closes with the prayer that Fancy will "once again / Animate some chosen swain" to sing "mighty verse" that can control the passions, "o'erwhelm" his hearers, and make England the modern Greece.

Warton's lines on the "widows' shrieks" (the passage goes on to wounded horses "mad with pain") suggest the virtuoso intent of this poem, an intent it shares with Collins's more operatic code, *The Passions*. The rest of *To Fancy* can be read as a table of contents of sorts to the rest of the volume, which includes amorous poems, descriptive "nature" poems, melancholy poems, and so on; but war is not a subject Warton will treat again. It is as if Warton believes that the poet must be able to sing of war—to "rouse with revenge" as well as to "melt with love" (138)—and so he does so. But the feeling that war represents the epitome of a public history and political ambition which are antithetical to pure poetry is as much a part of Warton's sensibility as it is of what I have called the politics of melancholy generally. The most telling evidence of such tension between the literary attractions of violence and ambition and the repudiation of them is a poem not part of the volume of 1746, the ode *On Reading Mr. West's Translation of Pindar* (published in 1749).

We do not seem to have a place in our hearts or our anthologies for the *nearly* successful Pindaric, but Warton's most deliberately Pindaric ode is worth our attention partly for its spirited Blakean opening—

> Albion exult! thy sons a voice divine have heard,
> The Man of Thebes hath in thy values appear'd—

and for its fine second stanza:

122

The fearful, frigid lays of cold and creeping Art,
   Nor touch, nor can transport the unfeeling heart;
   Pindar, our inmost bosom piercing, warms
   With glory's love, and eager thirst of arms:
   When Freedom speaks in his majestic strain,
   The patriot-passions beat in every vein:
      We long to sit with heroes old,
      Mid groves of vegetable gold
      Where Cadmus and Achilles dwell,
   And still of daring deeds and dangers tell.

The association of Pindar with the defense of Freedom and
martial glory is common to Gray's Pindarics as well, and in fact
Warton's description of Pindar's poetry as a cataract roaring
down from the heights almost surely influenced Gray's "rich
stream of music . . . Now rolling down the step amain" at the
beginning of *The Progress of Poesy*. But because the connection
between Pindar and the more ambitious "patriot-passions" is so
conventional, Warton's retreat from that world, here of all
places, is arresting:

For the bless'd man, the Muses' child
    . . . . .
Seeks not in fighting fields renown;
No widow's midnight shrieks nor burning town,
   The peaceful poet please;
  Nor ceaseless toils for sordid gains,
  Nor purple pomp, nor wide domains,
Nor heaps of wealth, nor power, nor statesman's schemes,
Nor all deceiv'd Ambition's feverish dreams
Lure his contented heart from the sweet vale of ease.

                                   [53, 57–64]

Warton makes amends here to the widows he treated rather
academically a few years earlier, and as he does so he renounces
not only war but most of the conventionally masculine pursuits.
We have seen how in the middle years of the century the ideal
poem and the ideal woman grow increasingly alike: neither
should be very witty or very ambitious or very bright. There is a

sense, too, in which the poet as well as his poem now begins to have a stronger connection to a world of women than to most of the values still officially lauded in the period as "manly." To explore the fact and feeling of this suggestive shift, we need to turn to feminine personifications in several poets before returning to complete our comparison of Warton and Collins.

4

So frequent are descriptions of poetic "song" and "mighty mothers" in the middle years of the century that one sometimes has the uncanny feeling that the prophecies of *Dunciad* have been fulfilled. What was adumbrated ironically is now allegorized approvingly. A striking instance is the juxtaposition of the "Mighty Mother" of the Cibberian *Dunciad*—

> The Mighty Mother, and her Son who brings
> The Smithfield Muses to the ear of Kings,
> I sing—

with the lines from Gray's *Progress of Poesy* describing not Cibber but Shakespeare:

> Far from the sun and summer-gale,
> In thy green lap was Nature's darling laid,
> What time, where lucid Avon strayed,
> To him the mighty Mother did unveil
> Her awful face. . . .

[83–87]

Many contemporaries may have caught the unfortunate echo, through which, as Gilbert Wakefield noted, "Wicked memory brings into mind the *Queen* of the *Dunces,* and destroys all the pleasure of the description by an unlucky contrast.[16] Wicked memory is in fact jolted not only by the maternal phrase but also by the maternal lap resting in Gray's lines and elsewhere in the *Dunciad:*

[16]*The Poems of Mr. Gray* (1786), p. 88, cited by Lonsdale, *The Poems of Gray, Collins, and Goldsmith,* p. 172.

> But in her Temple's last recess inclos'd,
> On Dulness' lap th' Anointed head repos'd.
> Him close she curtains round with Vapours blue,
> And soft besprinkles with Cimmerian dew.
>
> [III, 1–4]

One naturally wonders why Gray's own memory, usually so extensive and scrupulous, failed to warn him from these echoing rocks. Joseph Warton's memory seems to have been even shorter. His description of Shakespeare in *The Enthusiast* is not as close to the Cibberian phrasing, but it is perhaps even nearer to the spirit of "soft" and "close" protection. Shakespeare here is the infant whom

> Fair Fancy found, and bore the smiling babe
> To a close cavern
>   . . . . .
> Here, as with honey gathered from the rock,
> She fed the little prattler, and with songs
> Oft soothed his wond'ring ears, with deep delight
> On her soft lap he sat, and caught the sounds.
>
> [171–79]

It appears that Gray was actually remembering Warton's image of mother and son rather than Pope's, though perhaps he did not consciously recall either one. At such moments generally the difference between the practice of Pope and his successors seems to be the difference between voluntary and involuntary allusion. More "allusions" of this sort occur elsewhere in Warton's *Ode to Fancy* and Akenside's *The Pleasures of Imagination* (1744). The pertinent lines in Pope are those describing mother Dulness's inspection of poetic incongruities, as with parental pride she sees

> How Time himself stands still at her command,
> Realms shift their place, and Ocean turns to land.
> Here gay Description Egypt glads with show'rs,
> Or gives to Zembla fruits, to Barca flowers
>   . . . . .
> In cold December fragrant chaplets blow,
> And heavy harvests nod beneath the snow.

All these, and more, the cloud-compelling Queen
Beholds thro' fogs, that magnify the scene.
She, tinsel'd o'er in robes of varying hues,
With self-applause her wild creation views. . . .

[I, 71–82]

Here is a portion of Akenside's invocation, inviting the assistance of "indulgent Fancy" and "Fiction,"

upon her vagrant wings
Wafting ten thousand colours through the air,
Which, by the glances of her magic eye,
She blends and shifts at will, thro' countless forms,
Her wild creation.

Joseph Warton's invocation to Fancy is in much the same spirit:

O parent of each lovely Muse,
Thy spirit o'er my soul diffuse . . .
. . . . .
Waving in thy snowy hand
An all-commanding magic wand,
Of pow'r to bid fresh gardens blow,
'Mid cheerless Lapland's barren snow. . . .

[1–2, 13–16]

In the case of Akenside, one's first guess might be that the young poet was blithely unaware of the *Dunciad*'s "wild creation" and the ironies of an optical extravagance that "blends and shifts at will"; however, he knew and liked Pope's poem enough to borrow considerably from its second book for the satiric section of his own (III, 78–240) and probably from the more recent *New Dunciad* as well. The conceptual differences are conspicuous and are epitomized simply in the fact that Akenside can use the adjective "wild" with positive value, whereas for Pope it is likely to be at best neutral. A similar difference can be measured in Warton's *Ode to Fancy* when that "Parent of each lovely muse" is praised for her power to "bid fresh gardens blow" in snowy Lapland, a generosity which she shares with Dulness and her sons in their pastoral efforts to gladden Zembla with fruits and December with blossoms.

126

But since these conceptual differences can be studied as profitably in critical essays of the period, the more interesting poetic problem lies in the fact that important images should remain the same even while the theoretical emphases are reversed. The constant is the Mighty Mother who singles out a poetic son (Cibber or Shakespeare), nurtures him, protects him, holds him on her lap, and is also the mother of a new and wild creation or, as in Gray, the veiled source of "awful" power. She is thus the mother not only of the chosen poet but of the world at large, and in some instances there is a broader resemblance between the sublime figure and Dulness as the *general* mother, the gentle parent capable of "soothing" an entire nation, uniting all under one "imperial sway." The concluding lines of Collins's *Ode to Liberty* may recall several of the *Dunciad's* more prophetic unisons in Book IV and earlier (especially I, 311–18, and III, 123–26). Liberty, in Collins's account, will herself be apocalyptically "soothed" into the figure of Concord, a millennial female:

> whose myrtle wand can steep
> Even Anger's blood-shot eyes in sleep;
> Before whose breathing bosom's balm
> Rage drops his steel and storms grow calm;
> Her let our sires and matrons hoar
> Welcome to Britain's ravaged shore,
> . . . . .
> Till in one loud applauding sound,
> The nations shout to her around:
> 'O how supremely art thou blest,
> Thou, lady, thou shalt rule the West!'

It is not surprising that straightforward "progress pieces" should continue to have been written for some years after the *Dunciad,* which seems in retrospect the ironic epitaph of the mode, any more than it is surprising that the *Rape of the Lock* did not somehow prevent *Leonidas.* What is surprising is the tenacity of this particular image in the works of poets who have general reasons (and in these passages special reasons) to wish to avoid sounding like Pope. Why, in other words, should these versions of the Mighty Mother have such attractions for mid-century poets, attractions strong enough to outweigh or to suppress the obvious liability of arousing unintended laughter?

Some clues to an answer may lie in the relation of the mother figures examined here to memory and to the disruption of memory. It is interesting that while they are naturally symbols of continuity or permanence (Nature, Fancy as quasi-Platonic form, ideal Liberty, and so forth), they are each the mother of something so novel, "wild," "magic," or uniquely creative as to obliterate historical continuity and thus to obviate the traditional role of memory. The long-divided West is suddenly born into radical Concord, the infant Shakespeare suddenly unlocks the world of Nature, a new world is born in the sudden command of a magic wand or the instant blaze of ten thousand colors. "Indulgent Fancy," like Pope's reiteratively "gentle" Mother, encourages forgetfulness.[17]

To make Fancy the parent of each lovely muse is to divorce poetry from history, inspiration from memory, and the poet from the community. We need not attribute this tendency entirely to Joseph Warton to see in his poem the clearest emblem of the increasing concern with "pure poetry" in the writing of the Wartons generally, and in Collins, Akenside, and Gray, or to recognize that "pure" poetry tends more and more to mean "solitary" poetry. Critics have often noted that the aestheticism and lyric emphasis of the mid-century coincide with the image of the poet as an isolated figure.[18] The pertinent fact here is that the poet is frequently not merely isolated but also privileged and that his privilege derives from a special relation to a large, attractive, usually protective female figure. His isolation is that of an only son who is often a lover as well.

Perhaps most of the poems mentioned suggest this sexually problematic situation, but it will be helpful to explore some further examples of amatory and filial confusion. Thomas Warton's *The Pleasures of Melancholy* (1745; published in 1747) begins directly with an address to the "Mother of musings, Contempla-

[17]For "gentle" Dulness as the nurse of cultural amnesia, see *Dunciad* (1743), II, 34; III, 302; IV, 83, 509.

[18]E.g., M. H. Abrams, *The Mirror and the Lamp*, esp. pp. 84–94, and Martin Price, "The Sublime Poem: Pictures and Powers," *Yale Review*, 58 (1969): 194–213. For an interesting dissenting view which stresses the continuity of social orientation in eighteenth-century poetry, see Marshall Brown, "The Urbane Sublime," *ELH*, 45 (1978); 236–54.

tion sage," and eventually concludes with an invitation to Melancholy, the "queen of thought," to come

> From forth thy cave embowered with mournful yew,
> Where ever to the curfew's solemn sound
> Listening thou sitt'st, and with thy cypress bind
> Thy votary's hair, and seal him for thy son.
> But never let Euphrosyne beguile
> With toys of wanton mirth my fixed mind. . . .

It is in these last two lines that the sexual complications become apparent. The lines express not only a young man's reading of the young Milton but also a youthful protestation of erotic fidelity, a pledge which might be crudely but fairly rephrased as, "Mother, I will keep myself pure for you if you will let me be yours and only yours." In a slightly later and less well known poem, the ambitious *Ode on the Approach of Summer* (1753), Thomas Warton concludes by turning toward poetry herself, anticipating several maternal favors:

> She shall lead me by the hand,
> Queen of sweet smiles, and solace bland!
> Ambrosial flow'rets o'er my head:
> She from my tender youthful cheek,
> Can wipe, with lenient finger meek,
> The secret and unpitied tear,
> Which still I drop in darkness drear.

Then without transition, this final wish:

> She shall be my blooming bride;
> With her, as years successive glide,
> I'll hold divinest dalliance,
> For ever held in holy trance.

The feminine guardian, in other words, is to reward her youthful votary's devotion by conducting him by the hand through the dark to a point of sufficient sexual maturity—and sufficient forgetfulness of their former relation—to marry her and dally divinely ever after.

The conceit of divine dalliance figures more importantly in Akenside and Collins, where it begins to assume the proportions of myth in the reinterpretation of Creation, both heavenly and human. But before we turn to those developments, perhaps it is necessary to stress that the feminity of these powerful images is not incidental. Despite some provocative modern reconsiderations of personification and allegory, the implicit assumption in reading is still likely to be the romantic one, in which explicit allegorizing is "mechanical" rather than "organic." This response is all the more likely when the personifications occur in contexts or in poets regarded as particularly conventional. Certainly there is enough repetition of "hereditary images" in mid-eighteenth-century poetry to encourage frequent expression of the notion that muses and other sky-born maids are more mandatory than material. But the immediate problem with this view as a critical principle is that it necessarily assumes the priority of the idea to the situation. Thus one would need to assume that Thomas Warton addresses "Poesy" as a woman because what he really wants to say is that he wishes to devote himself to writing poems and hopes to be happy doing so. Or that poetry is feminine because he inherited the ideal of muses. Or that he is determined to apostrophize, apostrophizing requires a personified object, and personifications are usually feminine.[19]

But the argument for taking the situation more seriously (in this case, the situation of son-lover addressing mother-wife) than the "conventional' view usually allows is simply that more choice was open to the poet than it presupposes. It is quite conceivable, for example, to address the "idea of poetry" not only as the muses but also as Apollo—Shaftesbury thought *either* of these likely to be strained for a modern writer—and even the odd but unquestionably influential tradition of bestowing feminine gender on abstract nouns which have feminine endings in Latin was by no means unavoidable. Naturally one cannot avoid personifying "Mother Nature" as feminine, but one can avoid the personification or avoid elaborating it (as Pope generally does) without

[19]The "mechanical" view of allegory derives primarily from Coleridge's differentiation of allegory from symbolism; the problem posed by this critical tradition is the starting point for Angus Fletcher's massive reconsideration, *Allegory: The Theory of a Symbolic Mode* (Ithaca: Cornell University Press, 1964).

surrendering the topic. Nor do many nouns have traditionally inevitable associations. "Contemplation," the "mother of musings" in *The Pleasures of Melancholy*, need not be feminine unless Warton so decrees, and he chooses elsewhere to make this she a hoary he.[20]

Without such considerations the real significance of these recurrent "feminizations" may easily be overlooked.[21] It is not that they are born to their gender, or have it thrust upon them by precedent, but that they achieve it in remarkably similar filial contexts. Again and again the feminine image is used as a focus of withdrawal, a symbol of retreat from the harsh world of traditionally male history, "ambition," greed, London, politics, social strife—all of the things Joseph Warton lumps together in *The*

[20]*Ode on the Approach of Summer*, 11, 89ff. It is probably significant that Contemplation here is not the object of apostrophe, as she is in the passage from *The Pleasures of Melancholy*. In *Characteristics* (ed. John M. Robertson [1900; reprinted, Indianapolis: Bobbs-Merrill, 1964], I, 6), Shaftesbury remarks that "to be able to move others we must first be moved ourselves. Now what possibility is there that a modern, who is known never to have worshipped Apollo, or owned any such deities as the muses, should persuade us to enter into his pretended devotion and move us by his feigned zeal in a religion out of date?"

[21]E. H. Gombrich's remarks about discussions of classical and medieval personification are true for many later studies as well: "It seems to me sometimes that [personification] is too familiar; we tend to take it for granted rather than to ask questions about this extraordinary predominantly feminine population which greets us from the porches of cathedrals, crowds around our public monuments, marks our coins and our banknotes, and turns up in our cartoons and in our posters" ("Personification," in R. R. Bolgar, ed., *Classical Influences on European Culture, A.D. 500–1500* [Cambridge: Cambridge University Press, 1971], p. 248). Two mid-century texts which suggest how far from automatic the assignment of gender might be are Blair's *The Grave* (1743) and William Ayre's comment two years later on the *Dunciad*. For Blair, whether personifications are to be feminine, masculine, or neuter seems to depend more on immediate context than on classical or English conventions. Death is male, e.g., when pitted against the feminized soul (11.350ff.), but later this "great man-eater" emerges as female in opposition to Christ (710–12); even the presumably fixed "father" Time yields to a personification of Time as a female, "all-subduing," in opposition to the "columns" and other proud labors of masculine art (200–5). Of the personifications in the *Dunciad*, Ayre observes: "The Poet has not particulariz'd many Follies of the fair Sex; however he has not paid them any Compliment, as he made the *Sovereign* of Dulness a Female. . . . But then he has given to the Sex some of the greatest Excellencies human Nature is capable of possessing. The Description of Science, Wit, &c, Captives at the Footstool of *Dulness*, is a Picture so full of Imagery, that every Figure as much as presents itself to your View, as if drawn by the Pencil of *Le Brun*" (*Memoirs of the Life and Writings of Alexander Pope* [1745], II, 232).

Enthusiast as the "distant din of the tumultuous world" and from which he wishes to flee in poetry. What he flees to, in that extreme but characteristic conclusion, is total immersion in feminine security, a state of imagined repose where the poet's mind will fathom the submarine serenity of a sea nymph:

> So when rude Whirlwinds rouse the roaring Main,
> Beneath fair THETIS sits, in coral Caves,
> Serenly gay, nor sinking Sailors Cries
> Disturb her sportive Nymphs, who round her form
> The light fantastic Dance, or for her Hair
> Weave rosy Crowns, or with according Lutes
> Grace the soft Warbles of her honeyed Voice.

Warton did not invent the pieces of this image, but its whole and unqualified emphasis on withdrawal and refuge are new and, as suggested in the preceding chapter, as foreign to Pope's premises as to Hegel's. In part, the image is so arresting because Thetis is merely the most vivid of a whole gallery of feminine symbols in the poem—Virtue, Solitude, Contemplation, even Britannia, seen briefly while stooping to Vice, her "paramour"—which operate both as potential mother and as erotic focus for the speaker. By the end, the sensuous and submerged retreat in which Thetis sports, oblivious to the claims of other men, embodies both sexual attraction and sexual regression. The poet's mind turns to woman, the poet's body returns to the womb.

The feminine image serves in this way as a means of willed forgetting and avoidance. If to turn to the mother is also to turn *from* the father, then the father-as-image is not so much absent as excluded, suppressed—or, in plainer terms, conspicuous by his absence. When strong masculine images do enter the poems they are often nominally positive, representing "manly" action, fortitude, patriotism, or Arts and Industry (as opposed to "effeminate" passivity, in Thomson's *Castle of Indolence*), or the ethical energy of Pope (ibid.), or God, or the "bard." But there are nearly always problems with this division of attributes. Some of Thomson's best writing, for example, occurs when he is describing what he feels compelled to reject as unmanly and some of his worst when he is describing what he endorses. Akenside insists that all is ruled kindly by God the "Benignant Sire," but in his remarkable retelling of the fall (*Pleasures of Imagination*, II, 271–659), the only benign images are ministering females, and the only wholly malevolent one is male. Mother Nature is more accessible than God the Father, as Fancy is more "indulgent" than History. The feminine image forms a refuge in which poetic sensibility can exist; when male figures, even avowedly desirable ones, enter this area, they come as intruders, carrying destruction. The poetical character, thus conceived, cannot bear very much official reality.

If we consider only the Wartons this might be the essential story, or at least a crude outline for it. In their poetry the notion of poetry as refuge is most overt, the Augustan ideal of engaged Retirement most clearly rigidifying into a fantasy of Retreat. The retreat typically is from "Ambition," sometimes specified as "low" or "mean" ambition, but usually including most of the conspicuously masculine pursuits: fighting, seeking power, getting and spending, and competition generally.[22] But if poetry is frequently seen as the refuge from these values, it is also made the vehicle for them, in "higher" forms. Power, for example, is a central preoccupation, politically as well as prophetically. The "powers" of imagination form Akenside's real subject, as his "Argument" helps clarify, and Gray's ode was not published as "The Powers of Poetry" only because he found the title had been used a few years earlier. Poems are held capable of breaking "servile" bonds, instilling warlike valor, rousing fierce defiance of tyrants, bringing in the transformation of European politics, and letting out the "high capacious powers" which yet "lie folded up in man." Perhaps in no other brief span have so many poets made such competing and ambitious claims for their art and for themselves. Even, or perhaps especially, the oft-repeated gestures of humility before the great poets of the past imply competition and announce ambition.

[22]In an especially paradigmatic poem, John Scott of Amwell identifies the military recruiting drum with "Ambition's voice," whose "discordant sound" speaks to him of "burning towns, and ruin'd swains, / And mangled limbs, and dying groans, / And widows' tears, and orphans' moans; / And all that Misery's hand bestows, / To fill the catalogue of human woes" (*Recruiting*, in Thomas Park, ed., *The Works of the British Poets* [London, 1808], XXXIX, 89).

In theory distinctions might be made between worthy and unworthy ambitions, but these are more likely to be convincing from a safe distance—that shore where, in Keats's phrase, one might remain forever "taking tea and comfortable advice"—than in the currents of poetic practice. The lingering uncertainty of much mid-century poetry relates the problem of its own ambition. How is poetic ambition to be effectually distinguished, legitimized, chastened?

In part, by feminizing and internalizing it. An extremely important role is played here by the "convention" of speaking of the poet as masculine but of his inspiration or power as feminine—muse, fancy, mind, or soul. The convention, like that of "Mother" Nature, had of course long been available but had rarely been exploited, or strained, so consistently. Voicing one's ambition in the form of an apostrophe to a sky-born virgin-mother not only suggests purity by association (and dissociation from worldly ends) but also provides a means of excluding the father and avoiding the impiety of competition with him. This desire and the tendency to situate ambition safely in the privacy of the mind are strongly linked; therefore, the devices of feminization and internalization generally occur together. This double process unfolds to view most clearly in a lengthy passage from *The Pleasures of Imagination* describing the restlessly ambitious flight of the "high-born soul." The passage is deliberately long on the wing, so its effect requires fairly full quotation:

> Tir'd of earth
> And this diurnal scene, she springs aloft
> Thro' fields of air; pursues the flying storm;
> Rides on the volley'd lightning thro' the heav'ns;
> Or, yok'd with whirlwinds and the northern blast,
> Sweeps the long tract of day. Then high she soars
> The blue profound, and hovering o'er the sun
> Beholds him pouring the redundant stream
> Of light; beholds his unrelenting sway
> Bend the reluctant planets to absolve
> The fated sounds of Time. Thence far effus'd
> She darts her swiftness up the long career
> Of devious comets. . . .
> . . . . .

> Now amaz'd she views
> Th'empyreal waste, where happy spirits hold
> Beyond this concave heav'n, their calm abode;
> And fields of radiance, whose unfading light
> Has travell'd the profound six thousand years,
> Nor yet arrives in sight of mortal things.
> Ev'n on the barriers of the world untir'd
> She meditates th' eternal depth below;
> Till half recoiling, down the headlong steep
> She plunges; soon o'erwhelm'd and swallow'd up
> In that immense of being.
>
> [I, 185–97, 201–11]

Many of the details of this journey reflect eighteenth-century scientific discoveries, the "aesthetics of the infinite" to which they contributed, and particularly the space-intoxicated vocabulary of the contemporaneous *Night Thoughts*.[23] But a more revealing poetic alignment is with Milton directly; for the account Akenside gives is not merely a survey but an active voyage, and its closest model is the journey which Satan "tempts" through Chaos to the "calm Firmament" and eventually to Eden. The challenge in both cases is what Satan calls the "dark unbottom'd infinite Abyss," as he offers to "spread his aery flight / Upborne with indefatigable wings / Over the vast abrupt." The official difference between Akenside's high-born(e) soul and Milton's Satan is that *her* quest leads to heavenly contemplation; the imagistic difference is gender. The importance of this sexual fact can be felt in the simple experiment of rereading the passage and substituting masculine pronouns. If "her" soaring ambition were "his," the associations with illegitimacy and satanic overreaching would be too direct and too great.

It is difficult to know whether Akenside's own sexual substitution is so conscious. In him one catches the beginnings of a "romantic" reading of Satan, though there is no trace at all in his "chearful song" (I, 346) of a Byronic glorification of the outcast nor of the deliberately provocative transvaluation of Blake. But

---

[23]The phrase is Marjorie Hope Nicolson's; see *Mountain Gloom and Mountain Glory* (1959; reprint ed., New York: Norton, 1963), esp. pp. 271–323 and 363–67.

a romantic relation of particular significance is that between Akenside's Miltonism and Wordsworth's. Here the common element is primarily a matter not of style (though that deserves subtler attention than it has received) but of aspiration and attempted appropriation. If the flight of Akenside's feminized ambition recalls Satan, it also suggests and perhaps influences the ambitious journey described in the "Prospectus" of 1814, that massy fragment in which Wordsworth announces his intention to "breathe in worlds / To which the heaven of heavens is but a veil," to travel "unalarmed" past the angels and "empyreal thrones," past Jehovah, past Chaos, and presumably well past Milton. Beside these lines Akenside's ambition looks pale (as most people's would: Blake claimed the passage gave him a "bowel complaint which nearly killed him"), but it was genuine and potentially heterodox enough in 1744, both religiously and poetically, to need protection.[24]

As a protective sanction for ambition, the feminine image provides a means of approaching the father "unalarmed" but still properly "amaz'd" and without overt competition. In both Akenside and Collins the feminine image is in fact as old as the Creation and is the key element enabling the poet to equate his inspiration with God's. This is a loftier claim than even the insistence that the poet's inspiration is *from* God and a more complex one than the association of God and the poet as creators. Shaftesbury's "second Maker" or "just Prometheus under Jove" (*Soliloquy*, I, iii) now seems barely second or to under anything. Man and God are alike, at the close of *The Pleasures of Imagination*, because they are both in love with the same woman, Nature, who is also the "indulgent mother" (III, 615–33; I, 358). This female is not literally God's mother, of course, but she is the embodied form of a prior mother of Creation, the celestial "Wisdom" of Akenside's first account (I, 59–78) or "divinest" Fancy in Collins's *Ode on the Poetical Character*, to which, with Warton's *Ode to Fancy*, we will now return.

[24]Ll. 31–35, quoted from the text of the first printing (as the preface to *The Excursion*) as reprinted by M. H. Abrams in *Natural Supernaturalism* (New York: Norton, 1971), pp. 466–69. In his discussion of the *Prospectus*, Abrams (pp. 21–28) argues that Wordsworth is claiming that only his subject, not his ability, surpasses Milton's.

A recent critic of Collins has complained that Joseph Warton's work is, by contrast, a "poetry of the eye," committed to "theatrical dazzle rather to the labor of internalization," a "highly artifactual verse in which the personified agent exists for the sake of the visualization, the idea for the sake of the image." It is "patently a species of wit." There is no doubt that Collins's odes are much better than Warton's, but these do not seem to me the best terms in which to state the difference. They are too close to Warton's own: externalized description is suspect, bright light is suspect, and above all, wit is suspect. But in fact many of Collins's poems depend on a fine logic of wit and brilliant theatricality which, if recognized as such and not obscured by premises of romantic agony, should allow the odes to be read much less tragically or melodramatically or simply gloomily than has been fashionable.[25]

When we actually compare Warton's *Ode to Fancy* and Collins's *Ode on the Poetical Character,* we find the conception of the poems fundamentally different. Warton's preoccupation with Fancy as an "artless" power leads him to characterize her as the power of sympathy or projection, the emotional vehicle which allows the experience of the whole range of feelings described in the poem. But most of all Fancy is the sympathy of maternal melancholy, and the last image of her—

> O hither come,
> From thy lamented Shakespeare's tomb,
> On which thou lov'st to sit at eve,
> Musing o'er thy darling's grave—

suggests a Venus not of laughter but of sighs, mourning at the tomb of Adonis. The Fancy Warton is celebrating is a filter of feeling, and especially the soberer coloring, through which one

---

[25]Paul S. Sherwin, *Precious Bane: Collins and the Miltonic Legacy* (Austin: University of Texas Press, 1977), p. 64. Sherwin's vision of Collins is steadily tragic. "Engaged in a continual rite of passage, he becomes a prisoner of the passage, a liminal being vertiginously suspended between self-loss and self-presence" (p. 4). "More vulnerable than the great Romantics, Collins cannot freely offer up his spirit to a transforming visionary blindness" (p. 124).

is able to imagine the absent. This is not to say that the "idea" exists "for the sake of the image." The idea *is* imagery, and Warton's strategy in the poem is to conjure imagination by demonstrating his imaginative virtuosity.

Collins has no interest at all in making Fancy into an "artless" power and consequently leaves himself free to write a much more playful poem, for Fancy is here not simply an image-making faculty but a creator. The appropriate song for her, then, will be a creation hymn, one which does not seek to escape literary artifice but rather uses it (Spenser's weaving in this case) to recapture the original act of art. In Collins's version of the Creation, God was wooed by Fancy (the "loved Enthusiast") until he,

> Himself in some diviner mood,
> Retiring, sat with her alone,
> And placed her on his sapphire throne,
> The whiles, the vaulted shrine around,
> Seraphic wires were heard to sound,
> Now sublimest triumph swelling,
> Now on love and mercy dwelling;
> And she, from out the veiling cloud,
> Breathed her magic notes aloud:
> And thou, thou rich-haired youth of morn,
> And all thy subject life was born!
>
> [30–40]

The biblical-neo-platonic (and Spenserian-Miltonic) tradition leading to this sexual version of the Creation has been charted with great skill by Earl Wasserman, and Roger Lonsdale's extensive commentary adds further parallels, notably with Cowley and Akenside.[26] But despite its many respectable precedents, Collins's account remains shocking. Our surprise may not be as disapproving as Mrs. Barbaud's, in 1797, to "this strange and by no means reverential fiction concerning the Divine Being" (*The Poetical Works of William Collins*, p. xxiv), but her description contains a useful half-truth. The passage is not very reverential toward the male deity, nor even concerned with him directly; its real reverence and concern extend to the inspiring goddess the

---

[26]Wasserman, "Collins' 'Ode on the Poetical Character,'" *ELH*, 34 (1968): 92–115; Lonsdale, *The Poems of Gray, Collins, and Goldsmith*, 429–33.

poem has generously created to accompany him. With God's muse as his own muse, Collins works back through the Spenserian pretext of the poem's opening to a visionary share in the primal text.

The critical controversy as to whether the "rich-haired youth of morn" (39) refers to the sun or to the Poet is not likely to be settled, though one may feel it is unnecessary, since Collins seems careful to suggest both referents through the traditional associations of Sun-Apollo-Poetry.[27] Perhaps the urge to segregate these readings is part of a more general underestimation of Collins's wit in this, the ripest of his finished poems. Its wit derives largely from a newer decorum, one which is obviously not dependent upon restraint but which clothes its naked ambition in sexual playfulness. The poem begins with a coy but winning misreading of Spenser which immediately confuses the traditional associations of gender. The conceit of Florimel's "magic girdle" links the biblical girding of "prophetic loins" of the would-be chosen poet with a "Spenserian" has-she-or-hasn't-she virginity contest: for an instant it is as if Moses were trying on Cinderella's slipper. I exaggerate the burlesque, perhaps, but more than a trace of quaint amusement carries over into the exuberant rewriting of Genesis in the second stanza (quoted earlier), which manages the rare feat of taking gender lightly and seriously at once. This "strange fiction" transforms the biblical situation in two brisk steps. With the first Collins sees God and decides it is not good for him to dwell alone. With the second he appropriates for Fancy the "sapphire throne" of Christ (*Paradise Lost*, VI, 758), thus creating a feminine savior as well as a general mother.[28]

In both of these aspects she is the mediating figure who renders the father less forbidding, less "of rude access." The phrase

[27]The earlier disagreements are summarized by Lonsdale, *The Poems of Gray, Collins, and Goldsmith*, p. 432. Sherwin's reading (pp. 22–26) seems to me subtler and more accurate, but I do not share his view that Collins is "caught off guard" by his audacity and then retreats from it.

[28]In Akenside's philosophic heaven, Truth, Goodness, and Beauty comprise a loosely platonized Holy Trinity, and a feminized one, with Beauty in Christ's role: "Thus was Beauty sent from Heaven, / The lovely ministress of truth and good / In this dark world: for truth and good are one, / And beauty dwells in them, and they in her, / With like participation" (*Pleasures of Imagination*, 1744, I, 372–76).

is from the third stanza, where it begins the climbing description of Milton's "jealous steep," that hill on which "an Eden like his own lies spread" (62). This is the "scene" of Miltonic creation, the "inspiring bowers" of the conclusion, said to be "o'erturned" or "curtained close" now "from every future view." Because of these lines the poem is often read as a pessimistic statement about modern poetry or as a personal confession of inadequacy to reach the Miltonic heights. But it seems that the poem's ambition outweighs any gestures of diffidence. In more significant gestures Collins has rewritten not only Genesis but Milton himself by feminizing his heavenly hierarchy, and the third section grandly appropriates Milton's landscape as well by internalizing it, interpreting it as essentially a visionary condition rather than a historical one. Deferring to Spenser and then Milton, Collins proceeds to rewrite both of them, opening again the bowers officially closed to every future view.

With the poem's actual survey in mind, the final phrase leaves an odd note in the air; it suggests that perhaps the appropriate emphasis is "from every *future* view," that the ode now being completed, rather than *Paradise Lost,* is the last poetic glimpse of these lands. Whether or not this is so, whether Milton or Milton-in-Collins was really the last man out of Paradise, the full implications of ambition and optimism remain through the end of the poem. In either case, the Edenic stage of English poetry is *now* over, and there is no reason to assume that this fall need be any less fortunate than the biblical fall. The ground is cleared for poetry to assume its redemptive—or rather, *her* redemptive—role. For amid the hurry of retreating pieties in the closing lines, Collins firmly announces the implication of his myth, that the masculine "Heaven" and the feminine Fancy are "kindred powers."

To read the poem this way is to see its final ambition as less tentative than most criticism has considered it (following either a Johnsonian bias in which Collins is seen as "obstructed" or a modern one from which he is "doomed"),[29] but also as less di-

[29]In the "Life of Collins" Johnson characterizes his mind as "not deficient in fire . . . but somewhat obstructed in its progress by deviation in quest of mistaken beauties." Harold Bloom, in *The Visionary Company* (Ithaca: Cornell University Press, 1971), describes Collins as "one of the doomed poets of an Age of

140

rectly personal and based more on principle. To call the principle feminine is to oversimplify, but clearly the poem's argument
is meaningless, and its motivation obscure, without Fancy's insistent femininity and her elevation to godhood. Placing the emphasis here, on the claims made for the female, allows, too, a
reading of the ode which does not sever its connection with
Collins's odes generally or with the lesser odes of his contemporaries. Collins's habitual posture, like the Wartons', is that of
votary, and the characteristic "plot" of his poems is the "Assumption" of the feminized power, as in the promise to Mercy,
"Thou, thou shalt rule our Queen and share our / Monarch's
throne!" or to Liberty, "Thou, lady, shalt rule the West!"

Collins's *Ode on the Poetical Character* is clearly a more complicated piece of myth making than anything Warton had in mind.
Warton's ode *To Fancy* is in some ways closer to the more deriva-
tively Miltonic poems of Collins, such as the odes to Fear, Pity,
and Simplicity, where the let-me-dwell-with-thee pattern is relatively straightforward. By comparing two such poems, the odes
to Evening, we may be able to see the distinctive nature of Collins's imagination even in a more conventional lyric situation.
Collins tends toward impersonality the more he elaborates the
poem's central personification, as suggested by the revision of
these four lines between the first and second printings of the *Ode
to Evening:*

> Then let me rove some wild and healthy Scene,
> Or find some Ruin 'midst its dreary Dells,
> Whose Walls more awful nod
> By thy religious Gleams.

In 1748 Collins altered the lines to the less self-referential form
we now have:

> Then lead, calm vot'ress, where some sheety lake
> Cheers the lone heath, or some time-hallowed pile,
> Or upland fallows grey,
> Reflect its last cool gleam.
>
> [29–32]

Sensibility" (p. 14). Wasserman's view is less anxious, but like Bloom he sees the
ending of the ode as a doubt-ridden retreat, with Collins resigning himself to his
"merely human talents" ("Collins' 'Ode on the Poetical Character,'" p. 115).

The conclusions of the poems suggest the difference between Warton's and Collins's use of the role of "votary." Warton's final lines serve primarily to describe himself:

> A holy calm creeps o'er my peaceful soul
> Anger, and mad Ambition's storms subside.

> O modest Evening oft let me appear
> A wandering votary in thy pensive train;
> Listening to every wildly-warbling throat
> That fills with farewell sweet thy darkening plain.

Collins professes allegiance, too, but as he does so he steadily removes himself from the picture:

> But when chill blustering winds or driving rain
> Forbid my willing feet, be mine the hut
> That from the mountain's side
> Views wilds and swelling floods,
> And hamlets brown, and dim-discovered spires,
> And hears their simple bell, and marks o'er all
>   Thy dewy fingers draw
>   The gradual dusky veil.
> While sallow Autumn fills thy lap with leaves,
> Or Winter yelling through the troublous air,
>   Affrights thy shrinking train,
>   And rudely rends thy robes. . . .

It would be interesting to know whether the "shrinking train" of Collins's Evening influenced the "pensive train" of Warton's, or vice versa. But whatever the priority, Collins is clearly trying to embody Evening herself, relegating his own portrait and the landscape to secondary roles. The *Ode to Evening* is a secular hymn and just possibly the eighteenth century's best love poem. Collins's opening eagerness to find the right voice—"If aught of oaten stop or pastoral song / May hope, chaste Eve, to soothe thy modest ear"—dramatizes the sexual solicitude which he extends toward the females of virtually all of his poems. This solicitude is a fusion of two kinds of concern, the protectiveness of the courtly lover toward his idealized woman and the anxiety of the son concerning his mother's innocence. The fusion attains (in Stevens's phrase) the delicatest ear in the *Ode to the Evening*.

But sexual solicitude is also essential to the more resolutely
political and sublime odes of Collins, and a brief comparison of
passages from his and Warton's poems to Liberty will illustrate
the role of imminent violation in Collins's minature myths. As in
the odes to the Evening, the passages are close enough to indi-
cate almost certain influence, and as in the case of Warton's
"pensive train" and Collins's "shrinking train," the difference is
between a faint picture and a vivid drama. Warton:

> Britannia watch!—remember peerless Rome,
> Her high-tower'd head dash'd meanly to the ground;
> Remember, freedom's guardian, Grecia's doom,
> Whom, weeping, the despotic Turk has bound. . . .
>
> [51–54]

The corresponding lines from Collins's *Ode to Liberty* are these:

> No, Freedom, no, I will not tell
> How Rome, before thy weeping face,
> With heaviest sound, a giant-statue, fell,
> Pushed by a wild and artless race
> From off its wide ambitious base,
> When Time his northern sons of spoil awoke,
>   And all the blended work of Strength and grace,
>   With many a rude repeated stroke
> And many a barbarous yell, to thousand fragments broke.
>
> [17–25]

The statue is Rome, but since Rome is Liberty's creation, the
conflict is essentially between the feminine principle and the
"wild" sons of Time. Like Winter "rudely rending" the robes of
chaste Evening, the destruction of impious sons is felt in "many a
rude repeated stroke," an image which in turn might recall a
famous moment of metaphoric sexual violation in *The Prelude:*
"as I rose upon the stroke, my boat / Went heaving through the
water like a swan / . . . I struck and struck again."[30]

The sexual concern which leads Collins to take his personifications more seriously—and more playfully—than Warton and

[30]*Prelude* (1850) I, 373–80, in *The Prelude,* ed. Jonathan Wordsworth, M. H.
Abrams, and Stephen Gill (New York: Norton, 1979); cf. *Nutting* for a more
explicit violation of a virginal landscape.

most of the mid-century poets also leads him more decidedly away from the "descriptive" and into the "allegoric" subjects which the title of his collection promises. Description remains, of course, but it tends to focus on the archetype Collins is addressing rather than on its manifestations in daily or historical life. The departure from conventional mimesis of which Goldsmith would later complain in Italian poetry is apparent in many of the mid-century English lyricists; it is simply truer of Collins: "Poetry is no longer among them the imitation of what we see, but of what a visionary might wish."[31]

Even in the *Ode to Liberty*, which virtually demands a historical survey, Collins gravitates toward the realm of prehistory. Collins handles his history very deftly, sometimes charging a single couplet with both processional impersonality and a lyric counterpoint suggestive of Hopkins, as in these lines on the Medicis' role in Florence:

> Till they, whom Science loved to name,
> (O who could fear it?) quenched her flame.
>
> [35–36]

But he quickly turns from history and geography to seek a world out of normal time and space:

> The magic works, thou feel'st the strains,
> One holier name alone remains;
> The perfect spell shall then avail.
> Hail nymph, adored by Britain, hail!
>
> [60–63]

Collins maintains this magic spell by telling the story of England's legendary "blest divorce" from the European mainland and then locating at that same discontinuous instant a primal scene of the sort he envisioned in the *Ode on the Poetical Character*:

> Then too, 'tis said, an hoary pile
> Midst the green naval of our isle,

---

[31]Goldsmith, *An Enquiry*, in Friedman, ed., *Collected Works*, I, 276–77.

Thy shrine in some religious wood,
O soul-enforcing goddess stood!

[89–92]

History will not be of any use in approaching the archetypal truth represented by such a scene: "Though now with hopeless toil we trace / Time's backward rolls to finds its place," it is up to the visionary poet to recognize that the "beauteous model still remains" and to build the timeless temple anew.

We have looked earlier at the ending of this poem, in which Collins projects into the future as timeless and happily catastrophic a moment as he had imagined in the primal past. Liberty has been converted into Concord, and

> Our youths, enamoured of the fair,
> Play with the tangles of her hair;
> Till in one loud applauding sound,
> The nations shout to her around:
> 'O how supremely art thou blest,
> Thou, lady, thou shalt rule the West!'

In a recent discussion of the *Ode to Liberty* which seems to me otherwise very perceptive, Paul Sherwin finds Collins "hopelessly adrift" at this point and sees his sudden "shift in allegiance" from Liberty to Concord as further evidence of the "seductive power of Milton's influence."[32] But Collins's conclusion is in fact typical of a number of his odes and those of his contemporaries. It is the conclusion to a conversion, a sudden, radical transformation, after which nothing will ever be the same. In this case, since it is the whole culture which is to be converted, Liberty must be given her "social form," soothed from individual recalcitrance into the universal freedom of Concord. It is time to consider the prevalence of conversion experiences of several sorts in the broader range of mid-eighteenth-century poetry.

---

[32]Sherwin, *Precious Bane*, p. 90.

6

Earlier I suggested that the "Solitude" and "Innocence" that Thomas Warton singled out as instances of personification in recent poetry are not merely casual examples, for many of the poems Warton would have had in mind concern a conspicuously solitary figure turning his energies toward some representative of innocence. I believe it is now possible to describe the characteristic "plot" of such poems more precisely, while doing so in terms general enough to characterize a period phenomenon rather than idiosyncratic themes. The "plot" which seems to me most genuinely characteristic of mid-eighteenth-century poetry is a conversion story. We can see this story played out most often as a quest for radical innocence, at the end of which the poet (and perhaps everyone else) is taken out of the old historical order and is made the chosen son (or people) of the principle of purity being addressed. Although these are largely secular events and agents, in essence religious conversion becomes the model for what ought to happen in a poem. The dramatization of conversion thus replaces traditional historical material in much of the new poetry of the mid-century and figures strongly, though mostly unconsciously, in ideals of pure poetry which emerge then and are sometimes still felt today.

We have seen in Gray how the quest for radical purity is likely to lead to death (if the paths of glory lead but to the grave, so do the paths of pure poetry); in other poets the quest is likely to lead to a large feminine personification who represents maiden innocence, maternal protection, and a general alternative to the world of masculine history and striving. The atmosphere of such encounters tends to be hushed and critical, not necessarily melancholy but if cheerful, earnestly, single-mindedly, solemnly so. In this atmosphere three types of conversion can be distinguished, although the categories often overlap, and, in fact, their significance lies as much in their similarities as in the differences, which make it useful first to discuss them separately: (1) salvational conversions, that is, poems which enact the decisive adoption, after a period of error, of views necessary for salvation; (2) vocational conversions, that is, poems dramatizing or recalling the poet's *call,* his dedication to poetry and/or his decision to become the "votary" of a value seen as essential to poetry; (3) cultural conversions, that is, poems which announce the sudden transformation of the whole culture—generally England or "the West"—into something fundamentally different, operating on new principles, in accord with new but universally shared values, entering a harmonious era.

Salvational conversions are central to three of the notable long poems of the mid-century, *Night Thoughts, The Pleasures of Imagination,* and *The Castle of Indolence.* In *Night Thoughts* there is a sort of double conversion, the rescue of the freethinking Lorenzo to orthodoxy and the speaker's own movement from "Complaint" in Book I to "Consolation" in Book IX. In *The Pleasures of Imagination,* the youthful poet perplexed in doubt is suddenly and wholly translated into a realm of harmony where Virtue and Pleasure are reconciled. We shall look at these two poems more carefully in the next chapter. For the moment, *The Castle of Indolence* may be the richest example because it indicates how the claims of public orthodoxy (not necessarily religious claims per se) and the imperatives of poetic vocation can come into conflict. Officially, the saving conversion of that poem occurs when the poet-speaker and his associates are rescued from their bower of blissful indolence by the Knight of Arts and Industry and his rousing artist; but these two public men, the statesman and the poet, destroy Thomson's persuasive objectification of the poetic imagination. Before we return to this conflict between salvational and vocational poems, it will help to delineate the other types of conversion plot.

Vocational poems include any number of lyrics, primarily odes, which proceed by invocation and apostrophe to focus attention on the poet's relation to his muse, fancy, "poesy," or some other unworldly quality and which either enact or reenact a sudden turn from the profane and toward the imaginatively sacred. In addition to many of the odes of Collins, Joseph Warton, and Akenside which we have considered, we might readily include here Thomas Warton's *Pleasures of Melancholy* and ode *To Sleep,* Joseph's *The Enthusiast,* or Akenside's later and lovely ode *To the Evening Star* (which opens "Tonight retired, the queen of heaven / With young Endymion stays . . .") and his longer *Hymn to the Naiads* (which closes with the wish to exclude "all

profaner audience"), poems in which the speakers detach themselves from most of the ambition, strife, commerce—in fact,
from most of the social life around them—in order to become
filial votaries of something purer, more innocent, more unitary.

In cultural conversion poems the decisive turn is general
rather than individual, as in the optimistically apocalyptic vision
we witnessed at the end of Collins's *Ode to Liberty* ("Thou, Lady,
thou shalt rule the West!"), or his *Ode to Mercy* ("Thou, thou shalt
rule our Queen and share our / Monarch's throne!"), or the last
section of Thomson's *Liberty,* with its prospect of the English
futurescape. If we consider that such conversions can be dysto-
pian as well as utopian, then examples of the type would include
the visionary and virtueless England at the end of the *Dunciad* or
Joseph Warton's *The Enthusiast* or Goldsmith's *The Deserted Village.* The common element is the sudden, radical transformation
of the society into something single, with all its people and parts
united under one "sway," and presumably unchanging ever
after. Like the convert's soul, the converted country is borne out
of time and into eternity.

The kind of change described in the various conversion plots
of mid-century poetry is both deeper and more sudden than
conventional processes of education, maturation, or simply
changing one's mind. I suggested in chapter 2 that there are
parallels between the allegorical world of the poets and the emphasis on sudden conviction in the psychology of Law and
Hume. Law contrasts the mere "Act of Memory" with the genuine "inward change" which marks belief and results in a "new
State of . . . Existence." "The least Stirring of this inward principle, or power of life, is of more value than all the Activity of our
Reason, which is only as it were a Painter of dead Images, which
leave the Heart in the same State of Death, and Emptiness of all
Goodness in which they find it. Therefore, listen to the voice of
Grace, the Instinct of God that speaks and moves within you;
and instead of forming dead and lifeless Images, let your Heart
pray to God."[33]

---

[33]Law, *A Demonstration of the . . . Errors of a late Book, called, A Plain Account of
the . . . Sacrament* (1737), in *Works of W. L.,* 9 vols. (New Forest: G. Moreton,
1892–93), V, 19–20, 60–61, 73, 89–90, 93–94.

In his treatise on the subject of "new birth," *The Grounds and Reason of Christian Regeneration,* Law repeatedly stresses the importance of an intense "sensibility," an entire and "inward sensation," not rational assent, as constituting true belief.[34] Law's vocabulary is often close to Hume's. The comparison would have displeased both parties, but Hume as well as Law tends to describe belief as a sudden conviction, a momentary experience of intensity (in Hume's terms, an intensity which more or less converts an idea into a sensation). By the time of the second *Enquiry* (1751), Hume's description of the operation of "taste," in which more and more mental activity seems to be located, sounds like Warton on Fancy—taste has "a productive faculty, and gilding or staining all natural objects with the colours, borrowed from internal sentiment, raises in a manner a new creation"—and in fact it sounds like Hume himself on "superstition" ten years earlier, that faculty which "opens a world of its own, and presents us with scenes, and beings, and objects, which are altogether new." Here I want to suggest simply that toward the mid-century neither the fideist nor the skeptic was conceiving of belief as a matter of mere rational assent; the experience of sudden conviction, which is another way of saying a miniature conversion, became the model for the act of belief. It is just possible that Hume's famous conclusion to the infamous chapter "Of Miracles"—that Christianity not only must have been attended by miracles at its beginning but cannot be believed at present without one—is at some level less ironic than is usually supposed; for in Hume's psychology, *any* belief is virtually miraculous.[35]

---

[34]Law, *Works of W. L.,* V, 145, 152–53, 160–61, 163–65, 167–68.

[35]*An Enquiry Concerning Human Understanding,* ed. L. A. Selby-Bigge, rev. P. H. Nidditch (London: Oxford University Press, 1955), X, ii (p. 131). James Noxon, in *Hume's Philosophical Intentions* (Oxford: Clarendon, 1973), makes the most interesting comment on Hume's conclusion to "On Miracles" that I have found: "Whether one regards this finale as a 'volte-face', as did Taylor, or, like Flew, as 'blisteringly sardonic', it implies a very odd conclusion about religious belief. If Christian faith is a miraculous event, then no wise man would believe anyone who claimed to believe in Christianity. Whether this cryptic flourish of double talk was inspired by caution or by irony, it seems to have landed Hume in a dilemma. For now, apparently, he must either admit that miracles occur by the millions, or that millions of witnesses to their own beliefs are deluded or lying. In other words, he must either admit that beliefs are so frequently acquired in

The quest for intensity and the enactment of critical turning points in the poems are often ways of denying, or of attempting to deny, the significance of memory and the continuous past. The preoccupation with conversion models of truth during the period represents a strong interest in regarding as "poetic" isolated moments of intensity and innocence, an unusually strong sense of public memory as public guilt (and correspondingly of private memory as childhood purity), and a strong concern with validating conviction by means of the instantaneous force of feeling. Such force is what Hume means by its "vivacity" or "liveliness" and Law by the "life" or "living Sensibility of the Thing that is known."[36]

In Law's exhortation to turn from the mind's "dead and lifeless Images" and to "listen to the voice of Grace," we have the theological counterpart to the poets' habitual rejection of mimetic engagement and their desire to resolve their poems by the sudden and saving interposition of a voice of grace. At its best such a voice is a lyric grace, the external voice fused to the speaker's own and the entire poem built on confidence that the lyric structure can and will attain a "spell," work a "magic" transformation, invoke the necessary "power" precisely because it is a lyric. Such is the artistic confidence of Collins generally, of Gray in *The Progress of Poesy, The Bard,* and *The Fatal Sisters,* of the Wartons occasionally (especially in Thomas's *On the Approach of Summer* and *The Crusade*), and of Akenside.

But often the "voice of grace" intrudes in a quite literal fashion in mid-century poetry, and then it is likely to signal a conflict between competing conversions, the demands of conventional salvation jangling against those of vocation. In other words, many of the poems, including some promising ones, fall apart or end abruptly when salvational and vocational conversions are set against one another. For example, *The Enthusiast* by William

---

contravention of 'all the principles of human understanding' that his theory of the understanding has been disconfirmed, or he must autocratically reject the evidence of countless people who came forth testifying to their own beliefs" (p. 178).

[36]Law, *The Spirit of Love and The Spirit of Prayer,* ed. Sidney Spencer (Cambridge: James Clarke, 1969), pp. 115–16; for similar emphases in earlier works, cf. *Works of W. L.,* V, 90–93, 97, 117, 151–52.

Whitehead is nearly a miniature or epitomized version of *The Castle of Indolence*. The first half of the poem recounts a visionary moment in May when the poet was moved to profess, in "unbidden lay," his devotion to nature, contemplation and "serenest solitude." The second half of the poem consists of the voice of reason reminding him that he has social obligations and that "man was made for man." Having been first converted to the "poetic" or vocational world, the speaker must then be converted out of it. The distrust of poetry implied here and in *The Castle of Indolence* figures again in Joseph Warton's ode *Against Despair*, where similarly the first half of the poem contains a lively and at least conventionally persuasive exploration of melancholy pressures, which are then suddenly revealed as belonging to a past mood (*merely* a memory) since canceled out by the voice of Patience. And we find distrust again in Thomas Warton's *The Suicide*, where the speaker identifies with the despair of the suicide, who is imagined to be somewhat like the poet as seen by the swain at the end of Gray's *Elegy* and who in fact had vainly "sought the powers of sleep" in terms similar to Warton's own poem *To Sleep*. The speaker has even begun to build a poetic shrine to him when he is suddenly reproved by a voice from the clouds for the "specious" poetry he has bestowed on the "foul self-murderer." But to most ears this official dismissal is likely to sound more specious than the better part (in both senses) of the poem.

Another example of this conflict is Thomas Warton's *Written at Vale-Royal Abbey in Cheshire*, more poignant because in its evocative attempt to reconstruct by effort of historical imagination the meaning of the ruins, the poem is on its way to being one of the best of the period when Warton suddenly loses faith in his vision and in poetic vision generally: "Thus sings the Muse . . . ," but we need to pardon her: "Her fairy shapes are tricked by Fancy's pen: / Severer Reason forms far other views, / And scans the scene with philosophic ken"—and so on, to the praise of "new civilities" and the modern "social plan."

But exactly these distrusted "shapes" populate the abstract ode in the middle years of the eighteenth century. At moments these persons who are made, as Warton says elsewhere, of "abstracted things" allow for kinds of poetic representation not achieved in earlier or later poetry. The abstract ode is usually, in Akenside's phrase, a "suppliant song." By insisting both upon its personality—the apostrophe must be uttered by someone, and someone· in need at that—and upon its stylized, even choral formality, one is able to wring from the ode a representation of experience as at once unique and archetypal. The kinds of conversion experience enacted lyrically in these poems differ strongly, for example, from the recurrent "conversions" in some of the most memorable Renaissance sonnets. In sonnets such as "When to the sessions of sweet silent thought" or Milton's "When I consider how my light is spent," the surge of doubt is not a unique event, and "when" really means "whenever." Much of the force and appeal of these poems comes from the knowledge that their resolutions are re-solutions of familiar problems and that resolve comes and goes. But the "when" of a mid-eighteenth-century ode is "once" (even so in the sonnet, which Thomas Warton treats as an occasional poem), and the event it enacts is dramatized as having occurred at a discrete moment. On the other hand, the event typically involves an encounter with timeless powers, the personification or personifications of the poem, and the encounter thus has (or is just about to have) the effect of finality, moving the experience beyond a world of temporal process.

This very lack of process excludes the abstract ode from some of the resonances of resolution attained in the great sonnets. For different reasons, the denial of process also separates the mid-century poems from the greater romantic lyrics, which draw much of their music from the recognition that the timeless vision is temporary. But the "common task" (to use Cassirer's term again) of many mid-eighteenth-century poets seems to be, in contrast, the attempt to subsume personal and social change under unchanging but secular categories. These categories take the form of personifications and are capable of proliferating all too easily ("Come, Capitalization, heavenly pow'r," one expects to hear). Their proliferation is, however, a sign of their commonality. Mid-eighteenth-century personifications can be multiplied more readily than Renaissance or romantic "powers" because they are often neither deities nor forces of nature (pity, Solitude, Fancy, or Liberty are more plentiful than west winds or skylarks) but avowedly human constructs. Yet when we look at these mid-century personifications we find they have a good deal in common. I have tried to emphasize their femininity, which is usually taken for granted, and the way in which that attribute allows personification to function as an alternative to a world of men.

When we think in this context of Personification Herself, we may begin to perceive another facet of the "common task" of poetry during the period, the unconscious conversion of history into History. In the poets' various attempts to generalize the public past into War or Ambition or Luxury and in their attempts to dissociate themselves from it, we see glimpses of a new historicism, a crudely idealistic or "Hegelian" sense of history as a directive force—against which the poets must invoke forces of their own. Most of this is indeed less than conscious, and what we have is more like a photographic negative of the idea of history than the positive image of it. But we can in a sense develop the picture ourselves, seeing how History was beginning to be imagined by some of the people who, while by no means "world-historical individuals," tried to control it by abstraction or testified to its presence by seeking to get out of its way.

PART III

Narrative Diffusion

CHAPTER 5

The Long Poem Obstructed

To use the problem of the long poem as a guide to a period's discontinuities may be problematic itself. Successful long poems are so rare in the history of literature, the odds against their conception and survival so high, that investing them with normative value may be like trying to judge the ocean solely by analyzing whales. Always appearing on the verge of extinction, long poems fascinate largely because of their rarity, even improbability; as Thomson says of the literal (and amorous) whales, "They flounce and tumble in unwieldy joy."[1] If it is difficult now to imagine our literary inheritance without *Paradise Lost*, from a disinterested point of view it may be easier to imagine that it might never have been written. And if it had not been? Surely much that has been written about Renaissance humanism and epic continuity would then be pointless explication of the "inevitable"?

At the same time, we seem drawn to see the whales as more than improbabilities, feeling vaguely that they tell us not only the condition of the depths but the deep condition of areas nearer home. This feeling may well be founded on more than epic piety or nostalgia, since it is likely that a long, comprehensive poem will in the end be a poetic theodicy, whether because of Milton's influence or because long poems naturally imply a whole picture of the world which they figure. They will therefore present most of the intellectual uncertainties of a period as

[1] *Spring*, 1, 824. Quotations from *The Seasons* and *Liberty* refer to Thomson's *Poetical Works*, ed. J. L. Robertson (1908: reprint ed., London: Oxford University Press, 1965).

well as reflecting the ambitions of one of its actors. In the middle of the eighteenth century, the problem of the long poem is concentrated before us because the 1740s saw the completion of three very considerable blank verse poems which compete with the more familiar world order framed in *An Essay on Man*. Thomson's *The Seasons*, Akenside's *The Pleasures of Imagination*, and Young's *Night Thoughts* are poems of too much talent to be dismissed. But even as we recognize this fact, we recognize simultaneously that our recovery of them is fitful.

If we persevere to the point of asking patiently why we have so much more difficulty reading these poems on their own terms than *An Essay on Man*, or *The Prelude*, or *Prometheus Unbound* (to which we will return briefly), we may decide that their terms are in fact unclear, that the obstruction we feel in reading them is due in large part to conflicting appeals within the poems. Speaking very generally we could say that the leisure of length is at odds with the poets' desire for intensity or momentary sublimity. At best, as in much of *The Seasons*, we find the voice strong enough and the transitions sufficiently graceful to persuade us of the pleasures of variety and the appropriateness of a "varied God." At less than their best, the poems seem diffuse masses punctuated by unearned ecstasies or unaccountable stridencies. Intentionally and unintentionally, these poems present problems which *An Essay on Man* does not. If we can define the significant poetic differences, we may approach a coherent reading of major mid-century changes occurring simultaneously in ideas of order and in dominant poetic practice. To state the terms very broadly, the significant shift is from spatial to temporal theodicy, from proportion to process. Because the contrast is sharper between the poetic world of Pope and that of Young and Akenside, it will be helpful to begin with *Night Thoughts* and *The Pleasures of Imagination* before turning to *The Seasons*. But Thomson's poem, too, profoundly differs from Pope's; it insists upon articulating (and in this regard bears an interesting relation to Thomson's *Liberty* of 1735–1736) the fundamental problem confronting the poets: the secular but spiritual meaning of history or, in other words, the transformation of Providence into Progress.

1

Night Thoughts was written by an Anglican divine in his sixties and *The Pleasures of Imagination* by a suspiciously republican deist in his early twenties, but the works finally have more in common with each other as theodicies than either does with Pope's. *Night Thoughts* quickly became known by its subtitle, but its original title, *The Complaint* (leading to "The Consolation of Book IX"), reminds us that Young's general scheme is to pose and then to resolve various objections to Providence. The poem's contentions were long ago first studied systematically in relation to Christian apologetics, and more recently a strong case has been made for regarding *Night Thoughts* as a competitive answer to *An Essay on Man*, a reading which Young invites by comparing his subject with Pope's at the close of Book I: "Man too, he sung: *immortal* man I sing."[2] Akenside also draws attention to the relation of his argument in verse to Pope's recent precedent. While the comparison is respectfully and tentatively but explicitly made in the prose preface to *The Pleasures of Imagination*, the poem's opening lines immediately imply an ambition of more than Popean breadth:

> With what attractive charms this goodly frame
> Of nature touches the consenting hearts
> Of mortal men; and what the pleasing stores
> Which beauteous Imitation thence derives
> To deck the poet's, or the painter's toil,
> My verse unfolds.

This proposition actually breaks into two parts, and it is only the latter half which rests within the realm of *Spectator* modesty and the Addisonian psychology of the papers on imagination. The first subject Akenside proposes for himself is less suggestive of early eighteenth-century aesthetic treatises than it is of Words-

---

[2]*Night* I, 453. Quotations from Young refer to *Complete Works*, ed. James Nichols (London: n.p., 1854), vol. I. See Daniel W. Odell, "Young's *Night Thoughts* as an Answer to Pope's *Essay on Man*," in *Studies in English Literature*, 12 (1972): 481–501.

worth's providential scope in the "Prospectus" for *The Recluse,* a poem which was to have shown

> How exquisitely the individual Mind
> (And the progressive powers perhaps no less
> Of the whole species) to the external World
> Is fitted:—and how exquisitely too—
> Theme this little heard of among men—
> The external World is fitted to the Mind.[3]

The Pleasures of Imagination is in fact an extremely ambitious philosophical consideration of the "fitting" of the individual to his immediate and cosmic surroundings. Akenside's teleological argument even contains as its center a secular version of the Fall, Platonized and rather cushioned, it is true, but wholly intended to explain allegorically "the ways / Of heav'n's eternal destiny to man" (II, 670–71).

We have, in other words, two poems which are not specialized pieces with local aims—one a poem about graveyards at night, the other a verse treatise on the sublime—but which are instead comprehensive, encyclopedic poems designed to prove the world's design. In their broader purposes both works "fail," as Kant later said all theodicies were destined to, but what is interesting historically is that these poetic theodicies were attempted at all and were well received. It is difficult to imagine that two comparable "answers" to *Paradise Lost* or *In Memoriam* could have been written in the 1670s or 1860s, for example, and read attentively upon publication and respectfully for the better part of a century.

There are some obvious differences between the two poems; they would seem in fact to mark the "extremes" of religious doctrines which Pope had hoped to sail betwixt. Young's concentration on the redemption leads, for instance, to claims that "Religion's all" and that "Nature is Christian!" (IV, 550, 704), while Akenside's natural rhapsodies are as nondenominational as Shaftesbury's and generally as anticlerical. But without blink-

---

[3]"Prospectus" (1814), 11, 63–68. These lines do not occur in the first manuscript version; see M. H. Abrams, *Natural Supernaturalism* (New York: Norton, 1971), pp. 466–78, for the printed text and manuscript versions.

ing doctrinal differences, we can see less conscious and more instructive similarities in *Night Thoughts* and *The Pleasures of Imagination,* for the two poems are alike not simply in attempting to be unlike Pope but in several shared departures from the procedures of his theodicy. The term "procedures" is intended to suggest features of poetic argument which are as much a part of literary process as of paraphrasable "positions," and I employ it here in hopes of attending to kinds of meaning produced at the intersection of philosophic and metaphoric strategies.

At this level of meaning, then, the major differences between Pope's procedures and those of Akenside and Young may help us gauge the depth of change in poetry and philosophy during a crucial and admittedly problematic decade, the 1740s. The differences which seem most important are these: (1) Young and Akenside both depart from Pope's insistent commitment to empirical procedures, that is, to deductions based on observations; (2) both poems are more egocentric in perspective than *An Essay on Man;* (3) unbounded ambition, the desire to "soar," is treated approvingly rather than ironically; (4) both poems heavily base their proofs of providential harmony on reenacted conversion episodes; (5) both poems tend to make stronger appeals to "fancy" than to memory: (6) finally (and this difference may include the others), both poets rely more on solitary than on conversational voices. Each of these points requires some explanation.

Pope's empirical intention is signaled early—"Say first, of God above, of Man below, / What can we reason, but from what we know?" (I, 17–18)—and it is an orientation affecting not only the conduct of his argument but the poem's visual emphasis and texture as well. "What we know" for Pope means primarily what we can *see,* so that the mission he outlines involves beginning with the things at hand, placing them in sharper focus, and broadening the perspective until (and this is the ideal rather than the human condition for Pope) one can see with something like the sunlit clarity of God's "equal eye," which observes heroes and sparrows, worlds and bubbles, green myriads in the peopled grass, and the whole sea of matter in the same light. In *Night Thoughts,* however, the priority Pope had given to light is largely repudiated, and the change reflects something deeper than Young's straining for originality (in which spirit he solemnly boasts of being the first to invoke the moon as muse) or his cultivation of graveyard gloom. Darkness is valuable, in fact has "more divinity" than sunlight for Young, because "It strikes thought inward" and "drives back the soul / To settle on herself, our point supreme" (*Night* V, 128–30). While Akenside remains closer to what Martin Price has called the "light-centered world" and to metaphoric values of Pope and Milton, his poem is no less a transvaluation of Pope's empirically accessible "scene of Man."[4] Pope's subject lies in an "ample field" where two conversationalists can "expatiate free"; Akenside is drawn to a "fair poetic region" of "secret paths," and his real subject lies somewhere in the "laureate vale's profound recess, / Where never poet gain'd a wreath before" (I, 50–55). More significantly, the approach is exactly reversed: where Pope insists that the discussion begin from what is known or seen on the plane of "Man below," Akenside announces, "From Heav'n my strains begin: from heaven descends / The flame of genius to the human breast" (I, 56–57).

In speaking of the "egocentric" perspective of these poems, I wish to use the term as neutrally as possible. This is more difficult in the case of Young, whose manner George Eliot memorably characterized as "egoism turned heavenward"; but by it I mean the use of the self, and not the generalized "Man," as the measure of things.[5] The poems urge this measure in two ways. The first and more conspicuous lies in the value placed on self-absorption. At crucial rhetorical moments in the conversion of the doubting Lorenzo, Young issues the advice, "revere thyself," "Man, love thyself," and finally, "tremble at thyself" (VI, 128; VII, 170, 1004). Whatever the theological precedents, these comfortable admonitions recall only ironic statements of Pope's, as in Ariel's first address to Belinda: "Hear and believe; thy own

---

4Martin Price, "The Sublime Poem," *Yale Review*, 58 (1968): 203.

5Odell in "Young's *Night Thoughts*" characterizes Young as a "Christian anthropocentrist" (p. 493); Young's stress, however, seems to fall more heavily on the individual than on the species. For Eliot's renunciation of her "youthful predilection and enthusiasm" for *Night Thoughts* and her indictment of Young's "egoism," see "Worldliness and Other-Worldliness: The Poet Young," in Thomas Pinney, ed., *Essays* (New York: Columbia University Press, 1963), pp. 335–85, esp. pp. 358, 378.

The Long Poem Obstructed

Importance know." And if the advice to *tremble* recalls Belinda "trembling" at herself ("A heav'nly Image in the Glass appears, / To that she bends, to that her Eyes she rears"), Akenside's account of the mind's response to moral beauty is perhaps even closer:

> th' ambitious mind
> There sees herself: by these congenial forms
> Touch'd and awaken'd, with intenser act
> She bends each nerve, and meditates well-pleas'd
> Her features in the mirror.
>
> [I, 533–37]

But there is also a deeper egocentricity of perspective in both poems. We can see this perspective most quickly in Young, where the focus, literally, is on the self. Surveying the stars, he reflects that all the spaciousness of the night sky "streams to a point, and centres in my sight" (IX, 753). As if in reply to Pope's ironic question, "Can a part contain the whole?" Young writes:

> Those numerous worlds that throng the firmament,
> And ask more space in heaven, can roll at large
> In man's capacious thought, and still leave room
> For ampler orbs, for new creations, there.
>
> [VII, 1248–51]

The universe, known and unknown, is in the eye of the beholder. Akenside, for all his sunniness, is like Young in displaying less interest in the sunlight of assumed objectivity than in the light within. He invokes Beauty as "thou better sun" (I, 277), for example, and the phrase epitomizes both the Platonism absorbed from Shaftesbury (or, as Gray complained, from "Hutchinson-Jargon")[6] and his confidence in the redemptive power of imagination. A century earlier the "better sun" would likely have been a Metaphysical pun for Christ; here its function is still providentially mediating, but the incarnation evoked is primarily an affective or aesthetic reality:

[6]*Correspondence of Thomas Gray*, ed. Paget Toynbee and Leonard Whibley (Oxford: Oxford University Press, 1935), I, 224.

> Thus was Beauty sent from heav'n
> The lovely ministress of truth and good
> In this dark world: for truth and good are one,
> And beauty dwells in them, and they in her,
> With like participation.
>
> [I, 372–76]

The function of beauty, manifested alike in human and divine poetry, is an integral part of Akenside's argument because he begins from the premise that poets are the best interpreters of heavenly meaning:

> To these the Sire Omnipotent unfolds
> The world's harmonious volume, there to read
> The transcript of Himself.
>
> [I, 99–101]

The metaphor of reading which Akenside uses is as egocentric as Young's sight wherein all things center, although it is a less passive figure, since the order of the world, like the order of a text, takes shape from the reader's reading rather than in his retina. The metaphor also reaches past the familiar idea of the Book of Nature through its implication that the text is a difficult one, intended for gifted readers who are capable of tracing the "bright impressions" of God's hand in the creation and of finding "that uncreated beauty, which delights / The mind supreme" (I, 102–8).

This claim suggests the next point of departure from *An Essay on Man,* Young's and Akenside's approval of high ambition. If in Pope's scheme "aspiring to be gods" is evidence of ethical blindness, by the close of *The Pleasures of Imagination* it is a moral imperative:

> we feel within ourselves
> His energy divine; he tells the heart,
> He meant, he made us to behold and love
> What he holds and loves, the general orb
> Of life and being; to be great like him,
> Beneficient and active. Thus the men
> Whom nature's works can charm, with God himself

Hold converse; grow familiar, day by day,
With his conceptions; act upon his plan;
And form to his, the relish of their souls.

The mandate to be "great like him" reflects Akenside's distance both from Pope, for whom such logic is foolish, and from Milton, for whom it is satanic. There are many possible ways of saying that God speaks to Man through Nature, at least some of which are compatible with more "Augustan" or "Augustinian" positions. What is so highly personal in the terms of Akenside's "converse," however, is the emphasis on the power of nature to "charm" God and man alike. Man approaches God primarily not through a deductive understanding of created order but through his own capacity for creative ordering,[7] his ability to appreciate, as God does, the sublimity of nature. Although nature includes minute beauty as well as vast spectacles, and although the "pleasures of imagination" explicitly include both categories, Akenside is like Young in tending to attribute greater theological as well as poetic import to grandeur.[8] In *Night* IX, Young rationalizes this preoccupation by way of epigram: "True, all things speak a God, but in the small / Men trace out him; in great, He seizes man" (IX, 774–75). Akenside goes one step further, perhaps, by implying that God and man are "seized" aesthetically˙ by the same things and by similar emotions.

The ultimate seizure, so to speak, for both poets is conversion, the experience of a personal transformation after which all of one's former complaints against Providence are cast aside. (These are "salvational" conversions in the terms of the preceding chapter.) In *Night Thoughts* there are actually two conver-

[7]John Norton, in "Akenside's *The Pleasures of Imagination:* An Exercise in Poetics," *ECS* 3 (1970): 366–83, argues persuasively that the work is "not about the natural world" but about mental processes, and that "Akenside makes creative man . . . not God, the center of things" (pp. 369, 377).

[8]Samuel H. Monk, in *The Sublime* (1935; reprint ed., Ann Arbor: University of Michigan Press, 1960), first called attention to Akenside's preoccupation with vast objects and his use of the "affinity between the spirit of man and the vastness of nature" as a "symbol of man's divine origin and his ultimate attainment of perfection" (p. 72). David B. Morris cogently discusses Young's "interruptive and discontinuous" sublimity in *The Religious Sublime* (Lexington: University Press of Kentucky, 1972), pp. 145–53.

sions, the speaker's own, which can be considered a restoration of faith, and the conversion of a freethinker named Lorenzo, who plays a Hanoverian Earl of Rochester to Young's Bishop Burnet. Conversion in *The Pleasures of Imagination* is described, as one would expect, in more secular terms, but it is no less essential in "proving" the poem's conclusions, and its suddenness suggests the structure of conventional religious experience. The conversion episode that Akenside dramatizes locates the problem of evil in individual terms, the question becoming whether this is the best of all possible psyches. The young speaker is willing to grant that *some* of the passions implanted in man are evidence of providential care, but he doubts that *all* passions (such as anger, grief, or fear) can be truly necessary to achieve "Wisdom's artful aim" and "benignant end" (II, 123–25, 166–75). The question is answered by the abrupt entrance of "old Harmodius," kind sage and patron of the poet's toils, whose narrative reveals a visionary paradise and fall. The allegory is a refinement of the familiar "Choice of Hercules," in which the young hero weighs the charms of females personifying Virtue and Pleasure.[9] Akenside's youth eventually wins both ladies, but he first makes the mistake of pursuing pleasure alone and is racked by convulsions of guilt and despair. Since these personifications are also rather vivid women in Akenside's version, it is tempting to see the youth's fall as a loss of sexual innocence and his guilt as uneasiness at having rejected the more motherly Virtue in order to seek a female closer to his own age.[10] What is important for our purposes, however, is the fact that Akenside treats the fall as an inner event, a crisis in the individual's emotional development to be resolved by conversion. In their use of suggestively autobiographical conversion episodes, Young's and Akenside's

[9] In addition to Paulson's and Wasserman's remarks on the mid-century vogue of Hercules (cited in chap. 3, n. 20), see Maren-Sofie Rostvig, "*Tom Jones* and the Choice of Hercules," in Rostvig, ed., *Fair Forms* (Totowa, N.J.: Rowan & Littlefield, 1975), pp. 147–77.

[10] As I have tried to show in the preceding chapter, the femininity of many of the major personifications in mid-century poetry is not merely "conventional." The situation Akenside creates has little of the dramatic power of Keats's confrontation with Moneta in *The Fall of Hyperion*, but the interplay of erotic and ambitious paralyses seems at least distantly related.

theodicies bear more resemblance to the narrative resolutions of *The Prelude* and *In Memoriam* than to *An Essay on Man*.

The counterpart of the long poem of what we have elsewhere called a poetics of conversions is the tendency of both poets to sanction their truths in fancy rather than memory. Great importance is placed on the ability to achieve some new vision—a sudden and novel discovery rather than a recollection of something overlooked—which will radically transform the individual. It is true that "fancy" remains an equivocal term for both poets, who sometimes oppose its "maze" to "truth," as Pope had in the *Epistle to Arbuthnot*. But in its more positive aspect, fancy, or imagination, is seen as the necessary means to ideal truths. In part this priority appears in the self-conscious insistence of Akenside and Young on the wide-ranging originality of their works, a posture in sharp contrast to Pope's desire to make the few "certain truths" within everyone's reach more memorable. The contrast is evident, too, at the level of subject when we remember that a large part of Pope's vindication (epistle 3) is grounded in "remembered" history, a survey of civilization from past to present, while much of Young's and Akenside's teleology is based on a version of the future—religiously apocalyptic in Young, evolutionary and millennial in Akenside.[11]

Even within the present, imaginative truth is more important than accurate observation or recording. While the celebratory moments of *An Essay on Man* usually occur when the poet is reminding the reader of the external world's intricate beauty, Akenside and Young typically reach the highest pitch when appealing to the individual's ability to hold or make reality in his imagination. This is of course Akenside's declared subject, but much of Young's praise of the senses moved toward a celebration of fancy. The senses themselves not only enjoy nature's

[11]Young's poem ends with a vision of the Final Judgment, but the poem is oriented toward the future in a less dramatic way from *Night* I onward, where Young grounds all argument on "immortality." For Akenside the chain of being is a dynamic or progressive principle, and he writes as if on the brink of a new era in which the "high capacious powers" now "folded up in man" will be realized (1744, I, 222–23); cf. George R. Potter, "Mark Akenside, Prophet of Evolution," *Modern Philology*, 24 (1926): 55–64.

beauty but "far nobler, give the riches they enjoy" and, in a line echoed in *Tintern Abbey*, "half create the wondrous world they see." A few lines later the qualifying "half" is forgotten: 'Like Milton's Eve, when gazing on the lake, / Man makes the matchless image man admires." Richer than external nature is the "wealth / In fancy," especially the power of the individual mind "Commanding, with omnipotence of thought, / Creations new in fancy's field to rise" (VI, 420–69). The mirror image of an individual surrounded by objects of his own making might, in later hands, raise the specter of solipsism more insistently than it is allowed to here (see, however, *Night Thoughts*, VII, 954ff.), but for Young and Akenside the ability to see oneself in things is a gift of providential indulgence.[12] As Akenside warms to his theme, the ultimate subject of his natural rhapsodies is not "nature" itself but the "kind illusions" which God gives to man to make "all Nature beauty to his eye" and the "pleasing error" which protects the perceiver from doubting whether the green of the grass, the sky's blue, or the "music to his ear" are real. Illusory or not, these things cheer the human wanderer and "make the destin'd road of life / Delightful to his feet" (III, 487–515).

It is difficult to speak of a strictly solitary voice in two poems so clearly didactic, but the difference between Young's and Akenside's teaching and that of *An Essay on Man* can often be felt most strongly as one of imaginative situation—that is, the situation in which the reader is encouraged to picture the poet and in which he is presumably to imagine himself. Thus a large portion of the melodrama of *Night Thoughts* derives from Young's casting himself as a worn survivor, destined to tread funereal paths without a guide while less sensitive folk are asleep in their beds. But the solitary posture need not be melancholy, and Akenside cheerfully reflects the particular didactic premise of both poems when he invites the true lover of nature to read his poem and promises to "teach thy solitude her voice to hear" (I, 132–37). By the time

---

[12]Young returned to the image of Eve gazing at her reflection in *Conjectures on Original Composition* (1759, pp. 50–51), where it is a metaphor for the writer's recognition of his creativity. Robert Marsh discusses Akenside's argument in *Four Dialectical Theories of Poetry* (Chicago: University of Chicago, 1965), pp. 48–86.

this appeal is made the reader has already seen the ambitious poet setting out for "secret" and "untrod" paths, and later in Book I it is to the youth "whom solitude inspires" that Virtue chooses to appear (I, 553–59). Day or night, young or old, truth is something one discovers alone.[13]

So attractive is the idea of solitary wisdom to Young that he persuades himself that even Socrates might have preferred privacy to dialogues. The "famed Athenian" is pictured standing alone

> While o'er his head, as fearful to molest
> His labouring mind, the stars in silence slide,
> And seem all gazing on their future guest,
> See him soliciting his ardent suit
> In private audience. . . .
>
> [V, 184–88]

Young's Socrates suggests Wordsworth's image of Newton in *The Prelude* as a "mind for ever / Voyaging through strange seas of Thought, alone" (III, 62–63). For Pope, Newton was an example of human intelligence, either a humbling one, as when the angels "Admir'd such wisdom in an earthly shape, / And shew'd a NEWTON as we shew an Ape," or a liberating one, as when "God said, *Let Newton be!* and All was *Light.*"[14] In both roles Pope's Newton is preeminently a member of human society, and his achievement, exceptional but not lonely, is a gift to his species.

The difference between solitary voyages of Young and Akenside and the conversational or social procedures of Pope suggests the other departures their poems represent. For to prize intuitive vision over common observation, to value the individual's scope and soaring ambition, to find design in the crisis of conversion rather than personal continuity, and to define ultimate reality as what one's fancy can create rather than what

[13]John Dixon Hunt in *The Figure in the Landscape* (Baltimore: Johns Hopkins University Press, 1976), chaps. 4 and 5, discusses solitude and setting in Young and Akenside most perceptively.
[14]*Essay on Man*, II, 33–34, and "Epitaph Intended for Sir Isaac Newton," both written ca. 1730.

our memories can recall must involve a poet likewise in the idea that solitude is the essential human and poetic condition.

2

So far as I know, there is no case to be made for the influence of Hume on Akenside or Young, since like virtually everyone else in mid-eighteenth-century Europe, they may well have ignored *A Treatise of Human Nature* when it "fell dead-born from the press" in 1739–1740.[15] Nor can it plausibly be argued that Akenside or Young were essentially Humean beings before Hume; if so neither poet would have attempted to explain the ways of God to man, for Hume anticipates Kant in sensing the "failure of all attempted philosophical theodicies."[16]

But if we take the view that Hume defined rather than invented the uncertainties of his era—and Johnson, too, anticipates Kant's objections—then it is worthwhile to ask whether Hume's departures from Locke are in their implications analogous to the differences separating Young and Akenside from Pope. The question need not assume the possibility of constructing a paradigmatic "Humean poetic" which would inexorably dictate or account for the poems Young and Akenside wrote. All that need be assumed is that Young and Akenside were responding to something more complex than Pope's alleged neglect of "immortality" or their own raw ambition to write a long poem. If this is the case, it is likely that both poets were somehow answering a felt need to write a newer, more self-regarding poetry, one which would differ from Pope not only in form but also in its epistemology and in the shape of its arguments. Can we, then, see the relation at this particular historical moment of philosophic and poetic change?

Attempting to find some serviceable compass points, one can begin by considering the rough distance between the premises of Locke and Hume concerning personal identity and the

[15]See "My Own Life" (1776), reprinted in Ernest C. Mossner, *The Forgotten Hume* (New York: Columbia University Press, 1943), pp. 3–10.
[16]Kant's essay of this title is available in English in Michel Despland, *Kant on History and Religion* (Montreal: McGill-Queen's University Press, 1973), pp. 283–97.

knowledge of external reality—or in other terms, the truth of images, including that of the self. The distance is defined more roughly than it might be because my own concerns are those of the analytic amateur with synthetic interests, but perhaps the following reductions will serve.

First, identity in Locke rests ultimately on memory (the most important of the various senses in which he uses "conscious-ness"), while in Hume personal identity is a construct of the imagination.[17] The problem of identity is in fact an area of special doubt and hesitant qualification for both philosophers, but Locke's skepticism goes only so far as to allow that the self is perhaps a primarily "forensic" term, indispensable for legal and ethical sense making (II, xxvii, 26). Hume's self recedes further into doubt, with imagination as the real power uniting—or seeming to unite—the "bundle of perceptions" of which each of us consists into a single whole. The real existence of this whole or self is finally, Hume concludes, more a "grammatical" ques-tion than a philosophically arguable one (I, iv, 6).

The self's significant decline from "forensic" to "grammatical" status suggests many of the underlying differences between Locke and Hume. For Locke the "forensic" identity is essential (in both senses) because God's providence requires its existence; just as temporal justice must rely on the assumption that the Jones who stole Smith's chickens is the selfsame Jones who now stands in the dock, so divine justice requires that there be *a* self to stand at the Last Judgment (II, xxvii, 13, 22, 26). Similarly, Locke's assumption that our simple ideas are *"not fictions"* (Locke's italics) but "natural and regular" representations of the external world ultimately depends on the providential premise that God "ordained" certain objects to produce certain effects on

---

[17]The most pertinent part of Locke's discussion is II, xxvii ("Of Identity and Diversity"); Hume's explicit discussion "Of Personal Identity" is in the *Treatise* I, iv, 6. For Lockean consciousness as memory, see esp. *Essay* II, xxvii, 9 and 20, and Antony Flew, "Locke and the Problem of Personal Identity," *Philosophy*, 26 (1951): 53–68. Hume's treatment is discussed by Terence Penelhum, "Hume on Personal Identity," in V. C. Chappell, ed., *Hume* (Notre Dame, University of Notre Dame Press, 1968), pp. 213–39. For general surveys of the problem, see Penelhum's article in the *Encyclopedia of Philosophy*, ed. Paul Edwards (New York: Macmillan, 1967), VI, 97–105 and, with emphasis on Hume and modern philos-ophy, Godfrey Vesey, *Personal Identity* (London: Macmillan, 1974).

individual minds (IV, iv, 4; cf. IV, iii, 28). For Hume, not surprisingly, the providential premises have absconded—as part of
what we could call the "religious hypothesis"[18]—and with them
has departed the certainty of a single I in constant relation to a
substantial It.

Hume does recognize, however, that those mental events
which one believes to signal something externally real are separate in experience from those which one believes to be subjective
memories of inventions, and he accordingly begins the *Treatise*
(and later the *Enquiries*) by distinguishing between "impressions"
and "ideas." It is again indicative of the distance separating the
world of the *Essay Concerning Human Understanding* and the
world of Hume's *Treatise* that while Locke, too, had begun by
bifurcating, his twofold division is between the two *sources* of our
ideas, and that Hume begins more subjectively by distinguishing
merely between qualitative differences in mental phenomena.
As we have seen, the essential difference between Hume's "impressions" and "ideas," or on a larger scale, between belief and
mental suspension, is one of intensity: impressions are "stronger" than ideas, and belief is a more "lively idea" than fiction or
bare possibility (I, i, 1; I, iii, 7: I, iv, 7).

What Hume effectively does, therefore, is to transport the
quality of intensity of "liveliness" from discussions of aesthetic
reflection (where for Shaftesbury is signaled the Beautiful) and
from moral sense theory (where for Hutcheson it signaled the
Good) and make or extend it into the criterion of the Real.[19]
Hume's procedures lead him generally to situate reality in intense and simple impressions rather than in the larger structures
by which one seeks to unify them; he is readier to grant the
*un*imagined existence of atomistic dots than that of connecting
lines.[20] Although Hume never puts the problem in quite this

[18]Hume uses the phrase in his discussion "Of a Particular Providence and of a
Future State"; see *Enquiries* ed. L. A. Selby-Bigge, rev. P. H. Nidditch (London:
Oxford University Press, 1975, pp. 139, 146.

[19]The path from Hutcheson is charted authoritatively by Norman Kemp
Smith in *The Philosophy of David Hume* (London: Macmillan, 1941), pp. 23–51,
273–84.

[20]For a brief but penetrating application of Hume's analysis of experience to
Sterne's fragmentary presentation in *A Sentimental Journey*, see Richard Kuhns,
Structures of Experience (New York: Basic Books, 1970), chap. 2.

way, it seems that one of the "pleasures of imagination" is the quality of experience we call reality. Another is ourselves.

Two epigrammatic versions of reality which may illuminate each other in juxtaposition are Pope's "Whatever IS, is RIGHT" and Hume's "Whatever *is* may *not be*."[21] Hume's principle offers a provocative gloss for Pope's line by antithetically suggesting that it can be paraphrased to "Whatever is, is." The paraphrase is not as pointless as it might seem, since it does more justice to Pope's celebration of being than do quarrels over the validity of "right." Pope's proposition contains both a compressed version of the Augustinian solution to the problem of evil (evil is negation, is the thing which is not) and an injunction to look about and take the commonly observable facts of physical existence as the "givens" from which to begin any fully adult conversation. It is not coincidental that Pope's commitment to common empiricism is matched by a commitment in the *Essay* to conversation; from the Horatian and peripatetic opening to the final portraiture of friend and poet, we are meant to keep in mind the epistle's collaborative and corroborative function.[22] Hume's contrary principle, "Whatever *is* may *not be*," belongs only, as he points out, to the essentially solitary world of abstract demonstration and a priori reasoning, where the "non-existence of any being, without exception, is as clear and distinct an idea as its existence." Hume sheds his early skepticism by leaving his study—seeking "carelessness and inattention" in friendly talk, back-gammon (*Treatise,* I, iv, 7) or, in later years, the history of England.

But his ambitious work begins very much in the study we surveyed in chapter 1 and leaves it only in conclusion. Like Akenside and Young, he locates the "scene of Man" not in Pope's garden or maze, where the paths are wide enough for

<hr>

[21]*Enquiries*, p. 164.
[22]While it is true that when compared with Pope's later espistles, *An Essay on Man* may be seen as "more consonant with the hortatory, 'magisterial' mode associated with Lucretius than with one of 'well-bred good talk'" (Miriam Lerenbaum, *Alexander Pope's 'Opus Magnum,' 1729–1744* [Oxford: Clarendon, Press, 1977], p. 42), the *Essay* retains much of the conversational and tentative atmosphere which its original publication as separate "Epistles to a Friend" emphasized.

two, but in the isolated pursuit of individual attention. He is like them as well in portraying the pursuit as a difficult and original endeavor, and in each of these respects he departs as much from the premises of Locke's *Essay* as Akenside and Young depart from Pope's. Whereas Locke had begun with apologies for his lack of originality, with the hope that the reader will find the leisurely pursuit as pleasurable as he has, and with the reminder that the work began in sociable conversation with "five or six friends" ("Epistle to the Reader"), Hume begins with a declaration against indolence:

> For, if the truth be at all within the reach of human capacity, it is certain it must lie very deep and abstruse; and to hope we shall arrive at it without pains, while the greatest geniuses have failed with the utmost pains, must certainly be esteemed sufficiently vain and presumptuous. I pretend to no such advantage in the philosophy I am going to unfold, and would esteem it a strong presumption against it, were it so very easy and obvious. [Introduction, p. 4]

Hume's claim amounts to a sanction not only for "original composition" but also for obscurity. Hume has the good sense to stop short of saying that difficulty (rather than riddle) is the test of truth, but he strongly implies that anything which strikes us too familiarly is likely to be false. Against this background, the fondness of Akenside and Young for Obscurity, both atmospheric and stylistic, is perhaps less a thirst for novelty than a persuasion that the truth lies very deep, whether in night, in forested visions, or in the wandering syntax of unrhymed verse.

The verse arguments that Young and Akenside conduct resemble Hume's presentation of self and analysis of experience in very general but important ways. Like Hume, both poets dramatize individual isolation and inescapable egocentricity. In doing so, both define the self more in terms of moments of imaginative intensity than in terms of cumulative (and accountable) consciousness. Through their luxuriant descriptions and soliloquies, Young and Akenside pose more openly than Pope or Locke the question of where the putative I ends and the phenomenal It begins. Finally, they attempt to vindicate their "religious hypotheses" less through reminders of a visual scale which implies the "equal" eye of divine objectivity and more through selective visions of sublimity—as if only the sublime "impression" passed the test of liveliness firmly enough to be unequivocally real.

3

Thomson's *The Seasons*, which Pope was quick to call a "philosophical poem,"[23] is in many ways closer to *An Essay on Man* than are *Night Thoughts* and *The Pleasures of Imagination*. While the solitary moments and retreats from history which we considered in chapter 3 are very much a part of *The Seasons*, they are often balanced by postures of social engagement. Some of these appeals seem strained, like the compensatory good citizenship of the second half of *The Castle of Indolence*, but frequently Thomson's sense of the social nature of individual achievement and of his own relation to his community is less troubled than Young's or Akenside's. Thomson's Newton, we remember, is more like Pope's than Wordsworth's, and his Socrates is not the private stargazer of Young's fancy but an Athenian citizen, who taught in "every street" and "smiled the laughing race" of Greeks "into truth / And serious deeds" (*Liberty*, II, 226–31). If within *The Seasons* Thomson tends to portray himself as a philosophic wanderer (*Spring*, 11.101ff.) with a special fondness for the "haunts of meditation" (*Summer*, 1.502), he makes very few appeals of a specifically autobiographical sort. A crisis is suggested, but it is the general crisis of "these iron times," this momentous "now" when the passions "vex the mind"—everyone's mind—with "endless storm" and universal springtime has vanished (*Spring*, 11.272–300).

Moments of self-centered intensity tend for Akenside and Young to be versions of conversion, and the appropriateness of such resolutions is particularly clear in *The Pleasures of Imagination*. For Akenside the problem of evil is essentially the problem of emotional pain, and his solution of it is the decision that

[23]In the "Testimonies of Authors" prefacing the *Dunciad*, Pope quotes from Thomson's "elegant and philosophical poem of the seasons" (*Dunciad*, ed. James Sutherland, 3d ed. [New Haven: Yale University Press, 1963], p. 37).

emotional intensity is its own reward, that pleasurable or not, such sensibility is the "proof" of a higher nature. The terms of *Night Thoughts* are similar, though complicated by the poem's length and Young's more orthodox reliance on the afterlife as well. Perhaps the strongest temperamental link between Thomson and these poets is his tendency to treat "soaring" without irony (reserving his satire instead for timidity), to emphasize the possibility of original discovery and of a contemplative joy "divinely great" (*Summer*, 11.1714–56).

For each of these authors, the celebration of Lucretian expansiveness is self-consciously tied to the use of blank verse, the "rhyme unfettered" medium which Thomson equates with "British freedom" (*Autumn*, 11.646–47). Akenside chooses blank verse over the "closer and more concise" rhymed "conversation" of Pope because of "more open, pathetic and figur'd" manner better suits a subject rising "almost constantly" to "admiration and enthusiasm" ("The Design," par. 7). It is probably not wise to make too much of the issue of blank verse, since Pope and Thomson seem to have had no difficulty judging each other's work as real poetry. But it may be helpful to ask to what extent the choice of blank verse tended to trap mid-eighteenth-century poets into straining to maintain admiration and enthusiasm "almost constantly"—an attempt which would involve thematic as well as stylistic limitations—and whether its lure as an "open" style was not intellectually as well as technically beguiling. Clearly, blank verse can be concise, and it can be quietly restrained; but not until Cowper would these possibilities be apparent. At mid-century, the idea of blank verse, like the idea of the ode, seems to carry with it vague but insistent ideological associations of the sort often termed "Whiggish," associations which we could regard as extrapoetic but for the fact that they frequently have a strong effect on poetic procedures.

In the context of philosophical poetry the rhymed style of Pope appeared—and so to Pope himself—to have a particularly strong relation to memory and thus to the broadly conservative project of recalling man to ancient counsels. The poetry will function all the better to check individual indulgence if its formulas appear even less original than they are (Maynard Mack has described Pope's materials as "painstakingly traditional"), and Pope uses the couplet to achieve just this effect of repetition.[24] The naive and anachronistic reader who found *An Essay on Man* to be "all quotations" was responding partly in kind as well as in ignorance. But Akenside, Young, and Thomson are under great pressure to dress even their routine observations in an aura of originality, expanding reflections or descriptions which do not need expansion, save for the felt need to make them appear more "enthusiastic" or associatively improvisational, more self-generating and "open," than a decorum of conversational couplets would permit—or would demand.

I do not mean to suggest that these writers would have been better off with couplets. Young, the one who had most practice in the idiom (the Horatian satires comprising *The Universal Passion* are always competent and often strong), seems as a result to have striven overmuch for epigrammatic power in his blank verse, epigrams both of memorial familiarity ("Procrastination is the thief of time") and of the brand of self-conscious surprise which David Morris has nicely called the "exclamatory sublime."[25] Nor is it surprising that to a poet writing in the 1740s Pope should appear already to have appropriated the couplet, nearly to have "retired" it, in fact. If in the realm of philosophical verse Pope had succeeded in making the couplet seem a timely echo of timeless wisdom, a poet who followed the same path would all too probably sound like the echo of an echo.

Since *Winter* appeared several years before Pope emerged as a notable "ethick" writer, Thomson's choice of blank verse rests, so far as we can infer from his preface of 1726, on a more general dichotomy between the "little brightnesses" of social verse and the "unbounded greatness" of prophetic imagination. Such a differentiation of poetic sensibilities and styles stands behind Collins's choice in the *Ode on the Poetical Character* of Milton's high cliff over Waller's myrtle shade, as most likely does Akenside's contrast of Shakespeare's imagined taste for the "wild" lightning and clifftop with Waller sighing to the groves of slighted vows and love's disdain (*Pleasures of Imagination*, III, 546–67). But for all Thomson's tendencies to equate the vast

---

[24]Mack, ed., *An Essay on Man* (New Haven: Yale University Press, 1950),p. xlii.
[25]Morris, *The Religious Sublime*, p. 153.

with the poetic, his sense of scale and measure is fundamentally closer to Pope's than to Young's or Akenside's, primarily because *The Seasons* is in essentials an empirical poem, appealing to the norm of a firmly external world for its poetic argument. It is true that Thomson, like the other blank verse poets, is fond of what David Mallet rhapsodized as

> th' Immensity of Space,
> That infinite Diffusion, where the Mind
> Conceives no Limits; undistinguish'd Void,
> Invariable, where no Land-Marks are,
> No Paths to guide Imagination's Flight. . . .
> [*The Excursion*, 1728, p. 74]

It is also true, and not coincidentally, that these talismanic terms are close to Johnson's complaint of Akenside's "gay diffusion," which allows the reader to leave his long poem much as he came in because "he remarked little, and laid hold on nothing . . . , and as nothing is distinguished, nothing is remembered" (*Life of Akenside*). Nevertheless, once we have acknowledged similar tendencies in Thomson (and Young and Akenside derive more of their blank verse from Thomson than from Milton) to luxuriate into diffusion and to gravitate toward things "undistinguish'd," we are likely to remember as well passages that now seem to have cinematic clarity. When Thomson moves over a landscape, the landmarks are not always as specific as they are, for example, in the description of a summer storm crackling its path through North Wales (*Summer*, 11.1144ff.); but they are easily supplied in kind by the reader because the scene unfolds sequentially as it might to any observer who let an eye sweep along its contours.

Thomson's original sense of his poetic task is, like Pope's, largely visual. If one can see broadly and vividly enough, if one can bring the world into focus, then the relation of man and heaven will be clear as well. The ways of Providence require vindication because physical nature is now deemed "vindictive" by humans who have not observed it closely. The fundamental assumption for both Pope and Thomson is that the "out there" is an objective theater in which human actions (including misjudgments) take place and that therefore to see the theater steadily and to see it whole will be the best corrective to vindictive interpretations of reality. Pope's and Thomson's poems thus belong to physicotheology more consistently than do Young's or Akenside's. Whatever the limitations of our vision as a result of pride or inattention or simple human astigmatism, the world is there to be visualized and written about. *Night Thoughts* and *The Pleasures of Imagination* are not "about" the world in the same way. According to Young himself, *Night Thoughts* consists more of "reflections" than of description, and we should not take "reflections" merely to mean "maxims." Akenside assumes, by his very choice of subject, a discontinuity between nature and the individual mind, which lives surrounded by "kind illusions," gazing during charmed moments at its own reflection.[26] Young and Akenside do of course continue to use what has been called the period's "rhetoric of science" and to invoke the marvels of the physical world to prove their own designs.[27] But they do so at the expense, finally, of iterative indecision about whether matter matters beside the powers of the individual mind. If the mind is seeking its own reflection, is "nature" the best place to look?

In fact, even Thomson seems to have wondered whether the physical world in all its presence could lead to answers deep enough concerning the ways of God to *men*. If we consider Thomson's poetic career and take seriously his aspirations as a philosophic poet, we need to give more witness than usual to *Liberty*, his second longest poem and the work which occupied many of his best years. *Liberty* was published in 1735–1736; Thomson seems to have begun it shortly after completing *The Seasons* in 1730, and many of the more than 1,000 lines added to *The Seasons* in the editions of 1744 and 1746 reflect Thomson's political preoccupations. Thomson may well have thought, as

[26]John Norton, in the introduction to his "Critical Edition of *The Pleasures of Imagination* (1744)" (Ph.D. diss., University of Pennsylvania, 1967), argues that "Akenside's main interest was not writing 'nature poetry'" but "describing the operations of the human mind" and that the poem is, "in many ways a psychomachia" (pp. 15, 50, 51).

[27]William Powell Jones, *The Rhetoric of Science: A Study of Scientific Ideas and Imagery in Eighteenth-Century Poetry* (Berkeley: University of California Press, 1966); for Thomson, Akenside, and Young, respectively, see pp. 107–15, 150–52, 153–59.

McKillop has suggested, of his new subject as the outcome of a
Virgilian maturation from pastoral to a more overtly political
and epic undertaking.[28] We may think of it, less consciously and
generically, as Thomson's transfer of the problem of theodicy
from "nature" to history.

Perhaps before we go further it will help us to recall the persistence of the mid-eighteenth-century problem of theodicy,
which is essentially the loss of physicotheological confidence, by
considering some of its modern formulations. Its starkest statement in recent literature may be the memorandum Walker Percy's "moviegoer" writes to himself:

> Starting point for search:
> It no longer avails to start with creatures and
> prove God.
> Yet it is impossible to rule God out.[29]

Thomson's problem is not the same as that of Percy's narrator,
puzzled by "invincible apathy," although the later *Castle of Indolence* is in some sense a similar attempt to make meaning out of
apathy's pathos; but he has a similar literary problem in trying to
find the "signs" that will carry conviction. William James, lectur-
ing in Thomson's old university at the beginning of our century,
described the problem more fully:

> That vast literature of proof of God's existence drawn from the
> order of nature, which a century ago seemed so overwhelmingly
> convincing, to-day does little more than gather dust in libraries,
> for the simple reason that our generation has ceased to believe in
> the kind of God it argued for. Whatever sort of being God may be,
> we know to-day that he is nevermore that mere external inventory
> of "contrivances" intended to make manifest his "glory" in which
> our great-grandfathers took such satisfaction, though just how we
> know this we cannot possibly make clear by words either to others
> or to ourselves. I defy any of you here fully to account your per-
> suasion that if a God exist he must be a more cosmic and tragic
> personage than that Being.[30]

[28]Alan Dugald McKillop, *The Background of Thomson's "Liberty,"* Rice Institute
Pamphlet, 38, no. 2 (July 1951): 9.
[29]*The Moviegoer* (New York: Noonday Press, 1967), p. 146.
[30]William James, *The Varieties of Religious Experience*, lect. 3 (New York: Longmans, 1912), pp. 73–74.

It is *Liberty*, of course, that gathers dust in libraries, while *The Seasons* is regularly studied and is occasionally even read. But if Thomson's poetic capacity failed him badly in *Liberty*, his intellectual instincts were right. His active career spans exactly the years during which Vico was to declare a fundamental schism between our possible knowledge of natural science and our knowledge of history. Nature for Vico is finally a blank, but history is ours: made by men, it can be understood by men. Such understanding yields the "principles" of the "ideal eternal history traversed in time by every nation," and it leads Vico to a theodicy. "Our new Science must therefore be a demonstration, so to speak, of what providence has wrought in history, for it must be a history of the institutions by which, without human discernment or counsel, and often against the designs of men, providence has ordered this great city of the human race." To read this ideal history one must grasp the "language" of institutions; then it becomes possible to recognize, for example, that "all ancient Roman law was a serious poem. . . . , and ancient jurisprudence was a severe poetry."[31]

Vico's new science seems to have had virtually no influence until near the end of the century, but the intellectual dissatisfaction and curiosity which led to his brilliant historicism are reflected, however crudely and partially, in various "progressive" readings of history. Among these the most ambitious is Thomson's "progress" of Liberty, which is nothing less than an attempt to interpret Western history as an "ideal" history. We need to grasp the nature of this intellectualization in order to appreciate the genuine ambition of Thomson in *Liberty*, which is not simply a "progress piece" or a "Whig panegyric," and thus to understand the meaning of its failure for in relation to mid-eighteenth-century literature generally.

Thomson's *Liberty* begins and ends among the ruins of Rome, those monuments of vanished minds which Dyer would paint more melancholically a few years later. Thomson uses the scene to compare ancient and modern Italy and then to launch an intellectual survey of the progressive realization of liberty in Greece, Rome, and Britain, a survey which culminates in a

31 *The New Science of Giambattista Vico*, trans. Thomas Goddard Bergin and Max Harold Fisch (Ithaca: Cornell University Press, 1970), pp. 60, 342.

"Prospect" of the future. Thomson's poem is potentially more "severe" than the simple genealogies or pageants comprising most progress pieces because of his essentially idealist preoccupation with historical inevitability. Liberty moves like the sun, from east to west, as any self-respecting personification would have to in the period.[32] But Thomson goes further by addressing her as the "better sun! Sun of Mankind," as Akenside would address Beauty, and describing her course to "western worlds *irrevocable* rolled" (III, 326–27). The italics are mine, but the emphasis for Thomson is indeed on "irrevocable" rather than on "western," since Liberty will have veered north and then south before landing in Britain. She came to Rome and she left it with the "swift approach of fate" (III, 336; cf. III, 72–73). The Goths raged "resistless" because she "urged" them in necessary vengeance, and she herself is "by fate commissioned" to move on to England and oversee those struggles "educing good from ill" which make up its history (III, 527; IV, 407, 702). "Nought can resist your force," the poet says simply near the end of the poem.

But where in this hymn to resistless liberty is the place of the individual? Thomson's attempt to find order in history is an idealist one not because material things are undervalued (the paeans to Commerce are lavish) but because mind is regarded as prior. Physical changes occur in the course of history only after mental changes have caused them; Thomson insists upon this position even to the point of maintaining that "Ne'er yet by force was freedom overcome" (II, 494). So, for example, Greece fell not because of conquest but because it had already fallen in spirit, and thus "The Persian fetters that enthralled the mind, / Were turned to formal and apparent chains" (II, 488–89). And so in Rome the heroism of Brutus "burst the grosser bonds" of Caesar, but the "soft enchanting fetters of the mind" remained "And other Caesars rose" (V, 202–5). In such a world the individuals presumably have great responsibility for keeping their minds uncorrupted (Rome's fetters point the mor-

[32]Noted long ago by Reginald H. Griffith, in "The Progress Pieces of the Eighteenth Century," *Texas Review*, 5 (1920): 218–33. The full relation of English eighteenth-century progress poems to American nineteenth-century political mythologies of Manifest Destiny remains to be described.

al of a passage beginning "Britons! be firm . . ."), but it is not at all clear how their doing so would help their country resist, for better or worse, the resistless.

Thomson is hardly alone in not resolving the relation of the individual to history or in reconciling the values of personal freedom and collective destiny. Perhaps any attempt to make history more philosophic or poetic than Aristotle claimed it was, that is, any attempt to attribute to history relations essentially "logical" in which events "follow as cause and effect," is likely to encounter all of the problems of determinism and fatalism in combining claims of "historical inevitability" with, typically, hortatory morality. Moreover, since inevitable consequences are preeminently the property of tragedy, such an attempt is likely to yield a reading of history as tragedy, protestations of optimism not withstanding.[33] For Vico and later for Herder and Hegel, history would be the theater of that God whom William James called "more cosmic and tragic" than the Being of the old proofs. But Thomson really wants, not a brooding God, but an enlightened monarch, and his poem of history shows the strain at many points. One of Thomson's fondest progressive principles, the notion that liberal government leads to good art, is in trouble throughout the poem, especially so when Thomson ignores Greek and Roman slavery or attempts to distinguish between the Louis XIV who ruled despotically in hopes of "universal sway" and the good Louis XIV who encouraged arts (V, 484–531; cf. IV, 1074–85). Frequently the strain of competing views appears in imagistic infelicities, as in the climactic celebration of modern English liberty (IV, 1135ff.), when Thomson argues that the country is "often saved / By more than human hand" and then warns a few lines later of its vulnerability to the "felon undermining hand or dark corruption." When Thomson imagines the grand era of universal liberty as a time of British naval superiority so great that "not a sail but by permission

33Thus Croce in *History as the Story of Liberty* argues that the idea of progress is not an error, provided we speak of "eternal spiritual progress" and that we define such progress as an "ever higher and more complex form of human suffering" (trans. Sylvia Sprigge [London: Allen & Unwin, 1941], p. 52). The question is surveyed provocatively in the second of Isaiah Berlin's *Four Essays on Liberty* (London: Oxford University Press, 1969), "Historical Inevitability."

spreads" (V, 637), even patriotism may blush. When he praises the power of British commerce to "bind the nations in a golden chain" (IV, 438), we are more likely to think of the oppressive connotations of the image, as in the vocabulary of Pope or Blake, than of liberty. And when Liberty reveals that her purpose during the Roman era was to "diffuse / O'er men an empire" and so draw everything "into the vortex of one state" (III, 82–85), we are likely, once again, to think of the *Dunciad*.

Perhaps this last imagistic echo is, as Thomson would say, resistless. The *Dunciad*, after all, is the poem which takes a fundamentally idealist and tragic reading of Western history to a logical conclusion—a logic which Pope is freer to pursue because he is unencumbered with obligations to celebrate individual self-fulfillment under the inspiring protection of the British navy. We can grasp something of Thomson's poetic problem if we think of *Liberty* as in a sense an attempt to write an optimistic *Dunciad*. The fact that a majority of modern historians would probably regard Thomson as closer to being "right" about his period than was Pope may lead us to ask just what sort of historical verisimilitude is healthy for poetry.[34] But the more provocative fact is that a successfully "positive" *Dunciad* was historically rather than generically impossible, for *Prometheus Unbound* is such a work. A comparison of the two would take us too far afield, but one would begin with the observation that, like the *Dunciad, Prometheus Unbound* is a work "complete" in three parts but with a grand fourth movement operatically celebrating the effects of its cultural conversion. Yet an optimistically apocalyptic poem was not possible in either Thomson's moment or Thomson's manner. Shelley's theodicy works largely through subliminal appeals to revolutionary circumstances outside the poem and the elimination within it of historical material in favor

[34]The usual assumption, however, that the "gloom" of the Tory satirists does not do historical justice to the improvements in the lives of their countrymen during the period is occasionally challenged by the incisive gloom of less Whiggish historians today. Thus E. P. Thompson, e.g., draws a conclusion close to Pope's in the *Epistle to Bathurst:* "These great agrarian bourgeois evinced little sense of public, or even corporate, responsibility. The century is not noted for the scale of its public buildings but for that of its private mansions, and is as much noted for the misappropriation of the charities of previous centuries as for the founding of new ones"; see "Patrician Society, Plebeian Culture," *Journal of Social History,* 7 (1974): 396–404.

of myth, perhaps the ultimately appropriate vehicle for contests of nation-titans and historical forces.

Liberty failed to capture even Thomson's contemporaries—the press runs shrank steadily from part I to part V—but the ambitions of *Liberty* are strongly evident in *The Seasons*. As Thomson added to that lifelong work in progress, it became steadily more historical, broadening into political and anthropological surveys which attempt to show the various God's varied ways to man by reflecting on culture. Not every addition to *The Seasons* is political in any sense; the 1744 edition has more advice on fishing, for example, as well as a longer catalog of British worthies. But in general even Thomson's "nature" additions have either cultural implications—like the sixty lines added to *Summer* (371–431) which celebrate British industry—or implications for recognizing the importance of the unseen. And when Thomson extends his "vision" to things outside the speaker's immediate landscape, the description of natural phenomena, however sensational, turns eventually into discussion of cultural arrangements.

This development can be seen most clearly in Thomson's inclusion of the tropics in *Summer* and the far north in *Winter,* both of which provide occasions not only for descriptive extremes but for comparative history. The survey of northern nations (*Winter,* 11.794–903) culminates in a discussion of Peter the Great and the power of "active government . . . new-moulding man" (11.950ff.); Thomson's theme, in other words, is the Vichian-Hegelian one of the providence of institutions and the role of the "world-historical" individual in bringing about human freedom. Peter, like Henry the Navigator, is "heaven-inspired" to focus the self-interest of lesser men (*Summer,* 11.1006–12; cf. 11.1767–68). Thomson's longer foray into the "torrid zone" (*Summer,* 11.629–987) is an intriguing combination of lush primitivism and cultural imperialism. For all their sensuousness and fertile profusions—"and Ceres void of pain"—the tropical regions lack the "humanizing Muses," the "progressive truth," and the liberal "government of laws" which define European culture. Thomson is even prepared to deny these "ill-fated" inhabitants a capacity for true love. Sensibility grows in temperate zones. English culture is the providential compensation for English weather.

There is another emphasis which Thomson heightened by

expanding *The Seasons* to embrace more of the unobserved world, an emphasis on what he variously calls "fair forms of fancy" or "imagination's vivid eye" (*Summer*, 1.1974; *Spring*, 1.459). These phrases first appear in 1744, and the second of them comes at the end of the long addition on fishing mentioned earlier, which gradually slides from angling advice to a georgic of reverie:

> . . . let the classic page thy fancy lead
> Through rural scenes, such as the Mantuan swain
> Paints in the matchless harmony of song;
> Or catch thyself the landscape, gliding swift
> Athwart imagination's vivid eye;
> Or, by the vocal woods and waters lulled,
> And lost in lonely musing, in a dream
> Confused of careless solitude where mix
> Ten thousand wandering images of things,
> Soothe every gust of passion into peace. . . .
>
> [*Spring*, 11.455–64]

A complementary expansion occurs in *Summer* as Thomson muses on the evening clouds, "Incessant rolled into romantic shapes, / The dream of waking fancy." The dream of fancy includes the high work of the poet and the moral philosopher, a union described here more evocatively than in many of Thomson's declarations:

> Now the soft hour
> Of walking comes for him who lonely loves
> To seek the distant hills, and there converse
> With Nature, there to harmonize his heart,
> And in pathetic song to breathe around
> The harmony to others. Social friends,
> Attuned to happy unison of soul—
> To whose exalting eye a fairer world,
> Of which the vulgar never had a glimpse,
> Displays its charms. . . .
>
> [*Summer*, 11.1379–88]

Such changes ultimately make the landscape an object less of description than of reflection and thus shift the focus of poem toward the "pleasures of imagination." This is not a radical change but a cumulative heightening, sometimes apparent in small ways, as in the elaboration of a contrast between the forest's "solitude and deep surrounding shades" and the "giddy fashion of town," or the simile of a flower "unseen by all" which "breathes its balmy fragrance o'er the wild" (*Autumn*, 11.184–88, 209–16). Even Thomson's most scientific addition, some eighty lines on the "percolation" theory of underground springs (*Autumn*, 11.756–835), is an exercise in turning the unseen world into an imaginative reality:

> Let the dire Andes, from the radiant line
> Stretched to the stormy seas that thunder round
> To Southern Pole, their hideous deeps unfold!
> Amazing scene! Behold! the glooms disclose!
> I see the rivers in their infant beds!
> Deep, deep I hear them laboring to get free!
>
> [*Autumn*, 11.804–9]

Thomson's expansion of *The Seasons*, then, dramatizes a conspicuous tension: as the poem becomes more political and historical it also becomes more occupied with the contemplative joys of the solitary man and the "wondrous force of thought" available to the philosophic few. The tension often leads to flat contradictions and flat pronouncements. It also leads, for good or ill, to less reliance on the data of visual experience and more straining for "vision," more effort to render its theodicy in terms of private intensity. This is perhaps the major tendency which *The Seasons* comes to share with *Night Thoughts* and *The Pleasures of Imagination*, and the growing conflict between public and private claims of course becomes the subject of Thomson's last poem, *The Castle of Indolence*.[35]

35In a brief but extremely helpful reading of *The Castle of Indolence*, Morris Golden argues that Thomson develops "two competing roles of the poet, Magician and Knight, between whom the narrative persona must choose" (*The Self Observed: Swift, Johnson, Wordsworth* [Baltimore: Johns Hopkins University Press, 1972], pp. 17–20). What Golden refers to as the horror of the "self-imprisoned mind" may perhaps have been glossed historically by Croce: "During periods in which reforms and upheavals are being prepared, attention is paid to the past, to that from which a break is to be made, and to that with which a link is to be forged. During uneventful slow and heavy periods, fables and romances are preferred to histories or history itself is reduced to fable or romance. Similarly, men who shut themselves up within the four walls of their private affections and

The conflict plainly diffuses the rhetoric of each of these blank verse poems, from which we are separated finally not by their complacencies but by their uncertainties. When we think of the two entirely confident long poems of the mid-century, *A Song to David* and *Fingal*, we may recognize that they attain their certainties largely by shifting the burden of intensity wholly away from worldly argument and onto an act of identification with a great man. Smart's celebrant fuses himself for the space of his poem with David, a poet-king who is at once son and "father" of God. Macpherson's Ossian, the poet-son of a kingly father, makes no claims to explicating the present order but has special access to knowledge of how things were. In addition to all the usual explanations of the Ossian Sensation, we can attribute much of the popularity of *Fingal* (and it is paradigmatic enough to stand for the rest of "canon") to its success in reducing history to family romance, "nature" to a cloudily subjective force field, and the perspective of poet and reader to that of the sensitive son of a memorable father who belonged to another era. *Fingal* may be superficially pessimistic, but its pessimism is entirely unshaken by distractions from the outside world, much as its tendency toward diffusion is wholly unchecked by the obsessive cadences Macpherson substitutes for form. *A Song to David*, on the other hand, makes of its self-imposed, obsessive formal constraints a self-fulfilling prophecy. David's meaning and the poet's meaning are identical, as one validates the other by its very completion: an ecstasy DETERMINED, DARED, and DONE.

There is no question that Macpherson's work is not of the same order as Smart's. What is interesting historically is that in the early 1760s both writers should seek to order the world poetically by means of the hero. That, of course, is a most traditional way of summing up an interpretation of reality, but significantly, it was unavailable to serious poets of the preceding generation. The two best novelists of that generation do attempt, however, to locate the essential meaning of human experience in the exemplary lives of heroically representative individuals. It is a precarious attempt.

---

private economic life, cease to be interested in what has happened and in what is happening in the great world, and they recognize no other history but that of their limited anxieties" (*History as the Story of Liberty*, p. 45).

CHAPTER 6

The Final Novels of Fielding and Richardson

If for a moment we exclude the chronologically and generically problematic *Jonathan Wild*, the careers of Fielding and Richardson exhibit a crude symmetry: both wrote very good first novels, great second novels, and third novels which we rarely read.[1] *Sir Charles Grandison* has the distinction of being more profoundly neglected today than *Amelia* no doubt because of its length—it is one of the longest novels in the language and often seems even longer—but both novels figure too little in modern estimates of the period. We need them both, not only in the study of each author, but in understanding the problem jointly posed by these two careers. Clearly we are not dealing in either case with anything like Jonson's "dotages." Fielding may have been weakened somewhat by sickness, and Richardson by age, but *Amelia* and *Grandison* are intelligent books and partially

[1] The present consensus is that *Jonathan Wild*, which McKillop says is to be "judged as a satire rather than a novel" (*The Early Masters of English Fiction* [Lawrence: University of Kansas Press, 1956], p. 117), was largely composed before *Joseph Andrews*, with the Heartfree narrative added shortly before publication in 1743; see F. Homes Dudden, *Henry Fielding* (Oxford: Clarendon Press, 1952), I, 480–83, and Martin Battestin, "Fielding's Changing Politics in *Joseph Andrews*," *Philological Quarterly*, 39 (1960): 39–55. Although I am concerned here more with the impasses which Fielding and Richardson reach than with the general symmetry of their careers as novelists, another symmetry remains if we do include *Jonathan Wild* and the continuation of *Pamela* as second novels: i.e., a strong first novel, a less successful second, an undisputed "great," and an ambitious but problematic fourth work. Considering Fielding singly, it seems to me useful to regard the Heartfree story not as aberration or filler but as an experiment in the direction of urban melodrama and economic realism, explored more fully in *Amelia*. The edition of *Amelia* used here is the Everyman Edition (1962; reprint ed. in 1 vol., London: J. M. Dent, 1974).

very powerful ones. These are the final novels of immensely gifted fiction makers who were convinced that they were breaking significantly new ground.[2]

In an odd way they were extending their peculiar techniques and territories in these last and "lost" works, and in an odder way they were coming closer together, an approach of which we easily lose sight because so much of our understanding of Richardson and Fielding has been oppositional, sometimes barely subtler than the heated partisanship of their first readers. Perhaps this is a natural, if not graceful, legacy of the fact of Fielding's initial parody of Richardson and Richardson's settled antagonism toward Fielding, which Fielding's warm praise of *Clarissa* did nothing to shake. When it has not been invidious, the tradition of opposition has led to provocative criticism, from Coleridge to Ian Watt and later; but it can also easily obscure the deepening influence which Fielding and Richardson seem to have exerted on each other toward the end.[3]

The two writers almost trade places. After two "masculine" novels, Fielding attempts to create a heroine; with *Pamela* and *Clarissa* behind him, Richardson sets out to create a "Good Man." That Booth claims more of the reader's attention than Fielding probably intended only underscores the authors' similarity in practice, for so do Harriet Byron and her Italian counterpart, Clementina, in the book ostensibly about Sir Charles Grandison. In *Amelia* Fielding attempts something like Richardson's "writing to the moment," even, I believe, to the confusion

[2]The experimental rigor of *Amelia* has been noted most sympathetically by Robert Alter, *Fielding and the Nature of the Novel* (Cambridge, Mass.: Harvard University Press, 1968), chap. 5, "Fielding's Problem Novel," and Eric Rothstein, *Systems of Order and Inquiry in Later Eighteenth-Century Fiction* (Berkeley: University of California Press, 1975), pp. 154–207. The major appreciative readings of *Grandison* are conducted by Mark Kinkead-Weekes in *Samuel Richardson: Dramatic Novelist* (Ithaca: Cornell University Press, 1973), pp. 279–391, and Margaret Anne Doody in *A Natural Passion* (Oxford: Clarendon Press, 1974), pp. 241–367.

[3]For oppositions other than Ian Watt's in *The Rise of the Novel* (1957; reprinted., Berkeley: University of California Press, 1971), esp. pp. 260–68, see, e.g., Frank Kermode, "Richardson and Fielding," *Cambridge Journal*, 4 (1950): 106–14, and Howard Anderson, "Answers to the Author of Clarissa," *Philological Quarterly*, 51 (1972): 859–73. For Kermode, Richardson plays an intuitive Shakespeare to Fielding's Ben Jonson; for Anderson, Fielding (like Sterne) exemplifies stylistically a relationship of "mutual trust" as opposed to the "tragic self-reliance" of the Richardsonian individual.

of his omnisciently providential argument. In *Grandison* Richardson moves toward the temporal and spatial relaxation of Fielding (Coleridge's "open lawn on a breezy day in May"), while Fielding brings his story indoors (into the "sick-room heated by stoves") by plunging his Booth in jail, Amelia in small lodgings, and the family in continuous debt. *Grandison* comes closer to being a comedy of manners than anything else Richardson wrote, with the possible exception of *Pamela II; Amelia* is more melodramatic than anything of Fielding's except the Heartfree sections of *Jonathan Wild*. As these exceptions suggest, Richardson and Fielding did not need to learn everything of the modes of their last novels from each other, since their own earlier work contains hints of them. But it seems unlikely that they both would have pursued their least promising tendencies without the spur—and blinders—of emulation, or that they would have come so close to writing repudiations of the great works they had just finished.

Fielding's Fathers

While Richardson would wait until his last novel before doing away with his heroine's parents (and then only, as we will see, to give her many more adoptive ones), the recurrent situations of Fielding's main characters suggest an existential definition of man as a fatherless biped. This Fieldingesque condition is generalized and humanized beyond the legacy of romance or beyond the convenience of foundlings for fictions by two circumstances. When fathers do appear, they are likely to be comic or sentimentalized inadequacies, such as Squire Western in *Tom Jones* or Miss Matthews's irresponsibly "best" of fathers in *Amelia*, who are virtual children themselves. When fathers do not appear, as is more often the case in relation to sons, their absence is emphasized by the pervasive presence of a father surrogate, admirably adequate at times and clearly inadequate at others, Parson Adams and Allworthy play this role most famously, but perhaps it is Dr. Harrison in *Amelia* who, as a partial compound of these two earlier "fathers," offers the clearest glimpse of the type of Fielding's preoccupation with imagined fathers. To understand fully the clue which the theme of fatherhood offers to grasping the "logic" of Fielding's career as a novelist, we need to add to this list of father figures other, more effectual providential agents who interpose to set things right, the idealized magistrates of the last chapters of *Jonathan Wild* and *Amelia,* and other guides who watch their "children" with paternal solicitude, the narrators of *Joseph Andrews* and *Tom Jones.*

The subtlety of response and evaluation demanded of Fielding's readers has been recognized increasingly in recent years, and the demands are particularly great in the case of what have been called Fielding's "fallible paragons" or "disappearing exemplars."[4] Adams, Allworthy, and Harrison are all characters of this sort, men who serve as models of uncorrupted virtue and probity, who function at least part of the time as paternal guides, and who at other moments are too blinded by their innocence or the deception of others to live up fully to the expectations of the reader or to the mature needs of their "sons." Taken in sequence, they also represent increasingly complex and "realistic" types of characterization in Fielding's work, but the problems of judgment which they present are complex and real from the first. Even in *Joseph Andrews* we balance somewhat precariously, for the reader who would condescend too abruptly to the unworldliness of Adams finds himself Booby-trapped into repellent company. Preventing the reader from dismissing the exemplar for his naivete is a more self-conscious matter in *Tom Jones,* where the novel's decorum does not provide for the possibility of laughter at Allworthy's oversights. When that possibility seems to threaten, as in the case of Allworthy's unlikely choice of tutors for his charges, Fielding conjures, cajoles, and benevolently bullies the reader away:

> For the reader is greatly mistaken, if he conceives that *Thwackum* appeared to Mr. *Allworthy* in the same Light as he doth to him in this History; and he is as much deceived, if he imagines, that the most intimate Acquaintance which he himself could have had with that Divine, would have informed him of those Things which we, from our Inspiration, are enabled to open and discover. Of Read-

[4]Sheldon Sacks, *Fiction and the Shape of Belief* (Berkeley: University of California Press, 1964), pp. 110ff.; J. Paul Hunter, *Occasional Form* (Baltimore: Johns Hopkins University Press, 1975), pp. 207–8.

ers who from such Conceits as these, condemn the Wisdom or Penetration of Mr. *Allworthy,* I shall not scruple to say, that they make a very bad and ungrateful Use of that Knowledge which we have communicated to them.[5]

And yet, for all this, Fielding himself clearly condescends to Adams and Allworthy and even, I believe, to Dr. Harrison. Adams and Harrison are, of course, at opposite ends of at least one spectrum which Fielding himself establishes, a range of human experience or "penetration." Adams has virtually none, Harrison a great deal. Fanny's passion for Joseph Andrews would, despite her obligatory denials, have been obvious to "any one but Adams, who never saw farther into people than they desired to let him" (II, x). Before Harrison sets foot in Fielding's last novel, we hear Booth praising his "great penetration into the human mind," explaining in some detail how Harrison's benevolence is matched by "great experience" and insight to make him the "best of comforters" and "physicians of the mind" (III, ii). The contrast could not be stronger, as we recall Adams bound to the bedstead with Joseph, after the abduction of Fanny, failing as spectacularly in his role as physician of the mind as the comforters of Job. Other contrasts immediately come to mind, most of them having to do with worldly capacity and experience, and in most of them Allworthy would appear somewhere between Adams and Harrison. Allworthy, for example, can be a tough judge of character in the final stages of the novel and knows something, once pointed in the right direction, of how to cross-examine a witness. On the other hand, Harrison, is a man of enough property and a sufficiently able estate manager to carry something of Allworthy's temporal substance, and he is able to address shrewdly both rural and urban people of all ranks. That he is relatively impotent in dealing with those at the "upper" end of the scale—as when he attempts to secure a nobleman's favor for Booth (XI, ii)—reflects more the profound corruption of the political system than his lack of discernment or rhetorical sophistication.

Here, a further contrast with Adams may suggest both an

[5]*Tom Jones,* 3:v. I have used the Wesleyan Edition (Middletown: Wesleyan University Press, 1975), ed. Martin C. Battestin and Fredson Bowers.

important difference and a major continuity between the worlds of *Amelia* and *Joseph Andrews*. The most melancholy moment in all of *Joseph Andrews* occurs when Adams, in Fielding's phrase, "appears in a political Light." The chapter (II, viii) consists entirely of Adams's virtual soliloquy (his auditor is a coarse braggart who soon after reveals his cowardice) on a quiet hilltop just at sunset. He recounts his political history as a "man of consequence" due to his influence with his nephew, the alderman of a corporation. For refusing to urge his nephew to vote for Colonel Courtly, Adams was relieved of his cure by his former rector. The man for whom Adams had stood on principle—"for it was at a season when the church was in danger, and when all good men expected they knew not what would happen to us all"—in fact cared nothing for the church and soon gave up his seat in Parliament for a place in the government:

> At last, when Mr. *Fickle* got his Place, Colonel *Courtly* stood again; and who should make Interest for him, but Mr. *Fickle* himself: that very identical Mr. *Fickle*, who had formerly told me, the Colonel was an Enemy to both the Church and State, had the Confidence to solicit my Nephew for him, and the Colonel himself offered to make me Chaplain to his Regiment, which I refused in favour of Sir *Oliver Hearty*, who told us, he would sacrifice everything to his Country; and I believe he would, except his Hunting, which he stuck so close to, that in five Years together, he went but twice up to Parliament. ... .

Adams next supported Sir Thomas Booby, who was elected,

> and a very fine Parliament-Man he was. They tell me he made Speeches of an Hour long; and I have been told very fine ones; but he could never persuade the Parliament to be of his Opinion.— *Non omnia possumus omnes.* He promised me a Living, poor Man; and I believe I should have had it, but an Accident happened; which was, that my Lady had promised it before unknown to him. This indeed I never heard 'till afterwards; for my Nephew, who died about a Month before the Incumbent, always told me I might be assured of it. Since that Time, Sir *Thomas*, poor Man, had always so much Business, that he never could find Leisure to see me. . . .

I quote from this chapter at such length because commentators seem generally to overlook it, perhaps due to the difficulty of doing justice to Fielding's tone. But under the delicate shading of this twilight piece rustles a tale of victimization, dependent impotence, and political orphanage. Only if we ignore its implications altogether does the systemic disillusionment of Fielding's last novel appear to have been revealed to him wholesale and late.[6]

Even in the pastoral world of *Joseph Andrews,* Adams is too much the child at the mercy of exploitative grown-ups to provide fatherly protection for Joseph once the hero is about to leave the personal pastoral of his own childhood. Mr. Wilson's emergence as Joseph's true father is as necessary as an emblem of Joseph's maturity as of his legitimacy; his parentage provides Joseph with a link to a community of adults, bearing at least some resemblance to the experienced world of the narrator and the reader. Although he is nearly as impotent as Adams in the face of political caprice—there is nothing except the matrimonial merriment of the ending to suggest that the tyrannical squire who shot his daughter's dog will not do so again—he is a "man of consequence" in a way Adams seems incapable of imagining: he has penetration enough to draw consequences from his experience.

To say this is not to foreclose Adams's amiability or to forget that penetration is an equivocal value in Fieldin's fiction. It is a quality which blurs easily into suspicion or cynicism, so that the "prodigious Superiority of Penetration which we must observe in some men over the rest of the human Species" is often proof of nothing better than the fact that it takes a knave to understand knavery (*Tom Jones,* V, vi). Heartfree cannot understand Jonathan Wild instinctively without ceasing to be Heartfree.[7]

---

[6]Hunter (p. 205) sees *Amelia* as a departure from Fielding's "earlier Augustan faith in institutions as a check on human depravity." Battestin, in "Fielding's Changing Politics," however, does discuss the passage quoted from *Joseph Andrews* and finds in it evidence of Fielding's new and deeper political disillusionment with the Opposition. The quoted passages are from *Joseph Andrews,* ed. Martin C. Battestin (Middletown: Wesleyan University Press, 1967), pp. 133–34.

[7]The problem has been well stated by Morris Golden in *Fielding's Moral Psychology* (Amherst: University of Massachusetts Press, 1966): "Theoretically, the worthy person must acquire an awareness of evil through experience, since he has almost none of it within; he can easily enough recognize good, which is his own reflection. . . . But in his fiction, where he assumes the responsibility of showing full human nature at work in society, [Fielding] is no more hopeful than Johnson's Nekayah, who explains that marrying old is bad, marrying young is

Nonetheless, when Fielding reaches for a simile to characterize the ideal conscience animating Tom Jones, he describes it "as sitting on its Throne in the Mind, like the Lord High Chancellor of this Kingdom in his Court; where it presides, governs, directs, judges, acquits and condemns according to Merit and Justice; with a Knowledge which nothing escapes, a Penetration which nothing can deceive, and an integrity which nothing can corrupt" (IV, vi). This passage of course seems to describe God and the narrator more than any character in the book, but it comes closer to matching Tom than Allworthy, whose judgments on and off the bench we have witnessed well before the judicial simile is drawn.

Readers of *Amelia* invariably note its distance from the sunlit country of *Tom Jones,* although they vary somewhat in ascribing the change in method as well as scene to a failure of artistic confidence or to new concerns. However one might regard the real differences, it is instructive to remember that the novels share a major theme, that of paternal estrangement. As in *Tom Jones,* the father-son relationship which matters in *Amelia* is a metaphorical but functional one,[8] and the relation of this theme to the plot as a whole is the same: an adoptive father is found, lost, and found again. This is by no means the whole story of either book, but it is coextensive with the larger plots of each. The large difference is the displacement of the sequence from the childhood of the hero to his adulthood. In this sense, as well as in the more obvious fact that *Amelia* concerns a couple *after* their marriage, the latter novel beings where *Tom Jones* stopped. Booth first finds his "father" at just the point where Tom is reunited with Allworthy, that is, at the beginning of the courtship of the heroine, and the success of each courtship depends upon not only the sanction of the foster father but his active intervention on the hero's behalf as well.

---

bad, expecting to seize an optimum middle time for marrying is chimerical, and not marrying is worst of all. Prudence, Fielding's middle ground on which the good mind can meet reality, never seems available to the virtuous until authorial fantasy—'romance'—has provided them with perfect felicity" (p. 10).

[8] For a provocative argument that paternity is the metaphor which discloses the narrative and historical structures of *Tom Jones,* see Homer Obed Brown, "*Tom Jones:* The 'Bastard' of History," *Boundary* 2, 7 (Winter 1979): 201–33.

The alienation of paternal affection which dominates the middle of both books is deepened by misrepresentation and misunderstanding. Even while they are present, the fathers are distant and legendary figures, and once they have literally been distanced from their sons, they become emotionally as well as physically inaccessible, hardening into postures of indignation and credulous recrimination. We need at this point to distinguish as clearly as possible between versions of the father-son plot which Fielding consciously endorses and those which seem less intentional though just as strong. Officially, Tom might have avoided Allworthy's ire had he been more prudent; for in fact Fielding comes close to defining prudence, for his younger readers' benefit, as making sure one's virtue is conspicuous enough for a father to recognize it (*Tom Jones*, III, viii). But as soon as we apply any realistic criteria to the chain of events, it becomes difficult to understand how a man who is all the things Allworthy is said to be could misjudge Tom and Blifil so badly after years of daily contact. On the other hand, when we abandon realistic considerations, we are left with a parable of parental inaccessibility and unconscious antagonism.

Booth's separation from Harrison in *Amelia* is not the direct result of anger (Harrison is called away to accompany his patron's son on the grand tour), but they are suspicious opponents before they are allied initially, and the relationship is never easy. As soon as they are divided, miscalculations multiply, Booth making several errors of conduct and Harrison several of interpretation. Fielding never arraigns Harrison, just as Allworthy's misjudgments are moralized as cautions to the young and impetuous rather than to the old and precipitous. In fact, like Mr. Wilson in *Joseph Andrews*, who attributes misfortunes to his "early introduction into life, without a guide" (III, iii), Booth sees his "many errors" as originating in his separation from Harrison:

> "By this means I was bereft not only of the best companion in the world, but of the best counsellor; a loss of which I have since felt the bitter consequence; for no greater advantage, I am convinced, can arrive to a young man, who hath any degree of understanding, than an intimate converse with one of riper years, who is not only

able to advise, but who knows the manner of advising. By this means alone, youth can enjoy the benefit of the experience of age, and that at a time of life when such experience will be of more service to a man than when he hath lived long enough to acquire it of himself." [III, xii]

Through much of the novel Harrison does seem to be Fielding's proxy, a spokesman for strenuous virtue, expressing monitory views like those, for example, of "An Essay on the Knowledge of the Characters of men" and "Of the Remedy of Affliction for the Loss of our Friends."9 And there seems little reason to doubt that he speaks Fielding's own last word on the subject of human nature: "The nature of man is far from being in itself evil; it abounds with benevolence, charity and pity, coveting praise and honour, and shunning shame and disgrace. Bad education, bad habits, and bad customs, debauch our nature, and drive it headlong as it were into vice" (IX, v).

But while Harrison is often an effective companion and counselor to Amelia, he is of little real help to Booth. When they are on friendly terms, it is Harrison's unnecessarily rigid construction of Booth's debt to military honor which sends the young man off to war and wounding (III, i). When they are not on friendly terms, Harrison's posture toward his "son" is, like Allworthy's, one of mixed anger and prosecutory zeal. Harrison's jesting remark to Booth concerning Amelia—"You stole my little lamb from me; for I was her first love" (IX, viii)—perhaps offers an instructive gloss on some of the unhappier moments in the relationship of the two men. But the most dramatic gap between the descriptions of Harrison and his actual behavior in relation to Booth comes to light immediately following Booth's conversion. To Booth's explanation that his doubts concerning Christianity have been cured by reading Barrow's sermons, Harrison, his clergyman, physician of the mind, and "best counsellor" for several hundred pages, replies simply: "You say you have had your doubts, young gentleman; indeed, I did not know that" (XII, v).

9See *Miscellanies*, vol. I, ed. Henry Knight Miller (Middletown: Wesleyan University Press, 1972), pp. 153–78, 212–22, and Miller's *Essays on Fielding's "Miscellanies"* (Princeton: Princeton University Press, 1961), pp. 189–271.

Fielding does not ask us to blame Harrison because it is Barrow rather than he who causes Booth's conversion. The conversion itself is a sudden and mysterious affair (partly so, at least, because of Fielding's ambivalent attitude about it, to which I will return later); but the fact that Harrison did not realize that it was even necessary emphasizes the ultimate distance between the spiritual father and his son. In *Joseph Andrews, Tom Jones,* and *Amelia,* the overt plot centers on the maturation and education of the "son." But in each of the novels the "experience" of age proves to be more innocent than are the youthful heroes who presumably need its guidance. It is the education of the older man which constitutes the unofficial plot of the novels. For Allworthy and Harrison the education consists in the recognition of the past oversights and the reacceptance of a hastily rejected son. Parson Adams is so innocent as to be nearly ineducable, but in fact it is he, rather than Joseph, who needs and presumably heeds the concluding counsel of the novel, for it is he who had voluntarily left the world of retirement for that of "booksellers" and sought literarily to "make his appearance in *High-Life.*"

Adams's ignorance and innocence of the modern literary world is significant for our understanding because Fielding's other father figures share it and because they are, after all, innocent of the world in which Fielding and Fielding's readers live and laugh and learn. Fielding's fathers are relics. Much of the time they are venerable relics, whose lack of contact with modernity is part of their Edenic charm; but finally they remain ancestral antiques, representatives of another era whose function in this one is questionable and whose quaintness is unmistakable. Even Harrison, undoubtedly the most contemporary and realistic of Fielding's exemplars, belongs literarily to the past. While Booth discourses on the relative strengths of Swift and his contemporaries, and Amelia herself is well versed in English poetry and drama, Harrison has never "read a word" of Dryden or Pope. The one contemporary taste which Harrison shares with Fielding's narrators is his fondness for Hogarth; in all other respects he is nearly as proud as Parson Adams of his ignorance of the vernacular tradition. (III, xii; VI, vii; IX, iii)

In each of the three novels, then, Fielding creates an adoptive father who is ultimately inadequate for the role. *Joseph Andrews* and *Tom Jones* are distinguished from *Amelia* by the fact that in earlier novels the paternal role is assumed in large part by Fielding himself: in *Joseph Andrews* by a benign conspiracy between Mr. Wilson and the narrator (who tells us that those readers "who have as great an affection for that gentleman as ourselves will rejoice" at the prospect of seeing him again), and in *Tom Jones* by the more fully realized narrator himself, who regards "all the Personages of this History in the Light of my Children" (*Joseph Andrews*, III, v; *Tom Jones*, XVI, vi). In *Amelia*, however, the narrator does not assume the role of father toward his protagonist, and it may well be this absence which many readers feel when they miss the "old Fielding" in his last book and sense a lack of confidence or control. The interesting question is why Fielding was unable to play that role in *Amelia*. One sometimes still encounters the assumption that he was simply too old. But Booth's age would seem to be more to the point than Fielding's. Having begun with a mature hero, who is married, an army officer, and himself a father, the postures of affectionate condescension which Fielding's narrators had assumed toward heroes of fewer years and less rank would no longer be appropriate.

A further explanation for some of the problems of attitude and tone in *Amelia* lies, I believe, in Fielding's decision to put into his hero not only much of himself but also much of his own father. Like Edmund Fielding, Booth is a half-pay colonel, a man involved in money disputes with his wife's mother, a failed farmer, a prey to debt, and a dupe for conspiring gamblers.[10] These are not all the facts that matter in the novel, and indeed many of Booth's circumstances pertain more to the direct experience of Henry than to that of Edmund Fielding. (Although one at the same time senses something of Henry in Booth's oldest son, the most perceptive of the children and the one most affected by the father's absences.) But the economic circumstances common to Booth and to Fielding's father are some of the most significant ones in the novel in terms of its explicit and problematic theme, the role of "fortune" in individual lives. The question of whether Booth's misfortunes are just that—so much bad luck—or the consequences of misdeeds for which he is

[10]These parallels have been noted by Dudden, in *Henry Fielding*, II, 857.

culpable is never resolved in *Amelia*. When Fielding announces at the outset that some of the "accidents" which befell Booth and Amelia are so painful that "they seemed to require not only the utmost malice, but the utmost invention, which superstition hath ever attributed to Fortune," and then begins to argue in the same sentence that a lack of prudence is the more probable cause of human calamities, we may reasonably wonder to whose eyes luck *seemed* to be the problem. But while Fielding appears to be setting the stage for a plot, like those of *Joseph Andrews* and *Tom Jones*, in which seeming explanations will give way to real explanations, what "seemed" to be the case (presumably to Booth and Amelia) in Book I is not canceled but underscored by the end of Book XII: "As to Booth and Amelia, Fortune seems to have made them large amends for the tricks she had played them in their youth."

One wishes for a more confident and conscious epilogue than *Amelia* to the career of such a great fiction maker as Fielding—with great luck something like a *Tempest* or, even if disillusionment prevail, his *Billy Budd*. But perhaps it is too short a career after all for that. If we think for a moment of *Amelia* not as a summing up but as a middle work, which it could easily have been had Fielding lived to the age at which Richardson wrote *Clarissa*, it is interesting to ask what direction his writing might have taken after this "problem" work. The providential and magisterial fathers who dominate Shakespeare's and Melville's last works are reflected in Fielding primarily through the paternal and judicious narrators of his earlier successes. Once this narrative posture is abandoned, Fielding's novel is as orphaned as Booth and Amelia themselves. This most vulnerable of Fielding's novels has been called a "flight into the interior,"[11] and insofar as it reflects a collapse of the rhetorical structure which enabled Fielding to range in and over the political structure, so it is. But it is also a narrative *advance* toward more challenging conventions of adult characterization, toward a more complex syntax of cause and effect, and toward a more open surrender of paternal omniscience. Unless Fielding were to retreat from

[11]This is the title of Hunter's chapter on *Amelia* in *Occasional Form*, pp. 193–216.

these new rigors, which in retrospect seem more clearly emergent in the epistolary novel, his next problem would have been the large one which *Amelia* poses but does not resolve, that of how to establish fictive authority without authoring a father.

Richardson's Readers

While Fielding quietly turns his back in *Amelia* on the achievement of *Tom Jones,* Richardson draws an explicit and official relation between *Sir Charles Grandison* and *Clarissa.*[12] Early in the novel when Sir Charles's sister Charlotte is teasing her ardent suitor, Harriet Byron reaches for an allusion to rebuke her. "— A very Miss Howe, said I," and Charlotte replies in kind, "To a *very* Mr. Hickman" (I, 229). Richardson's characters not only read modern literature, they read Richardson. The theme of reading is one I wish to discuss further, but for the moment the importance of this allusion is simply that it invites the reader to compare the two novels.

Once we make the comparison, many of the circumstances of the later novel take on new interest. The plot is not complex, but it is complicated and may bear repeating for the reader who happens not to have given recent days and nights to *Grandison.* Harriet Byron, a young woman without parents but with family and fortune, is abducted by the most violent of her several suitors, Sir Hargrave Pollexfen. (As in *Pamela II, Amelia,* and *Tom Jones* sexual complications begin after a masquerade.) Before he can force her to the altar—this rather than the "last outrage" is primarily his intention—Sir Charles Grandison rescues Harriet and places her in the care of his sisters, Lady L. and Charlotte, later Lady G. (like Anna Howe, Charlotte does eventually yield to her man). During her stay Harriet falls in love with Sir Charles. Sir Charles feels himself previously committed, however, to Clementina della Porretta, a devout Roman Catholic whom he had tutored in English while living with her family in

[12]Parenthetical numbers in the text refer to Richardson's novel *Sir Charles Grandison,* ed. Jocelyn Harris (London: Oxford University Press, 1972). Although my reading of *Grandison* will appear in some respects less enthusiastic than the discussions of Mark Kinkead-Weekes and Margaret Anne Doody (see n. 2), I am greatly indebted to their studies.

Italy. The conflict between love and piety has driven Clementina temporarily mad, and much of the slight suspense in the plot hinges on whether she will recover her reason and be able to consent to marry a Protestant. When it is clear, after a lengthy second visit by Sir Charles, that she is well enough to make a "determined refusal," Sir Charles returns to England and proposes to Harriet. Clementina, meanwhile, is desperately trying to escape marriage altogether and finally flees her family by coming to England, where she engages the joint solicitude of Sir Charles, Harriet, Lady G., and Lady L., all of whom adopt her as their "sister." She is at length reconciled to her family, returns to Italy (and perhaps to eventual marriage to the Count of Belvedere), and the happiness of Sir Charles and Harriet is complete.

The most conspicuous way in which *Sir Charles Grandison* is an antithesis to the thesis of Clarissa is in its relentless presentation of a "good Man"; but there are less obvious and perhaps less conscious oppositions as well. Harriet's comparison of her friend Charlotte to Anna Howe implicitly draws an analogy between herself and Clarissa. Virtue, beauty, and intelligence, of course, they have in common. But beyond that their situations are in sharp contrast. As an orphan with benevolent guardians, Harriet is under no family pressure whatsoever. (Richardson could hardly countenance Ambrose Bierce's devilish definition of an orphan as a "living person deprived by death of the power of filial ingratitude," but he comes close, through Harriet and Sir Charles's ward Emily, to defining orphanhood as the power of marital freedom.) In place of Clarissa's tyrannical father, Harriet has both her uncle and Sir Rowland Meredith, a would-be father-in-law who cannot resist "adopting" her even after she has refused his son. In place of Clarissa's ineffectual mother, she has her sagacious grandmother, Mrs. Shirley, and another would-be in-law, the Countess Dowager of D., a woman of consequence and intelligent counsel. In place of Clarissa's mean-spirited sister, Harriet has the Grandisons, who speedily insist that she be their "sister," and in place of the grasping brother, she has Sir Charles himself (until he changes that role for a "yet dearer relation") and her various unsuccessful suitors such as Sir Rowland's son or the overly sensitive Mr. Orme. "We are," Charlotte tells Harriet, "a family of love. . . . We are true brothers and sisters." Sir Charles, according to Charlotte, is a "father and brother in one" (I, 133–38), and so he would seem to be for Harriet as well. Before long, Dr. Bartlett, Sir Charles's fatherly clergyman, has even become Harriet's "grandfather" (I, 228).

If this overdetermined "family of love" is decidedly unlike anything in *Clarissa,* there are other situations and characters which are analogous to the earlier novel, although generally sanitized and softened. Harriet's abduction replaces Clarissa's rape. Sir Hargrave takes the role of Lovelace. But then we see a process by which characters split in two so as to become less threatening or, as Johnson had recently put it in *Rambler* 4, so that they do not "mingle good and bad qualities" and "confound the colours of right and wrong." Thus Sir Hargrave has to share his Lovelace legacy with one of his rivals, Mr. Greville: Sir Hargrave inherits only Lovelace's audacity and lawlessness, while Greville assumes some of his attractiveness, theatricality, and occasional disinterestedness. Since Sir Hargrave lacks Lovelace's intelligence and Greville lacks his resolution, both Harriet and the reader are safe.[13] Harriet herself never really mingles good and bad, but she does have a quality which Richardson seems to regard as dangerous, a "satirical vein" which animates some of her early sketches in the novel and leads her to mimic several characters' styles quite archly. After her "rape," however, she is frightened out of her wit, and Charlotte assumes the satiric role.[14]

A deeper split occurs with the introduction of the Italian plot and the entrance of a second heroine. Clementina knew Sir Charles long before Harriet's involvement, but since we meet and sympathize with Harriet first, it is Clementina who seems to be what Harriet is afraid of being, a "second love." I think Rich-

[13]McKillop first noted the "splitting" of characters, in *Samuel Richardson: Printer and Novelist* (Chapel Hill: University of North Carolina Press, 1936), p. 212. Kinkead-Weekes aptly terms the abduction plot in *Grandison* "Lovelace-and-Water." (*Samuel Richardson,* p. 299).

[14]Doody in *A Natural Passion* (pp. 287–93) describes Charlotte in relation to the "witty, teasing, independent heroine" of Restoration and early eighteenth-century comedy. There is a chilling note, however, in Sir Charles's suggestion that wit and marriage will prove incompatible: "A lively heart is a great blessing. Indulge it. Now is your time" (II, 107).

ardson felt that he had to work out the Clementina plot so fully before allowing the central marriage to proceed because Clementina is in effect Harriet's more passionate self, or possible self, just as Olivia (a second Italian beauty whose frustrated passion impels her to attack Sir Charles with a dagger) is a Clementina with no repression. Whatever Richardson's motives or instincts, until Clementina's fate is settled, Harriet is unaccountably unable to fix a wedding date. "Heroines both," Charlotte Grandison says of Harriet and Clementina; "they are mirrors to each other" (III, 418). For Sir Charles they are "sister-excellencies." "My Harriet is another Clementina," and Clementina is the "Miss Byron of Italy" (III, 53, 343). Or, in one of the many *tableaux à trois* of the later part of the novel, "Sir Charles clasped his arms about us both. . . . Angels he called us" (II, 392). But it is the noble Italian who has inherited many of Clarissa's most interesting qualities: her spirited resistance to her family, her "wounded mind," her passionate yet slightly marmoreal grandeur, even the detail at one point of disordered typography which signals her turmoil "by the disposition of the lines."[15]

The problems with Sir Charles himself as a character were perhaps summed up most kindly by Anna Barbauld: "Perfection of character, joined to distress, will interest; but prosperous perfection does not greatly engage our sympathy."[16] We may add that in this case it does not engage our belief, either. Readers have since remarked that Sir Charles bears the faults (all too fictive!) of a character drawn up by a committee, as Richardson tried to bequeath upon him all the good qualities he and his admirers could think of together.[17] The reader's reaction is all too like Harriet's when she exclaims, "Had he but some faults;

[15]*Clarissa*, Everyman Edition (London: J. M. Dent, 1932), III, 209, and *Grandison*, III, 164.

[16]Anna Laetitia Barbauld, ed., *The Correspondence of Samuel Richardson* (London, 1804), I, cxxix.

[17]On the social composition of the novel and the encylopedic virtue of its hero see Kinkead-Weekes, *Samuel Richardson*, pp. 279–92, and Doody, *A Natural Passion*, pp. 241–74, 303–5; after reviewing Richardson's apparent reliance on works such as Allestree's *The Gentleman's Calling* and Steele's *The Christian Hero*, however, Doody remarks, "Yet this does not mean that Sir Charles does not exist as a character. He is not a man made after supper out of parings from the moralists; we are aware of his presence" (p. 274).

some great blemishes; I fansy I should be easier about him. But to hear nothing of him, but what is so greatly praiseworthy . . ." (I, 445). Lest there be any doubt as to the multiplicity of Sir Charles's exemplary virtues, Harriet twice summarizes the roles in which he has shone:

> I will endeavour to see with indifference, him that we have all been admiring and studying for this last fortnight, in such a variety of lights. The Christian: The Hero: The Friend:—Ah, Lucy! The Lover of Clementina: The generous Kinsman of Lord W.: The modest and delicate Benefactor of the Mansfields: The free, gay, Railler of Lady Beauchamp; and in her of all our Sex's Foibles! [II, 293]
>
> But could HE be otherwise than the best of HUSBANDS, who was the most dutiful of SONS; who is the most affectionate of BROTHERS: the most faithful of FRIENDS: Who is good upon principle, in every relation of life? [III, 462]

This final burst of praise is the same one in which Harriet describes Sir Charles as a "TRULY GOOD MAN" in contrast to "most of those who are called HEROES." It is here that one must turn from Richardson's failure with the character of Sir Charles to his intentions. Harriet's remark is merely the last chime of a theme which rings throughout the novel, the theme of true—and new—heroism.[18] Sir Charles is everywhere the "truly heroic" man. One of the many would-be duelists he disarms announces, "I never saw a hero till now" (I, 264). Harriet describes him as "The Friend of Mankind" rather than "The Conqueror of Nations" (II, 70), and Charlotte later sharpens the contrast by blaming heroic literature for instilling false honor: Homer begat Alexander the Great (III, 197–98). Richardson, on the other hand, begat Sir Charles Grandison, who is "great because good," who shows indeed that "goodness and greatness are synonymous words" (I, 388; II, 114).

The opposition of great and good is the one which Fielding had treated satirically in *Jonathan Wild* and Gray sentimentally in *The Progress of Poesy*, and it is not to be defined away by fiat. (The

---

[18]Both Kinkead-Weekes in *Samuel Richardson* (pp. 284–95) and Doody in *A Natural Passion* (pp. 252–74) discuss the strenuous moral idealism of *Grandison*, the former comparing it in this respect with *Daniel Deronda*.

debate over Alexander's heroism surfaces much later in the first chapter of volume 2 of *Caleb Williams*.) But Richardson attempts to create a greater goodness than the passive virtue embodied in Fielding's Heartfree or in Gray's solitary poet by insisting that his hero is a man of action, at large in the world. Sir Charles's "action" becomes a kind of choral theme, as character after character marvels at his efficiency. Harriet remarks that Sir Charles is "noted for his great dexterity in business. Were I to express myself in the language of Miss Grandison, I should say that a sun-beam is not more penetrating. He goes to the bottom of an affair at once" (I, 361). She had indeed caught Miss Grandison's language: "Light is hardly more active than my brother, nor lightning more quick, where he has anything to execute than must or ought to be done" (III, 114). Mr. Deane reports that "Lord L. said, that when he is master of a subject, his execution is as swift as thought. . . . Seas are nothing to him. Dr. Bartlett said, that he considers all nations as joined on the same continent; and doubted not but if he had a call, he would undertake a journey to Constantinople or Pekin, with as little difficulty as some others would . . . to the Land's-end" (II, 30). While Sir Charles is settling estates, executing wills, and reconciling families in two countries, Harriet says admiringly, "What an activity!" and in Italy Clementina's brother Jeronymo remarks, "The Chevalier Grandison speaks by *action*" (II, 333, 523).

On one level of fantasy Sir Charles is an idealized transformation of the mercantile hero, landed but ready to go to China if business beckons, a prototype of the international executive. On a second level he is a godlike savior whose mysterious "actions" awe and convert nearly everyone in the novel. Lord W., now resolved to marry his mistress, blames Sir Charles's father for "keeping so long abroad a son, who would have converted us both. Lessons of morality, given in so noble a manner by *practice*, rather than by preaching *theory* . . . , must have subdued us" (II, 59). During that absence Sir Charles's father himself had exclaimed from his death bed, "O save me! save me! my Grandison, by thy presence!" (I, 356). Characters whose essential virtue is hardly in doubt are similarly redeemed. Charlotte Grandison testifies that until "I knew my brother . . . as I now know him, I was an inconsiderate, unreflecting girl. Good and evil which immediately affected not myself, were almost alike indifferent to me" (I, 143). Even the pious Dr. Bartlett is not immune: "He preaches by *action*. Till I knew him, a young man as he then was, and still is, my preaching was by *words;* I was contented, that my actions disgraced not my words" (II, 667).

If readers felt anything like this power in Sir Charles's "action" the novel would of course be a much more successful work than it is. I believe that three large problems surround Richardson's effort to present Sir Charles as an interesting agent. First, there is simply the problem of modern business. Much of what Richardson shows Sir Charles doing is difficult to make vivid: the ordering of papers, the arrangement of legacies, the negotiation of familial treaties. One of the characteristics of Sir Charles's "divine philanthropy" is his ability to bring order out of disorder; but it tends to be order of a more clerical than tangible kind. Richardson's attempt to portray a literate, urbane protagonist at work—that is, doing those things which adults spend much of their time doing to preserve their economic, legal, and social identities—is an endeavor so rare in the history of the novel before George Eliot that it compels respect. Work has proven, however, to be even less tractable a subject for fiction than the city for poetry.

The second obstruction in the characterization of Sir Charles as a credible man of action goes beyond the dilemmas of verisimilitude to Richardson's conception of virtue as stasis. Richardson would not agree with this interpretation of his ethical vision and would argue that his good characters do not simply reject vicious actions but perform good ones. Still, in fact much of what we witness in *Grandison* is Sir Charles restraining his passion so that he may refrain from action. The modern epic is one of self-control. Harriet says as much as far as women are concerned when she explains just why the "affecting story" of her struggle to overcome her passion is important: "this case is one of those few in which a woman *can* show a bravery of spirit" (II, 259). Interestingly, and despite the fact that Richardson emphasizes different roles for men and women,[19] Harriet's de-

[19]Although *Grandison* contains an essay by Elizabeth Carter arguing for a recognition of feminine intellect (III, 243–44), Harriet speaks of a "natural superiority in the minds of men over women" (III, 181) because men are less

scription of a heroine applies just as well to the Richardsonian hero: "Sir Charles Grandison is used to do only what he *ought*," she reports, recalling that "Dr. Bartlett once said, that the life of a good man was a continual warfare with his passions" (II, 157). We may be reminded of the inwardness of Richardson's focus when we pair this dictum with Pope's remark earlier in the century that the "life of a Wit is a warfare on earth."[20] The idea that the exemplary man struggles with himself rather than with others is not in itself fatal to plot; but, like modern workaday fidelity, such rarefied stoicism makes it more difficult, as does the coupling of stoicism and the cultivation of "sentiment." What is fatal to Grandison's "action" is the impression that his struggles with his passions are so easy. He repeatedly refers to being a passionate man by nature, but Harriet's characterization of his safety of sentiment is more persuasive:

> Do you think my dear, that had he been the first man, he would have been so complaisant to his Eve as *Milton makes Adam* . . . —To taste the forbidden fruit because he would not be separated from her, in her punishment, tho' all *posterity* were to suffer by it?—No; it is my opinion, that your brother would have had gallantry enough to his fallen spouse, to have made him extremely regret her lapse; but that he would have done *his own duty*, were it but for the sake of posterity, and left it to the Almighty . . . to have annihilated his first Eve, and given him a second. [II, 609]

Like the life of a wit, wit itself must exist in social activity; but the life of Richardson's good man, or good woman, is a solitary condition—even in this social comedy.

A yet larger and more interesting problem surfaces in this novel than either the difficulty of dramatizing modern business or the limitations of Richardson's idea of virtue: *Sir Charles Grandison* is not a novel *about* Sir Charles Grandison but about people reading and writing about Sir Charles Grandison. In place of the plot summary given a few pages ago, we might construct a less

---

susceptible to superstitious fears. It is Sir Charles himself who offers the most "Victorian" differentiation of roles: "Male nurses are unnatural creatures! Women's sphere is the house, and their shining-place the sick chamber" (II, 58).

[20]Pope, Preface to *Works*, 1717, para. 7.

conventional but probably more appropriate one in which the significant actions might be the following.

Harriet writes the account of her "distresses and deliverance" while staying with the Grandisons, finishing it in a stretch of concentration during which she "overwrit" herself and was "obliged to lie down" (I, 193). She reads the history of the Grandison family and writes "almost night and day" to finish her own account of it to her relatives (I, 386). Harriet agrees to show the letters describing her abduction to the Grandisons (I, 392). Charlotte chides Harriet for being "eternally" at her pen and thus unavailable as a confidante (I, 396–403). Harriet declares her intention as a writer: "to let you into the character and sentiments of Sir Charles Grandison" (I, 430). Harriet distributes more letters to the Grandison sisters (II, 12). She spends most of her time reading the history of Clementina, while Dr. Bartlett begins to edit and transcribe Sir Charles's Italian letters for her—according to standards suggested by her own "manner or writing" (II, 160–82). Clementina writes down her "resolution" not to marry Charles, begins to keep and transcribe from a pocketbook, and tells her friends and family repeatedly to "read my paper" in order to know the "written determination" she regards as her real self (II, 527, 556, 597–618). Sir Charles gives Mrs. Shirley *his* letters as proof of his sincerity in courting Harriet (III, 17). Charles tells Harriet he loved her upon first reading her letters (III, 130). Clementina writes down, again, her attitude toward marriage and her acceptance of her parents' wish that she not enter the convent (III, 448).

This summary is not the whole of Grandison either, but it suggests how deeply the novel turns from experience to the presentation and analysis of experience. At the level of statement Richardson's self-consciousness is striking enough. Various characters remark throughout on "writing to the moment," on the importance of "minuteness," and on the difficulty of recording conversations aptly.[21] From the beginning of *Pamela* onward, Richardson seems to have enjoyed not only defending

[21]See, e.g., I, 34, 300, 362, 425; II, 89, 243; III, 24, 40, 47, 114. Harriet's plaintive desire, "I wish I could write as fast as we can talk" (I, 357), is later fulfilled by proxy when a shorthand writer transcribes verbatim a lengthy conversation on dueling.

his method but occasionally calling attention to it. In *Grandison*, however, the concern with technique becomes obsessive, as letters are evaluated, quoted, cross-referenced, and compared stylistically as character after character discovers the pleasure or necessity of writing. Because the letters in *Grandison* are not written with any of the urgency of Pamela's or Clarissa's, we do not read them (with the exception of Clementina's) as acts of survival and experiences in themselves. There is such leisure to compare them—as there is leisure for all else in this novel—that we read them as commentaries, reflections of offstage events and on each other, and finally as hypothetical propositions.

This last point requires explanation, since all fiction can be regarded as hypothetical by definition, as a series of what-if statements and situations. But conventionally fiction is hypothetical for the reader, not for the characters. In *Grandison* the characters appropriate the reader's role living their lives in a continual state of critical nicety. Harriet's assertion that Sir Charles is a man "that says nothing at random" (II, 293) becomes a rationale for close reading on her part as well as for "minuteness." When such attention is focused on one's own behavior, the result is a casuistry of conduct. "What, my dear Lady G. in your opinion, should we have done? Were we right, or were we wrong? Over-delicacy, as I have heard observed, is under-delicacy . . ." (III, 45). When it is focused on the heart it becomes a casuistry of compassion—again, hypothetical. "What say my Grandmamma, my Aunt, my Lucy? Shall I wish the noble Clementina may be prevailed upon in favor of this really worthy man? Should *I*, do you think, be prevailed upon in *her* situation?—A better question still—*Ought* I?" (III, 423). In place of the suspense of *Pamela* and *Clarissa*, the characters of *Sir Charles Grandison* move in suspension. Theirs is life in the subjunctive.

The concern with writing and with the reading of documents which is characteristic of Richardson's earlier novels becomes more general in his last, more self-congratulatory,[22] more tied to the pleasures of consumption than to a drama of definition. In *Pamela*, Pamela's ability to enter a world of letters is essential

[22]E.g., Harriet tells her aunt that she has written a letter "that no *man* . . . could write" (I, 217; cf. II, 70, 357).

to her character and to her upward mobility. For Clarissa her letters are her real identity, her "written mind," and from the spectator's point of view one of the deeper struggles in the novel results from Richardson's effort to shift the reader's sympathies from Lovelace's to Belford's "reading" of Clarissa.[23] In his last novel Richardson depends less on psychological selection and more on circumstantial accumulation. Harriet complains mildly that writing and experience may come into competition ("You must not, my dear Ladies, expect me to be so *very* minute: If I am, must I not lose a hundred charming conversations?" [III, 102]), and Charlotte had complained more strongly, (I, 396, 403) but neither woman is felt to be strongly affected by her partiality. Richardson has Mrs. Shirley speak for the presumed reader when she explains the pleasures of perfect spectatorship: "were I to be with you at Grandison-hall, I could not be everywhere: So that I should be deprived of half the delightful scenes and conversations, that you, your aunt, and Lucy, relate and describe to me by pen and ink: Nor should I be able perhaps to bear those grateful ones, to which I should be present" (III, 291).

The easy multiplication of minute details is finally what gives *Grandison* its soap-opera combination of verisimilitude and unreality. Its slow-motion fantasy is one where experience is something which can be halted, analyzed, replayed, like a daydream of complete knowledge. Richardson's greatest powers, however, rose from a darker dream of partial perception, fugitive truths, and urgent decisions. The world of *Clarissa* is a scene where, in Pope's words, "half our knowledge we must snatch, not take."[24]

[23]In *Reading Clarissa* (New Haven: Yale University Press, 1979), William Beatty Warner argues that "when readers 'misinterpret' the text, Richardson sometimes claims the position of the innocent and injured Lady for his text. . . . In a similar spirit, Belford . . . and all the 'true' critics of the text make the text into a beautiful and inviolable Lady they must protect from the 'false' critics who threaten to play the Serpent" (p. 261; cf. pp. 42–45, 91).

[24]*Epistle to Cobham*, 1.34. In a commentary on this poem (*Studies in English Literature*, 17 [1977], pp. 435–49), I have tried to underscore Pope's dramatization of an essentially artistic grasp "Of the Knowledge and Characters of Men," a topic to which Fielding returned with more monitorial emphasis in an essay of nearly the same title in his *Miscellanies* (1743); but fuller studies of mid-century epistemological concerns in fiction are offered by John A. Dussinger, *The Discourse of the Mind in Eighteenth-Century Fiction* (The Hague: Mouton, 1974) and Eric Rothstein, *Systems of Order and Inquiry*.

In the nearly timeless unfolding of *Grandison* we find a map approaching the size of the territory it depicts; drawn to such scale, the novel's presentation of detail is finally not an interpretation of experience but its replacement. This is not the achievement the book's defenders usually have in mind, but it is not a small one. In the following pages I will suggest that it belongs both to Richardson and to his time.

CONCLUSION

Literary Loneliness and the Historical Moment

Generalizations which do not embarrass are difficult to reach here because the discussion has been doubly motivated. One dogged conviction has been that generalizations can and should be made historically, even generationally, and that they will be truest as they are collective and impersonal. The other conviction has been that the proper subjects of our sympathetic reflection are writers writing, individuals whom we should not lose sight of in the delusive objectivity of literary periodization. I have tried in several ways to suggest that the period's meaning for literary study lies in its more interesting careers and personally experienced impasses and therefore in a large number of individual works, many of them relatively neglected. In one sense, then, if the tales told so far through and about those works are reasonably accurate ones, the trustworthiest conclusions now will be those the reader is willing to draw rather than those drawn by the teller.

Perhaps there is a deeper reason for mutual skepticism as well. One of the fundamental movements I see beginning to take shape in the mid-eighteenth century is a lyric flight from immediate history and a visionary approach toward History, a movement, in other words, from the details of contemporary life and toward a history sufficiently generalized or abstracted to serve as the ground of a broader theodicy. Because this is an attractively "modern" idea in itself, and because we like our histories to come out as they "had" to, it is particularly tempting in discussing it to let critical empathy replace critical distance and thus to extend what one thinks one has found to one's commentary on those findings. In this way we find the "inevitable"—or as Thomson would have it, the "resistless"—plot which links all we see. The seductions of story for historians have been painted most fondly by Hayden White.[1] This is not a problem I raise for solution but from candor. My own belief that a literary history attempting anything more connected than a chronicle will come at times to sympathize with idealist or rationalist projects is reflected, no doubt, in my "occasional conformity" to the positions of Cassirer and Hegel invoked at the beginning of the third chapter and the end of the fourth.

One last card hardly needs to be put on the table at this point. If in much of the rest of the discussion my intention has been to resist the "resistless" formulations in favor of pursuing diversity and eccentricity, my choice of people and problems throughout has proceeded from a conception of the period as unified by its heightened uncertainties about the relation of solitary writers and solitary readers to the theater of public life. It is this complex of voiced and unvoiced doubts which I have had in mind as literary loneliness.

We have seen these uncertainties worked out most demonstratively in Hume, who is characteristically the one both to articulate his doubts most rigorously and to find a happy solution to them, even though turning to the History of England meant retreating from the philosophical structure he had begun to build in the privacy of his chamber. The relation is problematic even for Richardson, who turns similarly toward the assurances of historical detail in his last novel—and there are moments when it seems that *Grandison* narrates as many treaties as Hume's *History*—only to wave those claims uneasily aside. For in the midst of all the public breadth and civic-mindedness of *Grandison* there is a countermovement toward private realities. After

---

[1] In *Metahistory: The Historical Imagination in Nineteenth-Century Europe* (Baltimore: Johns Hopkins University Press, 1973), White considers historical consciousness in terms of metaphor, synecdoche, metonymy, and irony, and historical narratives in terms of Frye's romance, tragedy, comedy and satire. White pursues some of these concerns further in several later essays collected in *Tropics of Discourse* (Baltimore: Johns Hopkins University Press, 1978), esp. "The Historical Text as Literary Artifact," "The Fictions of Factual Representation," and "Historicism, History, and the Figurative Imagination."

volumes of praise for his "action," Sir Charles says abruptly, "I wish not to be a *public* man" (II, 99).

Despite the apparent contradiction, his opposition of public to private claims and his renunciation of the more historically social role at last integrates Sir Charles Grandison into the world of the novel bearing his name, a world of individuals reading. Near the end of the work Richardson has Charlotte Grandison resist the role of even domestic historian, delegating the description of the long-awaited wedding to Lucy Selby. "My dear girl, take the pen—I am too *sentimental*. The French only are proud of sentiments at this day; the English cannot bear them: Story, story, story, is what they hunt after, whether sense or nonsense, probable or improbable" (III, 228). Richardson's defense of "sentiments" might be seen as a reversion to narrow didacticism, especially in light of the curious *Collection of Moral and Instructive Sentiments* from the novels which he published a few years later.[2] But perhaps it is more helpful to see it as an attempt to rescue the novel from the demands of plot and to define something we may provisionally call the pure novel. Like "pure poetry," it would move away from matter and from mere actions, even the "activity" of a Grandison. As Young had suggested in the preface to *Night Thoughts*, narrative would be subservient to "reflections."[3] An abstract ode may be a more attainable achievement

[2] The complete title is *A Collection of the Moral and Instructive Sentiments, Maxims, Cautions, and Reflexions contained in the Histories of Pamela, Clarissa, and Sir Charles Grandison* (1755). Nearly half of this collection (pp. 217–394) is devoted to extracts from *Grandison*, including Charlotte Grandison's sentiment upon sentiments (p. 377).

[3] In his preface Young states that his work "differs from the common mode of Poetry, which is, from long narrations to draw short morals. Here, on the contrary, the narrative is short, and the morality arising from it makes the bulk of the Poem. The reason of it is, That these facts did naturally pour these moral reflections on the thought of the writer" (*The Works of the Author of Night-Thoughts* (London, 1802), II, 210. A complex relation may be noteworthy: (1) Young uses "reflections" much as Richardson uses "sentiments," as a synonym for "morals" or moral maxims; (2) it seems to have been Richardson's suggestion that Young's prefatory note be moved from *Night* IV to the front of the collected edition of *Night Thoughts* which Richardson printed in 1750 (see Isabel St. John Bliss, *Edward Young* [New York: Twayne, 1969], p. 123); (3) Johnson's oft-quoted remark to Boswell (*Life*, 6 April 1772), that "if you were to read Richardson for story, your impatience would be so much fretted that you would hang yourself. But you must read him for the sentiment, and consider the story as only giving occasion to the sentiment," seems to be a direct echo of Charlotte Grandison's

than an abstract narrative, but the unfolding desire of *Grandison* is the same: to make a structure of words unburdened by history.

The depth of isolation which confronts us in mid-eighteenth-century writing is *literary* loneliness because it depends upon the tacit negotiations carried on between reader and writer. It is not self-evident that the social contract suddenly changed in this period, but it is clear that the literary contract did. This change is most conspicuous in poetry, where it is very nearly personified, but its problematic transformation in the novel also begins to surface in the final works of its two greatest practitioners. Again, I do not wish to exaggerate the convergence of the novel and poetry, for the increasingly divergent and specialized claims of each reveal one of modern problems emerging at mid-century. There is an important way in which novels assimilate "historical" material all the more hungrily as the poets avoid it. *Sir Charles Grandison* and *Amelia* do indeed have ready-made documentary significance for the social historian, while most of the poems we have been considering have very little. And this distinction holds when we compare the poems not only to the novels but to much of the best poetry of the earlier years of the century, such as Pope's epistles, Gay's *Trivia*, or Swift's "Hogarthian" progresses. Seen in this light the novel remains easily on the side of "history" and of the later Hume as opposed to that of the increasingly visionary world of Law and of resistless "magnetism." Yet there is another level at which Richardson and Fielding alike seem to share Law's distrust of the "fictions of behavior," the "table talk" reality of mere observation without a deeper vision of providential presence to make the inert details signify. In Richardson's last novel the putatively resistless virtue of Sir Charles exerts the essential magnetism, in Fielding's, the purity of Amelia does so.

Both characters are central, finally, not for the sake of their "actions" but because of their presence. They are catalysts for conversion, making possible, even "inevitable," the sudden, discontinuous transformations which occur in the lives of others. One reason *Amelia* remains a more plausible novel than *Grandi-*

"sentiment"—in which case Johnson is praising Richardson's novels not for the "feelings" but for the formalized utterances of their characters.

Conclusion

son proceeds from Fielding's decision to make fewer claims for Amelia's agency and to focus her power of conversion quietly upon the one character who is as close to her as the reader, leaving the rest of society largely unmoved by her presence. At the same time, the conversion of Booth sits awkwardly in Fielding's novel because his sense of the "conservation of character" extends to life as well as to the art of life. To the end Fielding's Methodists, for example, are stamped from the same mold as Swift's canting enthusiasts, while Richardson's remain converted and do not pick pockets.[4] Booth's conversion, however, is a particularly literary and Richardsonian one, recounted without irony and experienced while reading, and its mere presence suggests that the need to describe significant experience in terms of conversion respects neither persons nor creeds at the center of the eighteenth century. Here, briefly, Hume and Law, Akenside and Young, are members of the same congregation. And at the center of the last novels of Richardson and Fielding, we find a world not quite accounted for by the plot, one where the determining realities are unseen forces and the truest motions are regarded by the poets as the actions of spirits.

The importance of conversion in the period, not only as a recurrent theme but especially as a rhetorical motive and structural principle, suggests a strong desire to achieve a sudden purity, to enact a radical break from the temporal, mundane order existing everywhere outside the order of words in which writer and reader can meet. The emergence and articulation of this desire point to a broader sense of literary loneliness, that is, to the isolation of "literature" itself as a category. Raymond Williams has recently discussed the development of this specialization both in terms of semantic change—in which the word

[4]Near the end of *Amelia,* Fielding "converts" a character named Robinson, whose compassion and willingness to testify on behalf of Booth and Amelia convince Dr. Harrison that, despite having been "corrupted by his old master," he had "naturally a good disposition." Even this equivocal reformation apparently disturbed Fielding, however, for in the next chapter we learn that "the witness for some time seemed to reform his life, and received a small pension from Booth; after which he returned to vicious courses, took a purse on the highway, was detected and taken, and followed the last steps of his old master" (Everyman Edition [1962; reprinted. in 1 vol., London: J. M. Dent, 1974], XII, viii–ix).

218

"literature" shifts in meaning from (roughly) everything written to "imaginative" writing—and in terms of the economic specialization of industrial capitalism.[5] Whether the narrowing or "purification" of literature is as directly related to class changes as Williams believes is a question which properly requires a much broader historical and comparative study of readership and reception in the eighteenth century than has been attempted. Rather than try to establish the "cause" of the changes which occur in literary practice—and Williams himself recognizes the reductions of explanatory "determinism"—I believe it might be fairest to the limits of this study to conclude by arguing from effects. The assumption in this case is that the meaning of the changes we have been studying rests at least as much in their practical manifestation in the period and their critical influence at the present time as in their putative origin or origins.

We turn, then, to now. Much of what I have referred to earlier as the flight from history in mid-century poetry—an avoidance of particular external referents, especially political ones, and a preference for indefinite and static reification—seems to be re-enacted in modern criticism. Contemplating the similarities may suggest something of the current imagery of academic seclusion and may perhaps help refocus literary history.

Although contemporary critics of various persuasions routinely dissociate themselves from the formalism which attained its highest prestige in the 1940s and 1950s, the differences between New Critics and newer critics are often minor—differences, as Gerald Graff has recently argued, "between factions of the vanguard." Postmodernist perspectives have not, according to this view, demystified modernism so much as continued it. "The loss of significant external reality, its displacement by myth-making, the domestication and normalization of alienation" are all in Graff's view common features of earlier *and* later twentieth-century literature and criticism.[6] From a critical point

[5]*Marxism and Literature* (Oxford: Oxford University Press, 1977), esp. pp. 45–54.
[6]Gerald Graff, *Literature against Itself: Literary Ideas in Modern Society* (Chicago: University of Chicago Press, 1979), p. 62. Graff's reaction to recent critical theorists is sometimes extreme, as when he takes them to task for claiming that propositions in literary works "are not really propositions at all" (p. 26), a posi-

of view, the continuity might be simplified this way. Modernist ideology tended to stress the conception of literature as self-referential: literature is autonomous, poems are about poetry. Postmodernist criticism has extended the ideal of autonomy to criticism as well: criticism is, if it is pure criticism, about criticism. Most contemporary critics would not put that proposition so baldly, although in some circles such remarks are a way of establishing one's critical credit. So, in the pages of *Diacritics*, for example, it has been possible to encounter one theorist congratulating another on having survived the "heroic labors of metacriticism."[7]

More representative of the situation of criticism, however, is the tendency to differentiate literature from mimesis and—by silent analogy—to differentiate criticism from commentary. René Wellek and Austin Warren began their *Theory of Literature* from the position that in literature the "reference is to a world of fiction, of imagination." The "statements in a novel, in a poem, or in a drama are not literally true; they are not logical propositions. There is a central and important difference between a statement, even in a historical novel or a novel by Balzac which *seems to convey 'information'* about actual happenings, and the same information appearing in a book of history or sociology."[8] Northrop Frye later underscored the distinction between a literary work—a "structure of words for its own sake," an "autonomous verbal structure"—and the "assertive" or "instrumental" use of language. "In all literary verbal structures the final direction of meaning is inward," while in "descriptive or assertive writing the final direction is outward." Frye's eventual goal is "pure Literature," a self-contained and self-consistent world which "like pure mathematics, contains its own meaning." "We think of literature at first as a commentary on an external 'life' or 'reality.' But just as in mathematics we have to go from three

tion Sidney also found attractive. Other failures of patience are noted in George Levine's searching review of Graff's book in *College English*, 43, no. 2 (February 1981): 146–60. I am indebted, however, to parts of Graff's argument in several of the following paragraphs.

[7]Angus Fletcher, "The Perpetual Error" (a review of Paul de Man's *Blindness and Insight*), in *Diacritics*, Winter 1972, pp. 14–20.

[8]*Theory of Literature* (New York: Harcourt, Brace, 1949), p. 15 (my italics).

apples to three, and from a square field to a square, so in reading a novel we have to go from literature as a reflection of life to literature as autonomous language." Criticism must have "some measure of independence from the art it deals with," and it must have its own "conceptual framework" if the "autonomy" of criticism is to be achieved.[9]

Neither Frye nor many of the critics who follow him could be called formalist. What is significant is simply that formalists and antiformalists have tended to agree on emphasizing the self-containment of literature; the difference is whether one argues for the self-containment of the individual work or the whole of what Frye calls the "literary field." In either case, the criticism which ensues will seek and find essentially static or "synchronic" works, detached from political events and the truths or falsities of public life.

For Frye and for many theorists interested in "autonomy," the analogy of music is important, because music, like mathematics, comes closest to an ideal of "pure poetry" by being more clearly coherent than referential. Perhaps for the same reason Mallarmé tends to be invoked with uncommon frequency by French critics wishing to stress the nonreferential aspects of language. Frye attributes the formulation of the ideal of "pure poetry" to *symbolisme:* its conception of poetry as essentially centripetal in meaning successfully isolated the "hypothetical germ of literature." For all his interest, in other words, in romance and myth and archetype, Frye's norm for poetry tends to be the lyric, an "elusive verbal pattern" that avoids statement but which is unified by a "unity of mood."[10]

Whatever the problems of such a norm, the important thing to note here is that its articulation is, in England, the achievement not of the later nineteenth century but of the mid-eighteenth.[11] It is not just the fact of Joseph Warton's using the

[9]*Anatomy of Criticism* (Princeton: Princeton University Press, 1957), pp. 5–6, 74, 351. Commenting primarily on Frye and Cleanth Brooks, Evan Watkins argues that "Poetic autonomy is nothing but a fiction of modernism" (*The Critical Act* [New Haven: Yale University Press, 1978], p. 30).

[10]Frye, *Anatomy of Criticism*, pp. 80–81.

[11]See M. H. Abrams on "The Lyric as Poetic Norm" in *The Mirror and the Lamp* (1953; reprint ed., New York: Norton, 1958), pp. 84–88.

phrase in the 1750s that is revealing but the shared poetic practice of the period. The avoidance of history, controversy, verifiability, political particularity—these are all parts of the ideal of poetry as *essentially* nonmimetic, evocative, and unified by mood rather than a structure of descriptions of assertions. The world of a poem like Joseph Warton's *The Enthusiast*—with its final image of rosy crowns and according lutes undisturbed by sinking sailors' cries—is a synchronic, as centripetal in meaning, and as autonomous as Frye or any critic arguing for the radical separation of poetry and history could wish.

The poems most popular immediately after the work of the generation of mid-century writers under discussion here included the "Ossian" poems, the alleged translations of ancient poetry which were actually written by James Macpherson in the 1760s. It is an interesting phenomenon, an obvious cross-cultural symptom of a not so obvious period pathology worthy of more tolerant study. But briefly, we can add to the usual explanations of the popularity of Ossian (the poems' appeal to primitivism, to Gaelic pride, to notions of "sublimity," and so on) these further attractions: the Ossian poems tend to reduce history to family romance, to blur the external physical world to a cloudily subjective field of warring forces, and to generalize the situation of the poet to that of a sensitive son of a strong father who belonged to another era.

If Northrop Frye unwittingly echoed Joseph Warton, surely the paradigmatic Ossian of our generation is Harold Bloom. The connection is a shared rhetorical preoccupation with paternal predecessors, physical combat (lists determining the "strongest" poets), and the ghosts of dead bard-warriors. Many passages could serve, but two exhibits may suggest the family likeness.

Exhibit A

Ossian: "Lovely were thy thoughts, O Fingal! why had not Ossian the strength of thy soul? But thou standest alone, my father! who can equal the king of Selma?"

Bloom: "A poem is not an overcoming of anxiety, but is that anxiety. . . . Every poem is a misinterpretation of a parent poem. . . . Poetry (Romance) is Family Romance. . . . It is as though the final phase of great modern poets existed neither for last affirmations . . . nor as palinodes, but rather as the ultimate placing and reduction of ancestors."

Exhibit B

Ossian: "Dimly seen as lightens the night, he strides largely from hill to hill. Bloody was the land of my father, when he whirl-ed the gleam of his sword. He remembers the battles of his youth. . . . 'Raise, ye bards of other times,' continued the great Fingal, 'raise high the praise of heroes: that my soul may settle on their fame.' The dark winds rustled over the chiefs. A hundred voices at once arose; a hundred harps were strung. They sung of other times; the mighty chiefs of former years."

Bloom: "Every poem we know begins as an encounter *between poems*. . . . The father is met in combat, and fought to at least a stand-off, if not quite to a separate peace. The burden for a repre-sentation thus becomes supermimetic rather than antimimetic, which means that interpretation too must assume the experiential sorrows of a supermimesis."[12]

It would require a fuller and fairer treatment of both the eighteenth and twentieth centuries to see in just what geometry these parallels would meet; but perhaps one or two readings may be taken. If the parallels are more than accidental, then the common view that modern literary attitudes are essentially an extension of romantic ideas in misleading. Compared with the mid-eighteenth century, the romantic period in England con-ducted a significant repoliticizing of poetry, a resumption of the poet's public function, adversarial but not "alienated." It is largely because of this recuperation of roles that Pope and Blake often sound more like each other than either sounds like Collins or the Wartons and that Wordsworth objects less to the public voice of Dryden or Pope than to the refined withdrawal of Gray. (It was Arnold, contemporary of the *symbolistes*, who had the least sympathy with early Augustan poetics.) In short, many of the modern critical premises concerning poetry are closer to the

[12]The two quotations from Bloom are from *The Anxiety of Influence* (New York: Oxford University Press, 1973), pp. 94–95, 147, and *A Map of Misreading* (New York: Oxford University Press, 1975), pp. 77, 80. The first quotation from Macpherson is from *Carthon*, the second from *Fingal;* the edition followed is *The Poems of Ossian* (New York: John B. Alden, 1883), pp. 226, 325.

tendencies of "preromanticism" than to romanticism. An oscilla-
tion theory of literary history is admittedly no great boon, but
until we do better it may represent the last two centuries of
literary practice and reflection with less distortion than a linear,
evolutionary model.

If the similarities between mid-eighteenth-century poetic and
late-twentieth-century critical responses are illuminating, it is
because they exist neither at the level of merely quaint resemblances nor at the level of causes. Much of our recent effort
has gone into segregating poetry from history, and not because a
generation of minor poets attempted a homologous segregation
two and a half centuries ago. But it is a fact that such an attitude
is now part of the repertoire of responses available to students of
literature and that to study its emergence and implications in
various periods is to seek what we very much need, historical
understanding of our ahistorical impulse.

At the moment, claims for the historical study of literature are
frequently made most loudly at the edges of the political spectrum, and there are limitations on both fronts. Historical conser-
vatives tend to make the case for reconstructing authorial intentions and the suppositions of a work's original audience; such
literary history naturally tends in turn toward the biographical
and doctrinal—and, if sentimentalized, toward the reactionary,
which in English studies is often a diffuse Christian Toryism.
The history conceived by Marxist critics tends to be impersonally
mechanistic in theory and highly selective in execution; few
Marxist studies have dealt sympathetically with older English
literature apart from the novel. Between these edges suppler
possibilities exist, but ahistorical structures abound. It is simpler,
of course, to notice the gap than to fill it, but we need a richer
theory of the relation of public history and poetic production,
one which does not begin by assuming that poetry is above or
beneath other means of survival and celebration.[13] Such a theo-

[13]Michael Fischer states the dilemma neatly in a review of Pierre Macherey's
Pour une théorie de la production littéraire (Paris, 1966; translated as *A Theory of
Literary Production* [London: Routledge & Kegan Paul, 1978]). Noting Macherey's "condescension toward literature" in favor of "Marxist science," Fischer
concludes, "Marxism continues to offset inflated tributes to the autonomy of
literature with equally exaggerated assertions of its dependency"; see *Applied
Linguistics*, 1 (1980): 175–76.

ry will need, I think, to be "liberal" enough in its individualism to be concerned with personal authorial situations and with empathetic criticism and at the same time skeptical enough of bourgeois nostalgias to distrust any method which puts a proprietary fence around literary meaning or around the claims of single voices. More often than not, our pedagogy and our practical criticism will continue to move from individual to collected works. But our historical reflection should begin from the recognition of collective works. This premise, admittedly easier to honor in the study of unenshrined writers of writings, reminds us that literature is less lonely than we or some of its earlier votaries have made it.

Index

Abrams, M. H., 12, 80, 128n, 136n, 160n, 221n
abstract ode, 151–153
Addison, Joseph, 42
Akenside, Mark: *Odes*, 70, 104–105, 109, 112–21; *Pleasures of Imagination*, 125–136, 139n, 147, 158–170, 173–179, 182, 187
Alter, Robert, 190n
ambition as poetic theme, 103–111, 131–136
Anderson, Howard, 190n
Arbuthnot, John: and Hume, 31–36
Arnold, Matthew, 81, 223
Austin, J. L., 67n
Ayre, William, 131n

Baker, Eric W., 51n
Balderston, Katherine, 57n
Barbauld, Anna Laetitia, 138, 205
Bate, W. J., 80
Battestin, Martin, 189n, 195n
Berkeley, George, 27
Berlin, Isaiah, 183n
Blair, Robert, 131n
Blake, William, 51, 66, 69, 86, 136, 223
Bloom, Harold, 222–223
Boehme, Jakob, 52, 61
Boswell, James, 50
Boyce, Benjamin, 58
Brinton, Howard H., 52n
Brissenden, R. F., 45n

Bronson, Bertrand, 78n
Brown, Homer Obed, 196n
Brown, Marshall, 128n
Broxap, Henry, 61n
Byrom, John, 51n, 64n

Carter, Elizabeth, 208n
Cascio, Robert Jude, 51n
Cassirer, Ernst, 79–80, 152, 215
"Choice of Hercules," 91, 166
Coleridge, Samuel Taylor, 51, 66, 68
Colie, Rosalie, 22n, 37n
Collins, William, 68, 70, 96, 100, 105, 109, 112–114, 117, 120–124, 127–130, 136–148, 150–153, 177
"conversion" as poetic plot, 103, 146–153, 165, 217–218
Croce, Benedetto, 183n, 187n
Culler, Jonathan, 68

Daniels, Norman, 48n
Defoe, Daniel, 27
Descartes, René, 24
Deutsch, Helene, 71
Doody, Margaret Anne, 190n, 202n, 204n, 206n
Dryden, John, 83
Dudden, F. Homes, 189n, 200n
Dussinger, John A., 26n, 212n

Edwards, Jonathan, 70
Eliot, George, 162, 208

Fairer, David, 68, 81n, 109n
fancy vs. memory, 86–87
Ferguson, Adam, 54, 83, 90, 105
Fielding, Edmund, 200
Fielding, Henry, 107; *Amelia,*
189–202, 217–218; and develop-
ment during 1740s, 20; *Jonathan
Wild,* 100–101, 189–192, 195,
206–207, *Joseph Andrews,* 191–195,
197, 199–200; and Law, 50; and
Mandeville, 54; and narrative
problems, 13; *Miscellanies,* 198;
Tom Jones, 191–192, 196–199
Fielding, Sarah, 107
Fischer, Michael, 224n
Fletcher, Angus, 220n
Flew, Antony, 19, 34n, 171n
Frye, Northrop, 78n, 220–222

Gay, John, 84, 100
Gibbon, Edward, 50–51
Godwin, William, 207
Golden, Morris, 187n, 195n
Goldsmith, Oliver, 107, 144
Gombrich, E. H., 131n
Graff, Gerald, 219–220
Gray, Thomas, 68, 87–90, 96–102,
104, 115, 123–125, 146, 150–151,
163, 206–207
"greatness," 100–103
Green, J. Brazier, 51n–52n
Greene, Donald, 78n

Hegel, G. W. F., 100–103, 153, 185,
215
Hoadley, Benjamin, 53, 65–69
Hobhouse, Stephen, 52n
Hoyles, John, 64n
Hume, David, 11, 215, 217–218; and
belief, 35–37, 40, 46–49, 148–150,
174–175; and dichotomies, 33;
and "eloquence," 21, 37–43,
47–48; *Essays* (1741–42), 37–41;
on ethics vs. metaphysics, 41–43,
48, 65; on impressions vs. ideas,
23, 33–37; on memory vs. imagination, 35–37; and Law, 62–63,
72–73; *Letter from a Gentleman*
(1745), 28; on personal identity,
170–175; "Philosophical Essays"

vs. *Treatise,* 37–41; revision of
Treatise as *Enquiries,* 19–49; on
taste, 46
Hunt, John Dixon, 169n
Hunter, J. Paul, 55n, 195n, 201

Jackson, Wallace, 81n, 112
James, William, 180, 183
Johnson, Samuel, 20, 50–51, 57–58,
89, 104, 107, 140, 178, 216n
Johnston, Arthur, 81n
Jones, William Powell, 179n
Joyce, James, 84

Kant, Immanuel, 170
Keats, John, 166n
Kermode, Frank, 190n
Kinkead-Weekes, Mark, 190n, 202n,
204n, 205n, 206n
Kramnick, Isaac, 108n
Kuhns, Richard, 26n, 72, 172n

La Bruyère, 42, 50
Law, William, 11, 97, 217–218; *Appeal to all that Doubt,* 64, 67, 69;
Case of Reason, 60–63, 66; *Christian
Perfection,* 54, 56–57; *A Demonstration,* 53, 56, 63n, 64–69, 148; *An
Earnest and Serious Answer,* 64; *Letters to the Bishop of Bangor,* 53; *Of
Justification,* 71; *Regeneration,*
64–65, 67, 69, 149; *Remarks
upon . . . "Fable of the Bees,"* 54–56;
Serious Call, 54, 56–57; *Spirit of
Love,* 64, 150; *Spirit of Prayer,* 56,
64, 66–67, 69, 71; *Unlawfulness of
the Stage,* 54; *Way to Divine Knowledge,* 50, 64, 66, 71, 73
"literary loneliness," 215–225
"literature of Opposition," 108
Locke, John, 22–24, 34n, 37, 62,
170–174
Lockwood, Thomas, 82n
Longinus, 68

Macherey, Pierre, 224n
Mack, Maynard, 85, 176–177

Index

McKillop, Alan Dugald, 179–180, 189n, 204n
Macpherson, James, 188, 222–223
Malekin, Peter, 52n
Mallet, David, 178
Mandeville, Bernard, 51
Marsh, Robert, 168n
Miles, Josephine, 79
Mill, John Stuart, 31
Milton, John, 86, 117–118, 136–141, 145, 152, 157, 160, 165
Miner, Earl, 83n
Monk, Samuel H., 12, 80, 165n
Morris, David B., 165n, 177
Morrisoe, Michael, Jr., 19
Mossner, Ernest, 31n, 32, 38

Newton, Isaac, 45, 55, 72
Nicolson, Marjorie Hope, 135n
nonjurors, 61–62
Norton, John, 165n, 179n
Nuttall, A. D., 19

Odell, Daniel W., 159n, 162n
Overton, J. H., 52n

Paulson, Ronald, 13, 91n, 166n
Penelhum, Terence, 171n
Percy, Walker, 180
personification, 68, 86–91n, 114, 130–146, 151–153
Pittock, Joan, 78n, 81n
"politics of melancholy," 85–89, 106, 122
Pope, Alexander, 90–91, 223; *Dunciad*, 69, 184; *Ep. to Arbuthnot*, 119, 167; *Ep. to Cobham*, 212; *Essay on Man*, 158–169, 173–174; and Law, 50, 58–59; on motivation, 47n, 56–57; *Rape of the Lock*, 162–163; reaction against, 81–86; on *Seasons*, 175
"post-Augustan," 79–80; vs. "preromantic," 108
Potter, George R., 167n
Preston, Thomas R., 107
"preromantic," 78–79, 108, 224
Price, Martin, 68, 84–85, 128n, 162
Prodicus, 91
progress piece, 181–187

"pure poetry," 9, 12–13, 81–96, 107–111, 120–121, 128–146, 216

Rawson, C. J., 71n
Reid, Thomas, 48
retirement vs. retreat, 85–103, 133
reverie, 30, 186
Richardson, Samuel: *Clarissa*, 202–205, 211–212; *Collection of Moral Sentiments*, 216; *Grandison*, 189–191, 202–213, 215–218; *Pamela*, 210–211; and "sentiment," 13; and writing "to the moment," 26
Rostvig, Maren-Sofie, 166n
Rothstein, Eric, 190n, 212n

Sacks, Sheldon, 192n
Scott, John (of Amwell), 133n
Searle, John R., 67
Shaftesbury, Anthony Ashley Cooper, 1st Earl of, 22, 24, 130–131n, 136, 163, 172
Shelley, Percy Bysshe, 158, 184
Shenstone, William, 91
Sherburn, George, 81n, 111
Sherwin, Paul S., 137, 139n, 145
Sickels, Eleanor, 85–86
sight (vs. sentiment), 67–68
Smart, Christopher, 68, 188
Smith, John E., 70n
Speck, W. A., 61n
speech-acts, 67–69, 97
Spenser, Edmund, 138–140
Stephen, Leslie, 51n
Sterne, Laurence, 87
Swift, Jonathan, 20, 27–29, 84, 91–100

Talon, Henri, 52n, 64n
Tennyson, Alfred, Lord, 160, 167
theodicy, 91, 157–188, 214
Thompson, E. P., 184n
Thompson, William, 110–111
Thomson, James: *Castle of Indolence*, 93–96, 104, 132, 147, 150–151, 180, 187; *Liberty*, 70, 148, 158, 175, 179–185; *Seasons*, 90–93, 157–158, 175–187
Tindal, Matthew, 60–63

Index

Vesey, Godfrey, 171n
Vico, Giambattista, 181, 183, 185

Wakefield, Gilbert, 124
Walker, A. Keith, 51n
Walsh, John, 60n
Warburton, William, 53
Warren, Austin, 220
Warton, Joseph, 12–13, 53n, 80–87,
    93, 102, 105–106, 109–114, 118,
    120–128, 131–132, 136–137,
    141–143, 147–148, 150–151,
    221–223
Warton, Thomas, Jr., 68, 80,
    96–97n, 105–106, 129–131,
    146–147, 150–152; on "Romantic
    Kind of Poetry," 103, 109–110
Warton, Thomas (the Elder), 80–81
Wasserman, Earl, 33, 91n, 138, 141n,
    166n

Watt, Ian, 190
Weinbrot, Howard, 78–79, 98n
Wellek, René, 220
Wendorf, Richard, 105n
Wesley, John, 50–51
White, Hayden, 77n, 215
Whitefield, George, 50–51
Whitehead, Alfred North, 77n
Whitehead, William, 53n, 108,
    150–151
Williams, Raymond, 10, 218–219
Winn, James, 111n
Wordsworth, William, 39, 83, 88,
    136, 158–160, 166–169, 223
Wormhoudt, Arthur, 72

Young, Edward, 85, 89n, 135, 147,
    158–170, 173–179, 187, 217

Literary Loneliness

Designed by Richard E. Rosenbaum.
Composed by The Composing Room of Michigan, Inc.
in 10 point Linotron 202 Baskerville, 2 points leaded,
with display lines in Bakserville.
Printed offset by Thomson/Shore, Inc. on
Warren's Number 66 Antique Offset, 50 pound basis.
Bound by John H. Dekker & Sons, Inc.
in Joanna book cloth.

Library of Congress Cataloging in Publication Data

Sitter, John E.
   Literary loneliness.

   Includes bibliographical references and index.
   1. English literature—18th century—History and
criticism.   2. Loneliness in literature.   I. Title.
PR448.L66S5   820'.9'353   82-5105
ISBN 0-8014-1499-7   AACR2

DATE DUE